THE MAN AWAKENED FROM DREAMS

Liu Dapeng. Used by kind permission of Liu Niuzhong, Chiqiao.

The Man Awakened from Dreams

One Man's Life in a North China Village, 1857–1942

HENRIETTA HARRISON

STANFORD UNIVERSITY PRESS

STANFORD, CALIFORNIA

Stanford University Press
Stanford, California

Printed in the United States of America
on acid-free, archival-quality paper

Library of Congress Cataloging-in-Publication Data
Harrison, Henrietta.
   The man awakened from dreams : one man's life in a north
China village, 1857–1942 / Henrietta Harrison.
      p. cm.
   Includes bibliographical references and index.
   ISBN 0-8047-5068-8 (cloth : alk. paper) —
ISBN 0-8047-5069-6 (pbk. : alk. paper)
   1. Harrison, Henrietta—Travel—China—Chiqiao Village.
2. Chiqiao Village (China)—Description and travel.   3. Liu
family.   I. Title.
   DS797.75.C45H374 2005
   951'.17—dc22   2004018647

Original Printing 2005

Last figure below indicates year of this printing:
14   13   12 • 11   10   09   08

Typeset by Classic Typography in 10/14 Janson

CONTENTS

Acknowledgments   vii

Preface   I

1. Writing   9

2. The Confucian Scholar   21

3. The Filial Son   51

4. The Representative of the People   83

5. The Merchant   113

6. The Farmer   136

Epilogue   159

Notes   173

Bibliography   191

Index   203

roughly plastered over. Lifting a bamboo screen we come round the corner into a paved courtyard with four rooms round it. The old man calls out to the family and jokes that this was the only courtyard in the village whose stone paving was laid by graduates. Standing here we are facing the main rooms, which were once inhabited by Liu Dapeng's parents and now belong to the family of his eldest son. On our left is the slightly smaller south-facing building where Liu himself lived all his life. An old woman dressed in black comes out, introduces herself to me as Liu Dapeng's fifth daughter-in-law, and takes us inside. It is a long narrow room with a wide brick bed at one end and cupboards and tables set against the back wall. The far end is separated off to provide a small inner room, which once had a heated brick bed like the main room but now has two iron bedsteads. Directly facing us as we enter is a large portrait of Liu Dapeng: a serious man—his solidity and stature emphasized by a thick padded silk jacket—frowning slightly down at us.

Liu Dapeng's home was not what I expected. When the old man joked that the paving stones had been laid by graduates, I did not believe him. Surely Qing dynasty degree-holders did not lay paving stones. I was also surprised at the size of the house. My notes on the occasion record a string of questions: Was this the only courtyard Liu lived in? Did all his sons live here as well? Liu's daughter-in-law and a young woman who had married into the family of his eldest son were surprised in their turn but quite clear: Liu, his wife, parents, five sons and their wives and children all lived in the one courtyard. I knew that Liu and his son had both held prestigious provincial degrees in the last decades of the Qing dynasty. Although neither ever achieved the final national-level degree that provided access to official employment, even the holding of provincial degrees made them both members of what Chang Chung-li, writing in the 1950s, described as the upper gentry.[1] Below them were the many holders of the preliminary degree who had never been able to progress further. Together these degree-holders formed a group that writers of Chinese history have traditionally referred to as the "gentry" and described as taking a mediating position between the state and the general population.[2] This group is seen as being infused with a Confucian culture acquired through the education and examination system. Later studies have emphasized the importance of other sources of power. They describe degree-holders and others, such as those who had made money through trade or banking but did not hold de-

Preface

These days one can get to Chiqiao village by bus. The first time I came, in 1996, the bus driver let me off at the end of the track that runs across the rice paddies to the village. Many of the buses are owned and operated by Chiqiao families, but the bus crew was surprised that I wanted to go there. The village lies on the edge of the plain and its main street, which winds up the hill, is the old road that ran from Taiyuan, the provincial capital of Shanxi, to the southern part of the province. Most of the houses along the road are low traditional courtyards and, like the long-abandoned shops, are much the same color as the dirt road along which they are built. One of these was the home of Liu Dapeng, which I had come to see. Before Liu's father bought it the house had been a pawnshop, and it is solidly built with a small gateway over the entrance. The talkative old man who took me into the house told me that hanging under the eaves of the gateway there was once a large board saying "Father and Son are both graduates." Today the board is gone and the elaborate carving on the wall behind the gate has been hacked off and

THE MAN AWAKENED FROM DREAMS

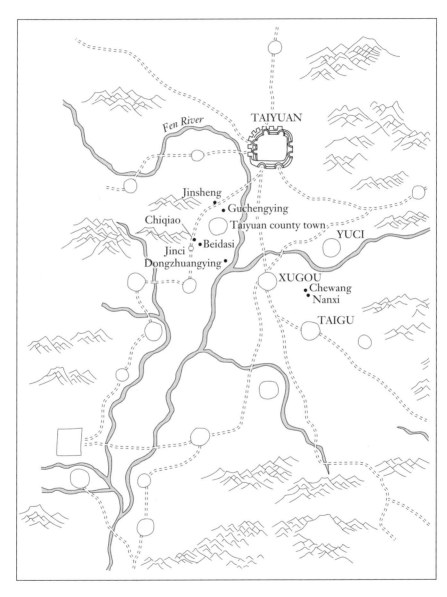

Central Shanxi. Source: ABCFM. Shansi Mission.
Adapted from Shen Guifen's map of Shanxi Province, 1881.

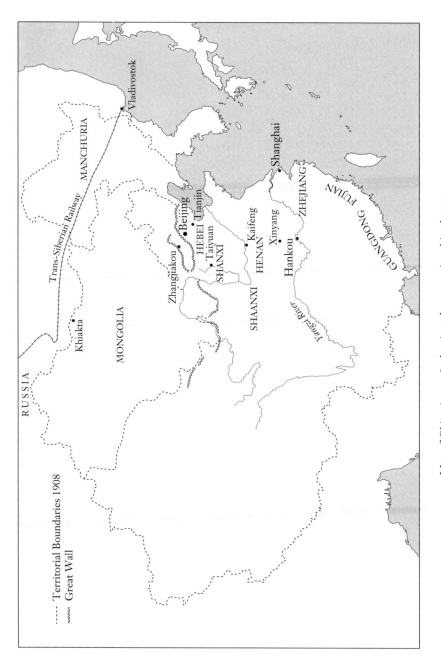

Map of China in 1908, showing places mentioned in the text

grees, as members of an elite.[3] Other scholars have looked at the lifestyles of this group and described how members of the elite differentiated themselves from other people through, for example, writing poetry, painting, and collecting rare books.[4] The effect of reading this literature had been to produce in my mind at least an image of the gentry as wealthy, cultured families living in large houses.

There is of course another image of traditional Chinese degree-holders: the impoverished schoolteacher. Penniless scholars desperately trying to pass the exams that would bring them an official position are famously satirized in the eighteenth-century novel *The Scholars*. This is the category into which my Chinese acquaintances invariably fit Liu Dapeng. Men like Liu Dapeng did not necessarily teach and the impoverished school teacher is a stereotype, but it is one that reflects a reality that has too often been overlooked. Educated but poor families do appear in the English-language literature on China, but their voices are often lost in the simplicity of the division between the elite and the common people.[5] This division appeals to us. We want to be studying either the power-holders or the subalterns. When we make that division we are making an alien society more comprehensible to ourselves, but we are also filtering out the difficulties.[6] Part of my aim in this book is to question some of the classifications we apply to Chinese society: gentry, merchant, peasant, elite. What do we mean when we use these terms? Does any individual, let alone a family, fit neatly into any one category? If identities are multiple and shifting, then how does this affect the historical narratives we relate?

Coming to Liu Dapeng's house and meeting his family also made me wonder about what happened to the degree-holding gentry after the 1911 revolution. On my second visit to the village, in 1997, I was introduced to the "landlord's son," an old man named Wu who had become a paper maker in the years after the Communist revolution of 1949. Despite his reputation as a skilled craftsman, he was nervous and avoided answering questions, an unsurprising result of his status since 1949. Liu Dapeng's family showed no such characteristics. Indeed, on one occasion Liu's elderly daughter-in-law took advantage of my presence to berate the village Party Secretary loudly and at length for the destruction during the 1960s of the carving on the decorated wall behind the main gate of the house. Family members were proud of Liu Dapeng and told me how many books he had owned (a whole cupboard full) but made no claims to school learning and clearly considered themselves to be quite ordinary members of the village community. Social mobility is known to have been an important characteristic of Chinese villages, but historians have tended to focus on those members of the elite who succeeded in preserving their status and in adapting to change. They see members of local elites becoming increasingly involved in social activism and in attempts to mobilize the population to support change and modernization.[7] It has also been suggested that traditional elites who had acted to protect their villages from government extortion lost their legitimacy as taxation increased in the early twentieth century, and that when this happened they migrated to the towns.[8] In all these scenarios traditional local elites still preserved some of their economic and social status. Liu Dapeng's case was much less positive. As his descendents' current situation suggests, the family had declined well before the Communist revolution of 1949. Given the picture we have of the preservation of existing elites, why did Liu's family fail? And how did men try to preserve the status they had earned as members of the gentry when the 1911 revolution destroyed any remaining hope that they might attain government office? These questions have led me to two stories, the first about Confucianism and the second about the province of Shanxi.

What role did Confucianism actually play in people's lives? And how did that change after the state abandoned its longstanding commitment to Confucian orthodoxy? Liu Dapeng was personally committed to the ideas he learned first as a schoolboy and later as a student in an academy in the provincial capital. He agonized endlessly over his failure to live up to the high standards he had learned, particularly what he saw as the inadequacy of his care and affection for his parents. His attempt to play out the role of a Confucian gentleman was unusual; his classmates in the academy, many of whom came from wealthier backgrounds, teased him for his earnest enthusiasm, while his neighbors in the village often disagreed with him over what constituted proper behavior. But even though few people shared Liu's personal commitment, they tolerated and even admired it because it was recognized and promoted by the state. Then, from 1900 on, the state gradually abandoned its Confucian values in favor of a new emphasis on nationalism and a vision of modernity tied to international trade and large-scale urban industry. The rhetoric of Confucianism lost its political currency to such an extent that officials would no longer even listen to arguments couched in those terms, and Liu lost the public voice that his education had once given him. But Confucianism was deeply embedded in local society and did not simply disappear. For Liu himself, the effort to behave like a Confucian gentleman was a crucial part of his identity, one that marked his status even after his educational qualifications became politically worthless. The ways in which he attempted to convert this identity into an income for his family suggest the extent to which Confucian ideas remained part of local institutions long after the state had abandoned them. In particular, in the absence of a strong legal framework, Confucian values continued to play an important role in business, where Liu found employment as a coal mine manager and investment manager. His status among the county's merchants was confirmed through his extensive work as a mediator in business disputes, where his value system was recognized and accepted. Confucianism continued to be part of many aspects of life: business, the family, agriculture. But in the absence of the state as a unifying force, Confucian values developed and changed in different ways in each of these institutions.

Throughout the book I use the word Confucianism as shorthand for the ideology promoted by the Qing government in the late nineteenth century, which Liu Dapeng usually referred to as "the principles of the sages and worthies" or "the way of Confucius and Mencius."[9] In his opinion this represented the authentic teaching of Confucius and his disciples. This view is not shared by modern scholars, who might prefer to call his philosophy "neo-Confucianism," emphasizing its origins in the thought of the twelfth century, but was shared by most of his contemporaries. I have used the term Confucianism partly because it reflects Liu's opinions, but also because Song neo-Confucianism, like Qing orthodoxy, was itself merely a moment in the great philosophical stream. Nor was Liu's Confucianism a pure version of twelfth-century ideas; it was shot through with ideas that came from the Daoist philosophical tradition as well. But both philosophies came to him through the same textual tradition, and he never explicitly differentiated between the two, accepting both as his heritage as a scholar and potential official and always referring to himself as following the way of the ancient sages.

In an earlier generation Liu Dapeng might have defined his Confucianism against some form of popular culture, but in fact he came increasingly to set it in opposition to what he refers to as the "new" policies. So, for example, he states,

> In recent years scholars have all been divided into two groups, called "those who hold to the old" and "those who hold to the new." Those who hold to the old cleave to the way of Confucius and Mencius, while those who hold to the new seek only after Western methods.[10]

From the 1890s through to the 1940s, he saw and lamented the inexorable political rise of "those who hold to the new" and their policies. I have chosen to refer to these people as modernizers and to their policies as modernization because in our language any government policy can be new, whereas what Liu saw was a particular political agenda, based on a Western-inspired vision of the future. He understood this agenda as being opposed to his own Confucianism, which looked back to the way of the ancient sages.

This brings me to the other story, which is about the Shanxi countryside and its gradual exclusion from commercial prosperity and political power as a result of changes that were closely linked to this vision of modernity. When I visited Chiqiao and then the village of Nanxi where Liu worked as a tutor for many years, it was immediately obvious that these villages had once been wealthy. The main street in Chiqiao is lined with buildings that were once shops but have long been bricked up for use as housing. Off the street the narrow lanes run into large yards with dilapidated chimneys and collapsing sheds that once housed the village's paper-making industry. In Nanxi and the neighboring village of Chewang, vast and once beautifully decorated halls and courtyards were locked up or inhabited by impoverished villagers who looked almost as if they were camping in them.[11] This was, of course, partly the result of Communist party policies of the 1950s and 60s, which redistributed wealth through land reform and the absorption of rural industry into the state; but it was also part of a longer process. In some cases Communist policies actually had the effect of preserving buildings of the kind that before 1949 were being broken up and sold for timber. The impoverishment of the once wealthy Shanxi countryside began well before 1949 and was the result of a series of political changes that transformed Shanxi's geography. Mongolian independence, the Russian revolution, and the refocusing of both national security concerns and trade from inland northwest China to the southeast coast—together these developments turned Shanxi from a major trading corridor into an isolated and inaccessible province. Meanwhile the vision of modernity shared by provincial and national governments emphasized urban industrialization and export-oriented commerce as the foundation for a strong nation.[12] Some parts of the country benefited from these changes; Shanxi villages did not. Between 1900 and 1980, the villages of central Shanxi were transformed from prosperous centers of commerce and industry into impoverished and largely agricultural communities.

These are large topics, but I have focused them round the story of one man, because that is how I came to them. This approach also allows me to focus on the details of everyday life where we can see how social structures and ideologies interacted in practice. Only at the level of the individual is it possible to see, for example, how the ideology of filial piety was put into practice and how this was affected by political changes; if we leap to the collectivity too quickly, we lose much of what is interesting. For the same reason I have by and large avoided narratives of the great political events of the day. Uprisings and revolutions punctuate everyday life, they add drama to it, and ultimately they may change it, but most people participate only as observers and the changes in their lives take place over a much longer term. Moreover, much of the book is based on Liu Dapeng's diary, which is missing the volumes for 1900 and 1908 to 1912. It seems that before the manuscript reached the Shanxi Provincial library, someone took out the years that he or she thought of greatest historical value: those covering the Boxer uprising in 1900 and the republican revolution in 1911. It is possible to reconstruct these events in some detail from Liu's other writings, indeed Liu is one of the major sources for the Boxer uprising in Shanxi; but I have chosen instead to take this as an invitation to focus on the everyday, the domestic, and the personal.[13]

This focus on a single person inevitably brings with it the question, was Liu Dapeng typical? The obvious answer to this question is no. It is not normal in any society to keep a diary for fifty years, let alone to leave the amount of other writing Liu did. Even in his later life, when he was laboring in the fields, Liu wrote about what was going on every day and sometimes several times a day. Nor was his devout commitment to Confucianism particularly widespread, though other people's reactions to it do give a sense of how it fitted into a broader community. The family's economic situation, on the other hand, was perfectly ordinary: in Liu's father's lifetime, that is to say up to the 1900s, they were comfortably off though never among the richest families in the village. They were the kind of people referred to as "the middling sort" by historians of early modern Europe and as "rich peasants" by Communist land-reform cadres. From the early 1900s on, the family declined and, by the late 1930s, when Liu ate sorghum porridge for breakfast, lunch, and dinner and could not afford coal for heating, they were poor by anyone's reckoning. Their decline was part of a larger process that involved much of Shanxi, and I have used their story to illustrate economic changes that have been discussed in greater detail by Chinese historians.

Liu Dapeng's situation was not unusual. He refers frequently to friends who shared his predicament, and his ideas and patterns of thought grew out of the social and cultural environment in which he lived. But I have not chosen to write about him because I think that he is typical. Real people are never typical. As I read his diary I began to feel a sense of commitment to him as a person, and when I talked to his family and neighbors that sense was strengthened. I admired his attempts to live up to his ideals, even though much of his thinking remained quite alien to me. (I doubt he would have approved of being studied by a foreign woman: he complained about the "endless streams of women from all the foreign countries who come to travel in China," since "women are supposed to be chaste, quiet, and secluded, and they cannot be that if they leave home and travel.")[14] Real humanity in historical accounts is all too often restricted to great leaders, famous writers, or original thinkers.[15] Liu Dapeng was none of these. As a young man he did indeed hope to be a great leader, but like most people he never achieved that goal. I have written about him because I hope that the very fact that he was a real person and not some abstract personification of a class or type may teach us to rethink our understanding of what it was like to live through some of the changes that transformed China in the twentieth century.

ONE

Writing

On 25 November 1925 Liu Dapeng was awakened by the sound of his baby daughter crying. She and her young mother slept in a small inner room that opened off the far end of the main room where Liu was sleeping. It was still completely dark, but the village cocks had begun to crow so morning was on its way. Liu got up and went into the little inner room where the baby and mother were now sitting up on the big brick bed and the baby was smiling and laughing. A short time later Liu's youngest son, Hongqing, who was seven, called to his mother that he wanted to get up. Then, as the first thin rays of the sun were just appearing, two grandsons, Quanzhong and Jingzhong, who slept with Liu on the big brick bed in the outer room and must have been awakened by all the activity, also got up and began learning their lessons. They were at school in the nearby town of Jinci, where they studied from the new modern textbooks, but Liu also occasionally taught them the old texts at home. In either case learning their lessons meant chanting the texts aloud. Another grandson, Shuzhong, heard the noise from the small room across the courtyard where he lived with his father, Liu's younger son Xiang, and his family. He came in to join his cousins in reciting their texts.

Surrounded by his children and grandchildren and the sound of their recitations, Liu was delighted. This was the time of day when he usually wrote his diary. He sat down alongside them on the big brick bed and got out his brush, ink stone, ink stick, and diary from the big wooden cupboard that stood on the end of the bed. The brush was old, but it would have to do. (A few days later he dreamt that he had been given four new writing brushes; when he woke up he meditated on the sad fact that people never did give him writing equipment.) He had made the notebook for the diary earlier in the year from scraps of whatever paper he could come by: a few plain white sheets, but also sheets of newspaper (which were flimsy but only printed on one side), the backs of funeral announcements, flyers advertising medical stores in the nearby town of Jinci, and advertisements for patent medicines. He cut them to a regular size, pasted them together, and folded them up in a concertina ready to write on. At the end of the quarter when he finished this notebook he would back it with stronger paper, fasten the edges of the concertina together with little twists of paper, write his name in elaborate seal script on the front, and add it to the hundred or so earlier volumes accumulating in the cupboard. He ground the ink stick on the ink stone, adding a little water to make a thick black ink, and took up his brush to describe the domestic scene, ending with the words "This is one of the pleasures of having a family. What else is as delightful as this?"[1]

Liu had begun the diary more than thirty years earlier, in 1891, when he was working as a tutor in the household of a wealthy banking and trading family in Taigu county, about a day's journey by cart from his home village of Chiqiao. When he started there was nothing particularly unusual about the project. Scholars at the time disagreed over when diary writing had begun in China, but the latest date they suggested was the Tang dynasty (seventh to ninth centuries). They discussed diary writing because it was a popular activity. Many diaries were also published, though naturally these tended to be those of the famous or wealthy. The content of these diaries was quite standard: entries usually began with a brief description of the weather, went on to the author's activities for the day often listing the names of those he had met or dined with, and included descriptions of scenic sites the author had visited and poems he had written.[2]

Shortly after he started writing the diary, Liu Dapeng was reading the published letters of one of nineteenth-century China's great statesmen Zeng Guofan, who had died some twenty years earlier. Liu hugely admired Zeng Guofan and copied into his diary a set of rules for everyday life that Zeng had suggested to his son. Zeng Guofan told his son to be respectful and serious in all his dealings, to sit in meditation for a while every day, to rise early, never to start reading one book before he had finished reading another, to read ten pages of the dynastic histories daily, to keep a diary, to jot down what he had learned that day, to write several poems and essays each month to preserve his literary skills, not to talk too much, not to get angry, not to exhaust himself, to practice his calligraphy every day after breakfast, and absolutely never to go out at night. He also gave some specific instructions on keeping the diary: "You must write it in the formal script. You should include all the sins you have committed during the day, that is to say sins of the body, the mind, and the tongue. You should continue to write it all your life without any gaps."[3] Liu Dapeng valued these rules and they made the diary part of his daily routine. He rose early, lit a lamp in the winter, and then sat in meditation for a while. Then he read a section of the dynastic histories, or in later years a newspaper, and wrote the diary. He wrote it neatly in the formal script and used it to reflect on his behavior. From time to time he copied into it poems and essays he had written. Before he read Zeng Guofan's instructions his diary had been intermittent, but afterward he wrote it every day.

Initially the diary was almost entirely concerned with moral reflection of the sort that Zeng Guofan envisages in his instructions. Liu reminds himself to be patient, to step back and reflect, not to argue, and not to criticize others.[4] The faults he selects shed some light on his character but tell us little about his everyday life. Soon, however, he begins to include anecdotes to illustrate his reflections. By the summer of 1892 he is recollecting his time studying at the academy in Taiyuan city, recording a dream, and recounting an uplifting conversation he had about the weather with some men hoeing the fields ("I said to them 'The Emperor on High loves living things so there is bound to be a good rainfall soon. He will certainly not send the scourge of drought to distress people. As long as we do as Heaven wishes, the land will naturally be moistened and every family will be happy.'")[5] These ways of writing are characteristic of the diary as a whole. Liu's practice of writing the diary first thing in the morning and meditating and reading the histories beforehand meant that many entries begin with his reflections on his own failings. The tendency to provide a moral frame to events also continues. More than a convention of diary-writing, this moral frame is an important part of the way Liu understands himself and what is going on around him. Thus the diary becomes part of the way in which he makes himself into the kind of person he wants to be.

When Liu began writing the diary, he still hoped that one day he would be famous so that the diary might be published as Zeng Guofan's had been. Writing it was also good practice for his calligraphy and for the examinations generally. But as time went on the diary developed a momentum of its own, tied to his personal experience of downward social mobility. Over the years it became a detailed record of Liu's daily activities and its writing spread through the day. So, for example, on that day in the late autumn of 1925 he wrote the paragraph describing his family first thing in the morning and made another entry that evening to record the fact that the county tax office had invited him to attend an opera performance in the county town. A man who was the same age as Liu's youngest son remembered seeing Liu writing the diary in his old age. He joked that Liu would sit on the brick bed looking out the window over the top of his spectacles, see airplanes flying past and write down "Three airplanes went past today."[6] Entries like this were very far from Zeng Guofan's instructions for diary-writing and Liu felt the need to justify them. In 1901, after a year in which many entries had been concerned with the local Boxer movement, he wrote:

> In the past people said that it was not appropriate to put news in a diary, but there is a lot of news in my diary. This is because I live in a time of political disorder and there is nowhere I can relax except in my diary, where I can put down all the things I am worried about.[7]

The diary was undoubtedly a comfort to Liu in times of trouble or anxiety, but much of what he noted down was neither moral reflection nor political news. A fairly typical entry, written when Liu was back in Chiqiao in 1915, reads:

> 11th day of the 2nd month.
>   At first light I was thinking about how I cannot make a living by farming. I am not making any progress toward high office and wealth, but on the

other hand I think that those who are officials today are acting wrongly and scorn their failure to remain loyal to the dynasty.

It was freezing again this morning.

I found a laborer to plant the fields. I too got wet and muddy because I was repairing the banks between the plots while the hired man did the ploughing. I did not rest all day and in the evening I felt exhausted because the work was so heavy.[8]

Liu gives his agricultural work a certain value by putting it in the context of his loyalty to the fallen dynasty. But the detail of his account goes beyond this. When Liu describes the way the work was divided between himself and the hired laborer, he is making a claim for the importance of his daily life simply by writing it down. This is especially true in a society where the written word was highly valued in itself. Liu is still remembered in his village for his practice of "respecting the written word": when he was out of the house and saw a scrap of paper or anything with writing on it, he would pick it up and take it home to burn it respectfully.[9] By writing down the humdrum events of his everyday life Liu made a claim for the value of a life that was otherwise very ordinary. By setting them against a background of national and local events he was rescuing himself from obscurity.

But the diary was not the only text Liu wrote. Members of his family say that at the time of his death there were more than 400 thin, hand-written volumes in the cupboard in his room. Half these volumes made up the diary and the rest contained other texts he had written. A stone inscription that was erected at the time of his death lists 263 volumes in addition to the diary. These include several accounts of the local area, diaries of various journeys, a plan for rebuilding local flood defenses, a collection of local superstitions, a family genealogy and a set of family regulations, a chronological autobiography, 48 volumes of essays, and a massive 93 volumes of poetry. The local histories and most of the diary survived in the provincial library, but no one was particularly interested in the poetry and essays. Chiqiao was a paper-making village and during the Cultural Revolution in the 1960s many old books were thrown into the paper vats and pulped. Even so the list of works inscribed at Liu's death was not complete: the Shanxi Provincial Library also holds a collection of petitions to the local government by Liu, entitled *A Glance at Present Conditions in Taiyuan County*, and 14 volumes of *A Brief Account of the*

Communist Bandits' Harassment of Shanxi, which Liu compiled in his old age and consists mainly of articles transcribed from the local newspapers.[10]

Of all of these writings the one that Liu Dapeng himself considered most important was his account of the local district, the *Jinci Gazetteer*. When, as he occasionally did, he listed his writings he put this first. Gazetteers were usually compiled by committees headed by acting or retired officials and were intended to be useful for administrative purposes. The first gazetteer for Taiyuan county, where Liu lived, had been published in 1552, and new versions were compiled in 1713 and 1826, with an appendix added in 1882. Liu's interest in gazetteers fitted with the general enthusiasm for practical scholarship that was a feature of the 1880s, when he was studying in Taiyuan city. He follows the standard format, writing about the temples and pavilions, mountains and rivers, historic buildings, religious festivals, inscriptions, schools, local residents, and plants; he transcribes essays and poems about the area, describes the irrigation system and historical events, and ends with a section on local myths and folktales labeled "miscellaneous." The conventional format makes the gazetteer look like the officially sponsored gazetteers of the period, but this is misleading. Liu's account is much longer than the earlier Taiyuan county gazetteers and only covers the part of the county that was considered Jinci township, so inevitably much of it is his own writing. Moreover, because he compiled the gazetteer entirely by himself without any official support, it was possible for him to use the text as a vehicle for his opinions and even at times his personal story. So when he describes the temples at Jinci, he reminisces about his father taking him round them as a child, something that would be unthinkable in a conventional gazetteer. Liu's *Jinci Gazetteer* is not only an unusually detailed description of a local area at a certain moment in its history but also a deeply personal document.[11]

But who did Liu Dapeng expect would read all this writing? Not one of his 400 volumes was published in his lifetime. Of course this did not stop manuscript copies from circulating. The *Jinci Gazetteer* was clearly intended as a work of local reference: Liu explains in the introduction that the section on the Jin river irrigation system was written because the villages that controlled the system would not allow outsiders to see their records and this gave rise to disputes. At the very least the manuscript would have been read by the three friends who wrote prefaces; Liu's father, who also wrote a preface; and his four eldest sons, who helped copy and check the drafts for the final version. Many years later Liu presented a copy to the county government. He clearly hoped that the *Jinci Gazetteer* would be published or at least circulated, but I doubt that in his later years he imagined that his diary could be published. It is written on the worst quality paper of any of his works: as late as 1936, when his family was almost penniless, he managed to find plain, if coarse, paper for his *Brief Account of the Communist Bandits' Harassment of Shanxi*, but the diary was written on scrap paper from as early as 1925. The children certainly used to steal volumes and read them when he was out of the house, but presumably Liu did not know about this. There is no mention in the diary of anyone's reading it, and little indication that he himself reread earlier entries. Nevertheless the diary was kept in the cupboard in his room alongside all his other writings and was listed along with his other works on the inscription set up when he died. Liu may not have expected that it would be read, but in his diary as in his other works, he was writing words that others could have seen, and might even have found morally uplifting.[12]

In fact the whole idea that there is a difference between books that other people read and a diary that is considered a private document would not have made much sense to Liu. When we look at two autobiographical essays he included in the gazetteer, we can see that he was not so much concerned with finding out who he really was as in finding a role for himself and overcoming the tension between his own feelings and experiences and the demands of that role. In these essays, as so often in his diary, Liu is not just writing a text but also creating an identity for himself that he can act out in his everyday life. The essays are placed at the end of his biographies of well-known local men and are titled "The Man of Wohu Mountain" and "The Man Awakened from Dreams." "The Man of Wohu Mountain" reads:

> I do not know who he is, but his home is at the foot of Wohu Mountain so it is used as his name. From his birth he was stubborn and stupid: he was six years old before he learned to speak. As he grew older he loved reading books, but he understood very little of them. Every time he read a book he put it down as soon as he had got the general outline and read something else, so he saw through a glass darkly and missed the subtle meanings and profound language. But in the writings of the ancients he read of the man who had met his death calmly adjusting his cap, the man who shot an arrow

bearing an important message into a besieged city, the friends who sang brave songs when parting in dangerous circumstances, and the men who willingly laid aside the seal of office. All these were heroes, men whose moral courage in situations of extreme danger was outstanding, men of determination and compassion who sang bravely even as the tears rolled down their cheeks.

He also came to like wine, but he is not a strong drinker. As soon as he drinks a little he gets tipsy, but never so drunk that he forgets to behave properly. His family is poor and he cannot often get hold of wine, but when he gets it he drinks it straight away. He prefers to drink alone so that he does not have to share the wine.

A few years ago, at the age of forty, he passed the provincial exams. He has been north to the capital twice but failed the national exams both times. Because he lacked the commitment needed to pass the exams, he just visited Qing mountain and Baiyun temple and did not care about success or failure, poverty or wealth.

He eats very simply and cares more about pleasing his parents. He loves the mountain scenery and likes to wander great distances. But because his family is poor and his parents are old, he cannot do exactly as he pleases, so he can only get this pleasure quietly by going for walks in the mountains near his home, drinking wine, writing poems, and spending the day reciting them to himself.

He most likes to work in the fields. Whenever he goes to the fields he falls in with the old farmers and fishermen. They talk about the mulberry trees and rice paddies, discuss the amount of sunshine and rainfall, and reckon the dates for ploughing and sowing. After chatting for a while he picks up his plough and starts work laboring alongside the hired men and contract workers. But although he is ploughing the fields, he has already forgotten what he is doing. Indeed he not only forgets that he is ploughing but even why he is ploughing; and not only why he is ploughing but the men working alongside him. If he were not living hidden away in the country-side, how could he have this pleasure? There is no greater pleasure than to forget both your actions and your thoughts, and there is also no greater pleasure than to farm the land to support your parents and bring up your children. Once, when farming did not provide enough money, he also taught to support his family. He does not like spending his time with rich people and he avoids all contact with Buddhist and Daoist priests. All his comings and goings are with woodcutters, fishermen, mountain farmers, and aged rustics. He knows nothing of government or disorder, never hears of official promotions or dismissals. His foot soldiers are the iris and cassia flowers and his subordinates the deer.

He is not desperate to make money or be tied up in worldly affairs. He has enough to live on where he is, is content with his lot, and enjoys the company of the people he meets. He wears simple clothes and eats only vegetables. He wanders between heaven and earth without a moment's worry: for him the honors and rewards of holding office are like things seen in a dream. The men who took the exams with him plot to become officials; he laughs but does not say anything, just excuses himself. His motto is the ninth section of the *Classic of Changes* passage on the hexagram called "The Worm," where it says, "Lofty is the determination of the man who does not serve the prince."[13]

This is Liu's own version of himself. It is based on the ancient ideal of the hermit, with images of fishermen and mulberry trees, neither of which existed in this part of Shanxi, and quotes a famous autobiographical essay by the fourth-century poet Tao Qian, who retired from the distasteful world of the court and officialdom to a rural idyll.[14]

But the biography of the Man of Wohu Mountain is also a quite straightforward narrative of the main events of Liu's life up until the time he wrote it in 1903. Chiqiao did indeed lie at the foot of Wohu Mountain. Liu had received a standard classical education, during which he had been much drawn to stories of heroic valor. After many years at the village school he had attempted the state examinations. He had passed the county exams in 1878 and the provincial exams in 1894. In 1895 and 1898 he traveled to Beijing for the national exams, but both times he failed. After that he lived with his parents, went for walks in the mountains behind the village, worked in the fields, and did indeed live a relatively humble life eating mostly vegetables. Interestingly, Liu scarcely mentions the ten years he had spent teaching. Working as an employee in someone else's home did not fit his image of himself and was left out, even though he was actually working as a tutor when he wrote the autobiography. He also omits his wife and children. He had been married in his teens to a young woman from a nearby village and had four sons. Family life was important to him, but did not fit the image that he was trying to convey.

The vision of himself as the Man of Wohu Mountain was important to Liu Dapeng. Images of himself as a hermit, a recluse who has rejected public office and chosen a life in the countryside, recur throughout his writings. Several years after he wrote the *Jinci Gazetteer*, he became involved in the local coal industry and wrote accounts of two of the mining valleys. In these he repeatedly uses the image of the valleys as a "Peach Blossom Spring," referring to Tao Qian's famous poem about an idyllic rural world cut off from history. When Tao Qian wrote poems about the joys of life as a farmer, he was playing with the tension between his life as a peasant farmer and his true status as a member of the ruling class. Tao Qian was a member of the ruling class who imagined himself as a farmer. It would be perfectly possible to read Liu Dapeng's writings in this way, but I wonder if it might not be more correct to say that Liu Dapeng was a farmer who imagined himself as a member of the ruling class. Tao Qian, like other hermits in this tradition, consciously rejected the life of a government official; Liu Dapeng failed the national examinations and therefore never had the opportunity. For him the image of the Man of Wohu Mountain is a consolation, a claim to status in his local community, and a way of maintaining his dignity in the face of failure.[15]

Liu Dapeng's second autobiographical essay in the *Jinci Gazetteer* describes the Man Awakened from Dreams. This is also the name under which he writes his own more personal contributions to the gazetteer. The Man Awakened from Dreams is a compulsive dreamer:

> When he was a child he often had dreams and when he grew up he had even more. At first he thought it strange that his dreams were so many and various, and afterward he was puzzled that they were so illusory.[16]

Eventually he realized that life was a dream, but it was a dream from which he was unable to awake.[17] He took the name The Man Awakened from Dreams after one particular dream that was to change his whole attitude:

> In 1893 in the month of the winter solstice on the night before His Highness's birthday, the Man Awakened from Dreams dreamt he saw a man with an aged face, slanting eyebrows, double pupils in his eyes, big ears, a big nose, a large mouth and dark moustache, a sleek and glossy complexion, and a tall and impressive physique. He looked severe but also gentle, and his

voice was stern. He might have been sixty years old or more. I do not know
who he was. As soon as the Man Awakened from Dreams met him he felt a
sense of deep respect. He approached and asked him for instruction saying,
"Since I began to study I have frittered away my good intentions and have
never really tried to be good or seriously attempted to reform myself. Nor
have I really tried to love and serve my parents, love my brothers, be loyal,
trustworthy, well-behaved, upright, and ashamed of my faults. I just spend
the days eating till I am full and whiling away the time. I am already thirty-
seven years old, and have not done a single good deed or had a single scholarly achievement. When I think about it I am very much afraid and full of
regret. I have realized that it is no use to complain about the past and that
I should look to the future. I have tried to be like the sages and worthies,
but I did not have sufficient motivation. Would it be possible for you, sir, to
teach me?"

The old man said, "So that is what you want! I am old, but in fact I have
never studied. For you to ask me to teach you is not just like asking a blind
man the way; it is also like asking a deaf man to listen for you. I have never
seen it work."

The Man Awakened from Dreams was now even more aware that this
was no ordinary person and he kept asking the old man to teach him. Then
the old man told him,

"If you wish to learn to be a sage, all you need to do is be sincere and respectful in your dealings, you do not need to search for anything else. There
was not one of the sages and worthy men of ancient times who did not succeed as a result of being sincere and respectful."

When the Man Awakened from Dreams heard this he felt as if cold water
had been poured over him. He woke up suddenly startled, leant on his pillow
and said to himself quietly,

"What a strange dream that was. There is no greater fault than failing to
be sincere and respectful because it causes so much damage. While I was
dreaming today I really learned something and have found a cure for my
troubles."

Then he knew that he had passed his life in a dream, and only on that
day had he finally woken up.[18]

Like the Man of Wohu Mountain, the persona of the Man Awakened from
Dreams grows out of the contradictions between Liu's vision of himself as an
educated man and potential government official and his actual situation. But

the image of the Man Awakened from Dreams is a much more complex and arresting one than the Man of Wohu Mountain. In the dream the strange appearance of the old man marks him as a divine figure, probably the Daoist immortal Lu Dongbin whose temple at Jinci was one of Liu's favorite haunts. In a well-known story, which Liu mentions a few lines later, Lu Dongbin met a student on his way to the examinations. The student fell asleep while Lu was cooking up some millet and thought that he had become a rich and successful official, then awoke and realized that it had all been a dream. Lu Dongbin explained to the student that all worldly achievement is merely an empty dream, a classic Daoist view. Liu Dapeng takes this idea but imbues it with Confucian moral values, for in his dream the immortal teaches him in words that were central to the moral vision of Confucianism as it was officially taught in the Qing dynasty: "All you need to do is be sincere and respectful in your dealings."[19] Receiving this advice Liu feels as if he has been suddenly doused with cold water. He awakens to the heart of the Confucian moral order at the same time that he awakens to the vanity of worldly ambition, and yet the Confucian moral order is based on the link between morality and power. When he calls himself The Man Awakened from Dreams, Liu is expressing his exclusion from political power, but he is also pointing up for us both the fragility and the complexity of the Confucian moral order.

TWO

The Confucian Scholar

In the family history he wrote, Liu Dapeng traced his ancestry back to Liu Zhiyuan, a tenth-century emperor of the short-lived Later Han dynasty. According to local tradition the emperor did not die but escaped to the mountains after the dynasty was overthrown and settled in the village of Wayao. He became a popular local deity worshiped not only by the Liu family of Wayao, who claimed to be his descendants, but also in at least one of the plains villages. To have an emperor and local deity as the founder of one's family might be prestigious, but the need to look so far back also suggests the lack of success of the family's more immediate ancestors. The first member of the family to settle in Chiqiao was probably a migrant laborer who came down from Wayao some time in the eighteenth century. The Chiqiao villagers specialized in making paper, an industry that provided regular employment for strong young men and made the village a magnet for migrants. Already in the nineteenth century the village had far more people than could be supported from its agricultural land. At the time Liu Dapeng's father, Liu

Ming, was born, in the 1820s, the family inhabited a small, tumbledown courtyard with two or three buildings. Like many other village families they did not own any land.[1]

Liu Ming did not go into the paper-making industry; instead, like many Shanxi men of all social classes, he left home to work as a merchant. Shanxi is cut off by mountains from the north China plain and the coast, but forms a corridor linking central China to Mongolia and the Russian steppes. From the fifteenth century to the seventeenth Mongolia was China's main strategic frontier, and the government licensed groups of merchants to provision the frontier armies, allowing them to operate the salt and tea trades in return. Shanxi men were well-positioned to obtain these licenses and used them to build trading networks that stretched from the tea farms of Fujian on China's southeast coast and the salt fields near Tianjin in the north to the trading posts on the Mongolian frontier where they bought horses and other livestock. Then in the mid-seventeenth century China, along with Mongolia, became part of the expanding Qing empire. This put an end to the licensed trade, but the great Shanxi trading houses were well-placed to take advantage of the new opportunities in Mongolia, which they entered in the immediate wake of the Qing armies. They sold tea, silk, and many daily items imported from China to the Mongols, often lending them the money to buy these things, and brought the Mongols' livestock to sell into China. The trade was highly exploitative and extremely profitable. Then in the early eighteenth century the Qing signed a treaty with Russia allowing for trade at the Mongolian border town of Kiakhta, where it rapidly came to be controlled by the Shanxi merchants. Tea and silk were exported to Russia, while sheepskins, woolen cloth, iron, leather, and livestock were imported. When the trade was at its height in the nineteenth century, Russia was China's second-largest trading partner after England, and 60 percent of Russian exports to China were passing through Kiakhta.[2]

The profits of this national and international trade flowed into Shanxi, where the great merchant houses were based, and created opportunities and wealth there. One Qing official famously claimed (when proposing a tax increase) that Guangdong and Shanxi were the two richest provinces in the country. This reflected the situation in the 1850s, when much of the central and eastern China was affected by rebellions, but it does give a sense of how Shanxi was perceived. Alexander Williamson, who traveled through north

China in the 1860s, wrote that the Shanxi cities were more numerous and prosperous than those anywhere else. The villages, too, he found wealthy and prosperous with many imported goods in evidence, including large quantities of Russian cloth and woolens. Liu Ming used to tell his son that the Chiqiao businesses had been wealthy enough to put on three days of opera each year. The importance of trade created a culture in which many young men expected to spend a large part of their working lives away from home and used the money they earned to support their families who remained behind. One Taigu village surveyed in 1935, after years of economic troubles, still had 36 men working in the county town, 14 in other villages in the county, 24 in other counties in Shanxi, and 28 in other provinces, primarily in the northeast and Manchuria. This was 17 percent of the total male population of the village, but over 30 percent of men in their late teens to their late twenties. Liu Ming went from Chiqiao to Limanzhuang village in Taigu county on the other side of the plain, to run a wood store that sold furniture and coffins. He worked there until he was in his seventies, coming home only for New Year and occasionally for other major holidays. Liu Ming comes across in his son's diary as a man of ambition and steely determination. His carpentry shop flourished, and the money he earned paid for a fine new house for the family and for the purchase of some land in Chiqiao. Although they were never as wealthy as Chiqiao's two leading families, the Lius were comfortably off and respected. Liu Dapeng's education was to be his father's crowning achievement.[3]

Liu Dapeng was born in 1857. In later years he remembered the prosperity of the village in his childhood and particularly the New Year celebrations, with lanterns, bright fires, and street performances by groups of villagers. He was the eldest son and his father, on his occasional visits home, took him to temple fairs and to see the great temples at nearby Jinci. But he also had a younger brother and a sister to play with. Afterward he thought of childhood as a time of laughing and crying, eating and drinking, dancing, singing, and jumping. Boys played together in large groups. They climbed trees, played on the ice in the paddy fields in the winter, played hide and seek, kept crickets in woven baskets, and went fishing. But most of their games were competitive games of skill: throwing pebbles into circles drawn in the dust, tossing jacks made from small stones or sheep bones, hitting the "fat pig," a small piece of wood that was flicked up from the ground and then hit with a bat (the batsman then had to guess exactly how many bat lengths away it had fallen), and playing checkerboard games on lines drawn in the dust with small stones for pieces. Like other children they also reenacted the adult world in their games. Sometimes the boys would play at being King Yan, the king of hell, and his judge and catch another boy to interrogate. Another popular game called "hitting the crowing cock" was more complex. Stones were laid out in a row at an increasing distance from a line where the boys stood. The stones were given names, with the furthest away being the Crowing Cock, then the Judge (or King Yan), and the closest being the Little Devil and, finally, the Pig. The boys took turns standing behind the line and throwing a stone to hit one of the stones laid out on the ground. Each boy took the identity of the stone he had hit and the game went on until the Crowing Cock was hit. Then the Judge, the boy who had hit the most distant stone, was allowed to order the Little Devil to extract a penalty from the Pig. Even before Liu Dapeng started school he would have been familiar with an image of the world in which contests of skill led to positions of power that were associated with government offices and ranks.[4]

Liu started school at the age of eight. His teacher was Liu Wuyang, a lower-degree-holder who ran a school in Chiqiao. This was an ordinary village school, where the teacher was paid a small amount by the parents of each of his pupils. The boys brought their own benches and tables, which they placed under the eaves of his house in summer or inside, on the heated brick platform, in the winter. Liu Wenbing, an acquaintance of Liu Dapeng's from nearby Xugou county, records how when a boy first entered a school his father brought him in, the boy carrying the book he was to study while his father brought gifts of food for the teacher. In the school was an altar where incense sticks burned before the tablet of Confucius. The new pupil got down on his knees to kowtow to the tablet and then to the teacher. He then bowed to each of the other pupils in turn. There was a meal provided by the father who then left. Liu Ming used to remind his son in later years that his aim in sending him to study was that he would be an honor to his family, but he also wanted him to have good relations with his neighbors, to respect his teachers and friends, to be upright and of good character, to be charitable to the poor, to be on his guard against greed, and to improve himself by learning not to want too much. With these words Liu Ming set up the tension that was to plague Liu Dapeng for many years to come between education as a means to social mobility and education as a form of moral indoctrination.[5]

Education brought honor primarily because it provided access to government office. Boys who did well at school could be prepared for the state examinations. The examinations for the lowest, licentiate, degree were held at the county level and passing them brought considerable prestige in the local community. Licentiate-degree-holders were qualified to compete in provincial examinations, and then, if they passed, to travel to Beijing for the final, national exams. Passing these would earn them a position in the state bureaucracy and thus place them at the pinnacle of the social scale and bring both wealth and honor to their families. Even as a child Liu Dapeng could hardly have failed to be aware of the importance of degrees to his father, who had passed the test for one of the less competitive military degrees, which required physical feats of strength and written tests on military texts. Military degrees were common enough in these Shanxi villages, where martial arts were a popular recreation, but were still a source of family pride: Liu Ming kept his bow, spear, and shield hanging on the walls of his house.[6] Part of the prestige came from the fact that the odds against success in the regular civil examinations were extremely high. Liu Ming presumably expected that his son would study for a few years, learn to read and write, and then leave school to be apprenticed to a business. So when he spoke to his son he balanced the honor to be won from a degree against schooling as a form of moral indoctrination that would make the boy into a good member of the community.

Education was seen as a form of moral indoctrination largely because of the nature of the textbooks. Like other boys of his generation Liu Dapeng would have begun his studies by memorizing one or two of the primers used for teaching introductory reading. From there Liu Wuyang moved his pupils straight to texts with a strong moral content: the *Classic of Filial Piety* and the *Elementary Learning*. Liu Dapeng then began to study the *Analects* of Confucius, which is the first of the *Four Books*, a compilation of earlier texts made in the twelfth century as a school primer. After the *Four Books*, he set to work to memorize the full canon prescribed by the government for the official examinations. Over the next fifteen years of his life he memorized the *Odes*, the *Documents*, the *Rites of Zhou*, the *Book of Rites*, the *Classic of Changes*, the *Spring and Autumn Annals* and its ancient commentary, the *Zuozhuan*, the *Book of Ritual*, and finally two more ancient commentaries, the *Gongyang* and *Guliang* texts. By the end of the fifteen years he could recite all these books, which he calculated contained 626,306 words. This massive feat of memorization occupied much of the time Liu spent in education. He would have brought his book to Liu Wuyang who would decide the day's task, punctuate the text, and read it aloud. As a small boy Liu Dapeng would have read the text after his teacher until he could read the characters correctly and then returned to his seat to start learning by reading the passage aloud. Education experts suggested that passages should be read at least two hundred and preferably three hundred times the day they were first learned. They were then constantly repeated to ensure that they remained in the memory: all his life Liu Dapeng would be able to remember and quote the texts he had learned as a boy.[7]

The syllabus Liu studied was formulated by the government for examination purposes, but the texts themselves comprised a body of learning that had long been associated with Confucius, either because he was said to have read and approved of them or because they were written by his disciples. (The only text that was claimed to be by Confucius himself was the *Spring and Autumn Annals*.) These canonical texts, known as the classics, were in fact only a part of a large body of material in a variety of genres, composed over many centuries, but by selecting them and imposing the use of a standard set of commentaries the Qing government limited the range of possible interpretations. The commentaries followed a style of interpretation that had been developed in the twelfth century and emphasized the moral content of the texts. The values of sincerity and respect that Liu Dapeng was taught by the divine figure in his dream are central to this interpretation of the Confucian texts.

Most boys in this area left school after three or four years, but Liu Dapeng must have been a promising student and Liu Ming decided that his son should continue his education. He would then have paid a new fee for "beginning explanations" so that the teacher would begin to give his son lectures on the content of the classics. As a lecturer Liu Wuyang emphasized the moral and philosophical content of the texts and tried hard to keep his pupils from limiting themselves to learning how to pass the government examinations. Many teachers used standard volumes of written lectures to explain the classical texts, but Liu Wuyang explained the context of the passage and used recent events and local people to illustrate the behavior of the "gentleman" or the "mean-minded man" as Liu Dapeng himself was to do in later years. The pupils were taught to judge themselves and those around them in terms of the values they learned from the texts. Liu Dapeng learned that memorizing a book should alter the way a person behaved in everyday life and that his reading and actions should be in concord.[8]

The formal, ritualized behavior of the schoolroom also inculcated certain values and attitudes. Later in life, when Liu became a teacher, he collected sets of school rules from his part of Taiyuan county. The physical behavior of pupils was an important part of these rules. One set, used in a school conducted in one of the Jinci town temples, required pupils to sit upright on their benches with their feet together, walk slowly, stand up straight with their hands together, speak quietly, and bow from the waist. The rules Liu later established for his own school included walking properly, speaking carefully and playing no games, for "the beginning of study is to keep the body still."[9] Similar rules inculcated a respectful attitude toward books: pupils should wash their hands before sitting down to read, should avoid touching the book as far as possible, keeping it a few inches from the edge of the table and using the index finger of the right hand to turn the pages. Books were of course valuable objects, but the respect with which they were treated also reflected the perceived moral value of their contents. A Western missionary tells a story of a Shanxi scholar of this period who "took up a book of the classics from the table and deliberately placed it on the floor."[10] He then claimed that no one else in Shanxi would have dared do such a thing. No doubt the claim was an exaggeration. Nevertheless the deliberate nature of the action, combined with the exaggerated tone of the comment, suggest that to students of this generation respect for the book, and especially the Confucian classics, was deeply ingrained by the time they reached adulthood.

But this moral content was always intertwined with preparation for the examinations and ultimately for official life. Liu studied alongside Wang Keqin, whose family lived up in the mountains, and Zhang Zhen, an older student who had succeeded in persuading his family to allow him to give up a commercial apprenticeship and return to his studies. Each month they attended practice examinations organized by the county academy and marked by its headmaster and the county magistrate. For this they received a small stipend.

Meanwhile the students continued to memorize texts and to practice their calligraphy, but they also learned how to structure an exam essay and write poems. Wang Keqin left the school after eight years, but Liu continued for sixteen. He and Zhang Zhen even studied some of the philological techniques that had become fashionable in the eighteenth century, though genuine familiarity with these ideas relied on large libraries of a sort unthinkable for a Shanxi village school. At an underlying level these techniques were philosophically opposed to the orthodox morality Liu Wuyang taught his students, but they had been one of the major intellectual fashions since the eighteenth century, and thus examination candidates might be expected to be familiar with them. The fact that Liu Wuyang taught them suggests the overriding importance of the official examinations in structuring even this village-level education. And beyond the examinations lay the ultimate aim: government office. Everyone knew the story of how some two hundred years earlier Yang Eryou from nearby Jinci town had passed the examinations and risen to hold some of the highest offices in the land. No one from the area had reached such dizzy heights since then, indeed no one had risen above the lowly post of education official, but even that was a government position and Liu, at least, believed in the possibility that he might become not only an official but a leading member of the court.[11]

As Liu prepared for the examinations the drought began. Drought is always a problem in Shanxi because not only is there little rainfall, but the farmers need the rain to fall at exactly the right times of year for their crops to succeed. Every year farmers looked at the sky and worried: if the rain fell too late they would not be able to plant the wheat; if rain fell for the planting but then did not fall on the seedlings, the wheat would wither and only the hardier (but less valuable) millet and sorghum would survive; in the worst scenario of all, the millet and sorghum too would fail. Later in life when Liu himself became a farmer, he spent a lot of time worrying like this; but even as a pupil in the village school he must have been aware of the villagers' main topic of conversation as the drought lengthened and the panic began. For three years the farmers prayed to the Dragon Kings, the deities who lived in pools in the mountains behind the village and were thought to control the rainfall. The Chiqiao men went as a group up into the mountains, where they heaped stones into a cairn, topping them with willow branches and sprinkling water over them. They also joined larger processions from the neighboring village of Guchengying. The men walked in their bare feet, with wreaths of willow branches on their heads, some of them carrying heavy iron implements to express their repentance and the sincerity of their pleas. In Chiqiao the families along the main street put little altars outside their doors with candles, bowls of water, and willow branches. As the procession approached they could hear the pleading "*Amitofo, Amitofo, Amitofo*," as the men called over and over again on the Amitabha Buddha to help them. When the procession passed slowly by, some knelt down, others burned paper money, while yet others dipped willow branches in bowls of water and waved them, scattering the procession with a sign of the rain they so desperately prayed for. The men went on up into the mountains to a temple of the Dragon King that stood beside a small pool. For three days they ate only thin gruel and prayed day and night; when no rain fell they made the gruel still thinner and repeated their prayers. But still no rain fell.[12]

Drought was always terrifying for farmers, who relied directly on agriculture to make a living, but in normal times the higher prices would attract imports and drought would not lead to famine. In fact Shanxi's commercial wealth had allowed the population to expand well above levels that could be supported from local agriculture; since at least the 1820s the center and south of the province had relied on large imports of grain from Shaanxi province to the west and the new lands being opened up in Mongolia to the north. But now these areas, too, had been affected by drought and production had declined. At the same time the trading networks, which usually brought so much wealth into the province, were suffering from the aftermath of the great Taiping rebellion, which had wrecked much of central and eastern China in the previous decade, and the other regional rebellions that followed it. When trade declined some Shanxi men came home unemployed, while others stopped sending money to their families. Meanwhile a big military campaign against Muslim rebels in the northwest of the country absorbed large amounts of neighboring Shaanxi's grain production. Thus while grain prices rose, buying power fell.[13]

Drought was not necessarily bad for farmers: in Chiqiao much of the farmland was irrigated by the Jin river, which did not dry up, so farmers must have profited from rising prices. But nevertheless the drought was a disaster. Chiqiao was one of many villages which specialized in industries that collapsed as food prices rose. Seventy percent of Chiqiao's population was primarily occupied in the paper industry. Many of the paper makers earned their living from day to day at the best of times, using the money they earned in the morning to buy food for the evening meal. Now as grain prices rose and the market for paper collapsed, they were the first to suffer. People began to leave the village. At some point, while Liu Dapeng himself continued his studies, his younger brother was sent away to find work; like many others, he never returned.[14]

In 1877, in the midst of the drought, Liu Dapeng sat for the government examinations for the first time and failed. That winter people suffered from the cold as well as the shortage of food. Normally coal was cheap and abundant, but the famine was even worse in the mountains, where the agriculture was totally dependent on rainfall. Carters did not dare fetch coal from the pitheads because they feared that if they went alone their pack animals would be stolen and eaten. In the mountain villages whole families died of hunger in their homes, but in the plains villages, though many fled, most of those who remained survived until the next summer, when the rains still did not fall and epidemics struck. The victims suffered from fevers and headache; in good times only the very young and the very old might have died of such fevers. Now, when people were weakened by two years of hunger, almost anyone could succumb, and since the diseases were highly infectious the rich died alongside the poor. By the end of the summer almost 70 percent of the population of Chiqiao village was dead. Liu was shut away in the schoolhouse studying; the dying, he said, was so ghastly it was "unbearable to look at."[15] Across the province millions perished, but each individual death was a tragedy that marked the lives of those who survived it long afterward. More than fifty years later Liu Dapeng's grandson remembers his grandfather going out to the crossroads at the Qingming festival to burn, as he always did, a purseful of paper money for his sister who had died young.[16]

That summer, at the age of twenty-one, Liu went to Taiyuan city to retake the county examinations. This time he scored in the top sixteen of the eighty taking the exam from Taiyuan county and passed.[17] He was now a holder of the licentiate degree. But what did it mean to pass the examinations in such a time? When news that relief was being distributed reached the village, a group of Chiqiao men gathered in the village office to decide what to do. According to Liu, someone said that he had heard that the emperor had given an order to provide relief aid and a lot of money had been issued to the magistrate, but it had not reached the village. "Aren't we the dynasty's commoners? How can they turn a deaf ear to us?" he asked. Then an old man spoke up: "If our Emperor has ordered that we should be relieved then we must surely receive the money. Now the magistrate has not come to give us aid, but how can we just sit and wait to die? We ought to go to the county town and beg him."[18]

A group of men went down to the county town but the magistrate refused to give them any aid and threatened to have them beaten. The men were terrified of what the consequences would be for them and their families; they fled and more than ten of them died or disappeared. Liu's teacher, Liu Wuyang, was furious when he heard what had happened. He took several of the older men with him and went down to the county town to speak to the magistrate. The magistrate was forced to issue them a small amount of millet.

The famine was a natural disaster, but most of those who wrote about it would have agreed with the Chiqiao villagers that it was also the government's responsibility. Timothy Richard, a British missionary who collected and distributed aid for famine victims in the worst-hit parts of the province, felt as Liu Dapeng did that he could hardly bear to look on. He wrote that "this last journey southwards made me so sick at heart that I wished I could return with my eyes closed and ears stopped."[19] When he also saw the difficulties the government had in getting grain transported into the province over the steep mountain passes to the east, he was convinced that railways would have prevented the disaster and devoted the rest of his life to promoting science and modernization in China.[20] Liu Dapeng's account of the villagers who were refused aid by the magistrate suggests that he saw the problem and therefore the solution differently. He emphasizes the culpability of district-level officials who failed to understand local conditions, claiming that there was no need to relieve villages irrigated by the Jin river.[21] They wrongly assumed that most villagers were farmers and any other activities were an agricultural sideline, whereas in fact in Chiqiao most families worked in the paper industry and did not farm at all, so when the market for paper collapsed and grain prices rose, they suffered terribly. But in addition to this Liu claimed that the reason many poor areas did not receive any relief was that "the local officials and gentry did not carry out the orders they received in a charitable way."[22] Some did not take the problem seriously and delayed taking action, others felt that they were beyond the reach of the law, and others actually embezzled the money themselves. The implied solution was for the dynasty to appoint upright and well-informed local officials who felt a genuine concern for the people. This was the role for which Liu felt that his education was training him, and seeing the catastrophic results of the famine can only have strengthened his determination.

But in order to be appointed to an official position Liu still had to pass both the provincial and national examinations. Three years after passing the licentiate degree at the age of twenty-four, he left the village school and moved to the Chongxiu Academy in Taiyuan city to prepare for the provincial examinations. Moving to the academy took Liu away from both his community and his family for the first time. Looking back on it, he remembered how some of the students recited loudly after everyone else had gone to bed (even if others had an examination early the next morning), kept the cooks waiting until late into the evening before eating, and slept through early morning lectures. His shock at these examples of selfishness reflect the extent to which most of the time the students lived and worked to the same timetable: they studied at the same time, slept at the same time, ate together, and rose at the same time for morning lectures. Not only was Liu separated from his family but he was living in a very different type of community: a community of elite men whose lives were focused round the structures of the state. He had grown up in the world of the village, where the family was the most important social structure. Men's and women's worlds were clearly defined and separated, but women were nevertheless a part of life.[23] As children boys and girls played different games and the school was an entirely male environment, but within the family men's and women's worlds intertwined. Liu's mother was the dominant figure in the family since his father was away in Taigu nearly all year. Liu himself had been married for several years and his wife would have been busy round the house cooking, mending, helping occasionally with any farm work that could be done without leaving the courtyard, and caring for their two small sons. When Liu entered the academy he left the family and entered the public world of the state. Family was important to the rhetoric of this public world: the proper understanding and expression of family relations was central to the Confucian ideas Liu was being taught. But in terms of everyday life the family played little part and women simply did not exist.

This elite male community bound students together in a way that both created and conferred social status. Lectures, which were often held at dawn, were attended by all the teaching staff who sat facing the lecturer while the students sat in rows at the side. All the students were licentiates while their teachers held provincial and sometimes even national degrees. Both students and teachers wore full formal dress, their hats topped with the decorations that designated their official rank. The formal dress reflected the fact that the purpose of the lectures was to train a new cohort of government officials. Almost all future Shanxi officials would be graduates of one of the three academies in Taiyuan city, and a few might go on to hold some of the most powerful positions in the land. In recognition of this potential future status, all students were addressed by the academy staff, despite their youth, as "your honor."[24] But the students' prestige was not a result only of their degrees and possible future careers; it also grew out of the wealth and social status of the families of many of the young men who entered the academy. Those who attended the Taiyuan city academies were drawn from much wealthier families than those who had sat the licentiate examinations alongside Liu. To get a son through the licentiate degree one had to forgo his labor for many years, but the actual costs of schooling in the village were low. Supporting a son to live away from home in Taiyuan and attend the academy so he could try to attain a higher degree was a much greater financial commitment.

The heady mixture of existing social prestige and possible future power was inevitably felt most strongly by those students like Liu who came from poorer backgrounds. For Liu even the most commonplace activities of everyday life in the academy were a reminder of how different his life here was from his life at home. This was a society in which food was the great marker of social status. At the bottom levels of society simply having enough to eat marked the comfortably off from the poor. Above that the crucial distinction was the type of grain eaten. The poorest of the poor ate only the cheapest grains, sorghum and maize, while those who were better off ate millet. Most Chiqiao people, including Liu's family, lived on a mixture of these grains and vegetable dishes. At holidays they ate wheat flour noodles and meat dishes. Really wealthy families lived on wheat noodles and ate rice for special occasions. They also ate meat dishes on a regular basis. Later, Liu remembered an occasion on which one of his friends at the academy had teased him saying,

> "You are good at being frugal, but why does your food and drink have to be as poor as this? Do you think your stomach is too fat?"

Liu replied,

> "The point of our studying here is to improve our morals, not our food. You say my food is too poor, but every day I eat noodles made of wheat flour or of mixed wheat and bean flour, and I sometimes have meat and vegetables with them. I often think of my parents at home who wouldn't know whether to eat food as good as this, so when I give myself this I feel very lucky. And since I am fortunate enough to be here because of my parents' kindness, I think your words are rather inappropriate."[25]

The friend could think of no reply to this and left. He thought the food Liu was eating was so poor Liu must be showing off his frugality, a virtue central to the Confucian ethics they were both being taught. But Liu was in fact eating food that was better than he would have had at home.

Liu knew that he wasn't good at being teased. He tells another story of how one day he and two friends were sitting in his study at the academy chatting, when a couple of other students came in and began to joke. One of Liu's friends said to him,

> "Do you realize that it's you they're making fun of?"

Liu smiled but did not say anything. Then his other friend said to the other students,

> "Old Liu doesn't usually joke around with us. It is really very rude of you to begin to tease him as soon as you see him."

The student replied that they had not been making fun of Liu and had always treated him with respect. But after that he did not tease Liu again.[26] We can imagine that Liu was probably being teased again for his attempts to embody the Confucian values he was being taught: he was after all the sort of student who could be suspected of eating poor food simply to demonstrate his frugality. Even the kindly friend who spoke up for him drew a line between "us," the people who joke, and Liu, the outsider. Wealthy young men did not need to take their studies particularly seriously. Their families had made an investment to allow them to compete more successfully in the examination system, but if they failed to pass the examinations, there were many other opportunities available to them. Liu's father had invested a far greater proportion of his wealth to send his son to the academy. As a result Liu's status was more dependent on his academic achievements and he was under more pressure to succeed academically. Moreover, the fact that the system had already allowed him to come so far encouraged him to internalize what he was taught to a greater degree than other students. Liu was teased at the academy because he took his studies so seriously; it seems likely that he did this in part because he came from a much less wealthy background than most of his peers.[27]

Liu Dapeng was becoming more and more deeply committed to the moral content of the Confucian texts he had studied from childhood, but that did not mean that he was immune to the intellectual atmosphere of the time. He saw himself as facing a choice between literary studies explicitly geared toward passing the examinations, and putting his efforts into practical studies that would prepare him for life as an official. This emphasis on practical studies was one of the main strands of eighteenth- and nineteenth-century thought and was very much in fashion in Taiyuan at this time. When Liu first arrived in Taiyuan city in 1881, there were two academies: Chongxiu, which had recently been set up for students from Taiyuan prefecture, and Jinyang the provincial academy. The Jinyang academy had been famous in the 1860s and 70s for its emphasis on essay-writing and literary skills. Yang Shenxiu, the head of the Chongxiu academy, on the other hand was interested in practical subjects like astronomy and geography and was an advocate of ending the rigid format of the examination essay. Liu chose to study at Chongxiu.[28]

A year after Liu arrived in the city, Zhang Zhidong, one of the rising political and intellectual stars of the period, was appointed to govern the province. Shanxi was a political backwater which did not often receive men of this caliber as governor; in fact Zhang Zhidong was sent there only because the famine had made reconstruction a priority for the central government.

Zhang was later to become one of the most famous supporters of Westernizing reform at the Qing court, but in 1882 when he arrived in Shanxi he was still allied with the court faction that opposed ideological change. He was committed to practical studies that would train more competent and better-informed officials, but did not yet see Western learning as part of this. When he arrived he set about founding an academy and commissioning a gazetteer of the province. The new academy was to train the province's top students as a new generation of Shanxi officials, while the gazetteer would provide readily accessible information about the province to the government and thus improve policy formulation and implementation. Teachers were invited to the new academy who would also work on the gazetteer. The head of the new academy and the chief editor of the gazetteer was a Shanxi man who had lost a position at court some years earlier when the reformist faction in favor of "self-strengthening" succeeded in ousting the conservatives. He was known both for the brilliance of his examination essays and for his commitment to morality, but he was also interested in such subjects as geography, mathematics, and ancient inscriptions. This concern with practical learning and especially gazetteer-writing, which was to influence Liu Dapeng greatly, was typical of the intellectual stars who now arrived in Taiyuan. Finally, Zhang Zhidong poached Yang Shenxiu, the head of the Chongxiu academy. Yang Shenxiu is known to history as one of the six martyrs who advocated radical Westernization and were executed in the aftermath of the Hundred Days reforms of 1898. His concern with Westernization seems to have emerged as a result of a later official position in the coastal province of Shandong, but his fiery temperament and commitment to effective government rather than essay-writing must have been exciting for a student like Liu Dapeng, who had arrived in Taiyuan after experiencing the great famine and who hoped one day to hold high government office.[29]

The alternative to practical learning was created by the structure of the academy and the examination system. The students lived together and, at least in Liu's case, associated almost entirely with one another. They were equals and regarded one another as friends, but the academy was a place of constant competition and testing. The students were tested twice a month, and each of these tests was merely a prelude to the examinations for government office that they were preparing to take. Not only were they brought together in a closed and competitive world, but each of them was there precisely to take part in a competition for a limited number of degrees. The rewards they hoped for would come only to those who gained such degrees, which were awarded to those who passed examinations in essay-writing and poetry on themes from the classical texts. In theory, according to teachers like Li Yongqing, who was head of the Jinyang academy and taught one of Liu's closest friends, excellence in essay-writing would grow naturally out of study of the classics and self-improvement. In his comments on his pupils' essays, Li encouraged them over and over again to live the behavior they described and to devote themselves to moral self-improvement rather than worrying about the examinations. But essay-writing was also a skill in itself. This was particularly true because the style and format of the essays required for the government examinations was severely restricted. All essays had to have eight sections, and each of these sections was required to carry forward the argument in a certain way. The topic given by the examiners had to be divided into two contrasting subthemes, which were elaborated by a chain of reasoning that eventually brought the writer to his conclusion. Moreover, each section had to be written in balanced phrases of exactly equal length. Not only were essays frequently graded by examiners (who had to deal with thousands of them) more on their exact adherence to the required form than on their content, but the form itself limited the ways in which candidates could write about the topic. These problems had existed for centuries, but could only get worse as the number of candidates gradually increased. Inevitably, preparing to write examination essays occupied much of the students' time in the academy and bore little relation to the moral self-improvement their teachers urged.[30]

Many of Liu's friends and contemporaries justified their study of essay-writing techniques on the conventional grounds of filial piety. Liu described meeting a couple of good friends who urged him to put more effort into practicing essays. When he replied unenthusiastically, they pointed out that the aim of studying was to pass the examinations. If all Liu did was read a lot of books and paid little attention to essay-writing, how would he pass the exams and please his parents? When he wrote this down, Liu admitted that for his first eight years at the academy he really had studied as his friends urged, and that he had done it because he knew it was what his parents wanted.[31] Nevertheless, Liu never really accepted filial piety as a justification for an amoral concern with essay-writing. Instead, he agonized endlessly over what he perceived as a conflict between ambition and personal morality.

Conflict between knowledge and survival skill [handwritten margin note]

Liu had begun to realize that the values of the institution in which he was living were very different from those that that same institution was teaching him. He was torn between the knowledge that in order to pass the examinations he should focus on the formalistic rules of essay-writing, and conforming to the content of what he was taught, which he believed would prepare him for life as an official. He also believed that the failure to emphasize the moral content of education was harming society and local government. When he heard of a local upper-degree-holder who was greedy and arrogant, Liu wrote that his failure to assimilate the values he had been taught must be due to the emphasis on essay-writing.[32] Behind his criticism of the emphasis on eight-legged essays lay the conventional thought that the examination system, which was supposed to embody the link between morality and power, was actually preventing people from studying morality. As Liu put it to a group of friends who were urging him to study essay-writing,

Liu chose what he have been taught [handwritten margin note]

> If you don't try to understand the underlying principles but only study essay-writing to try and get a degree, it will not be easy for you to do well in any exam, and even if you do, I fear that your words and deeds will not be principled.[33]

For Liu intellectual and ethical coherence demanded that he believe in practical learning and the study of classics and history as a way of passing the examinations. Yet year after year he failed.

So Liu was caught between his commitment to the texts he had been taught to believe in, his friends who urged him to study essay-writing for the examinations, and his own and his parents' disappointment at his failure to pass the provincial degree. The examinations were held every three years; by 1891 he had sat and failed them five times.[34] He had spent ten years in the academy, and over the last couple of years he had made a determined attempt to improve his essay-writing. He had invested personally much more heavily in his education than most of his peers; now it began to seem that this investment had been wasted. The purpose of this education, whether it emphasized self-improvement through reading the classics or essay-writing to pass the examinations, had been to prepare him for government office. Liu was now thirty-four and had spent 25 years of his life studying, to prepare for a career that he was beginning to fear he had no chance of entering.

His early education with Liu Wuyang, his experience of the horrors of the great famine, and the intellectual fashions of the time all led him to commit himself to practical studies, with their emphasis on local knowledge, and internalizing the moral core of the Confucian texts. Yet it was this commitment which appeared to be causing him to fail the examinations.

In 1891 Liu left the academy and accepted a position as tutor to the sons of a rich family in the Taigu county village of Nanxi. Afterward he remembered how desperately miserable he was when he first arrived in his new schoolhouse, hating the fact that he had been unable to continue his studies, but instead had to go out to teach "grinding down my life's ambitions" as he put it.[35] He had learned that it was in poetry that a gentleman expressed his deepest feelings, and his poetry at this time is full of his unhappiness.

> The red morning sun is bright in the east,
> I lie daydreaming idly in my study.
> Suddenly I hear the sound of sighing outside the window,
> And know that the courtyard is full of the autumn wind.[36]

Here his idleness lying in bed after the sun is up as much as the autumn wind reflects his frustration and depression. In another poem he is more specific about the causes of his misery:

> Teaching is indeed a lowly occupation;
> The ancients used to be ashamed to do it.
> The pupils come and go whenever they please,
> But the master is not free to go in or out:
> He is constantly with his pupils, diligently instructing them
> And must rise quickly at first light for his own studies and self-improvement.
> How can I make this my life's endeavor?
> I have laid down my pen, but still imagine being knighted with a distant
>   fiefdom.[37]

The first line of this poem half quotes a well-known eighteenth-century poem.[38] The sad lot of the scholar turned teacher was, after all, an inevitable consequence of the examination system as it had existed for centuries. Like many tutors over the centuries, Liu writes of the restrictions of living as an employee in someone else's family and the loss of his high hopes of government office. He followed his poem with some comments: teaching, he felt, was enough to destroy anyone's moral commitment and ambition, no one who was really determined to succeed would do it. He himself could do it only as a way of making a living in the short term and would look with horror at a lifetime of teaching. He ended by noting that it was not until he started teaching that year that he had realized how hard it would be.

Liu spent eleven years as a teacher in Nanxi and over that time he made many attempts to persuade himself that teaching was a worthwhile activity. Toward the end of his first year in Nanxi, he wrote a list of the hardships and pleasures of teaching. He began with the hardships: loneliness, lazy pupils ("I spend all day instructing them and telling them off"), interruptions whenever he managed to settle down to his own reading or recitation, and his pupils' lack of progress. He then commented that although really teaching was very hard, it was essential to think of some pleasures that arose from it. He decided on seven: he could spend all day reading the classics and writing essays and poems, there were few outside distractions, listening to his pupils reciting the classics prevented him from forgetting them himself, explaining the classics helped him to understand them better, he had to sit still and be formal and correct all day (which he found difficult but thought was good for him), he was training talented men for the country as well as training his employer's sons, and finally he had time to himself outside class when he could drink tea or wine, recite poetry, grow flowers outside his window, and look at the bamboo in the courtyard. There were positive sides to life as a tutor. In later years Liu made friends with other tutors in nearby villages, and as his pupils grew older and his duties gradually diminished, he spent more and more time going to temple fairs where he could meet his friends and enjoy the opera. He was no longer lonely, he occupied a courtyard that was larger and more comfortable than his parents' home, and he was waited on by a servant. He never seems to have had more than five pupils and was allowed to bring his young son to study with him and also one or two private pupils. His employer provided a generous salary and gave Liu the right to order the servant to prepare any meals he chose. Over the years Liu became increasingly close to his employers, who took him on occasional trips to see opera or local sights, entrusted him with distributing relief to the villagers during the drought of 1901, and even sent a servant with food to Chiqiao when Liu was ill there. But despite all this he was never really reconciled to his position. He liked to quote the proverb:

The man with three piculs of grain
Won't o'er children reign.[39]

In other words, no one with enough to grain to get through the winter becomes a schoolteacher.

Underlying Liu's unhappiness was the clash between his original ambitions for government office and his position as a tutor in a society where people with jobs in commerce and banking made a lot more money and had higher status. On one occasion when he was helping at a wedding, someone said, "These days no matter what class of society you are from, if you are wealthy everyone will respect you."[40] Everyone agreed that a wealthy man was respected and a poor man was not, however admirable he might be in other ways. Liu said that attitudes like this were vulgar and people should not be affected by them, but he knew perfectly well that this was how people thought and that as a result they looked down on teachers, even though they respected those who had succeeded in the examination system and become officials.

Liu's employer, Wu Yanqing, ran a business in Zhangjiakou, on the Great Wall, one of the main points for trade with Mongolia. Members of the family, which included most of the village's population, regularly traveled on business to Beijing, Manchuria, and the treaty ports of Tianjin and Shanghai. The family had been wealthy since the sixteenth century and had produced a holder of the highest national degree in the eighteenth century. The high walls, heavy gates, and two-story buildings of their mansions, which dominated the village, were far grander than anything in Chiqiao. When Wu Yanqing married in 1903, his wife brought a dowry of 1,000 taels, which was roughly what Liu would earn in his ten years working as a tutor for the family, and Liu knew that he was generously paid for the job he did. But the Wu family were by no means the wealthiest in the area: the Chang family of Chewang village a couple of miles to the north were richer and owned larger and more impressive properties. One of the men of the Chang family had passed the provincial exams in the same year as Liu, and Liu often visited Chewang for tea, or to go to the opera or temple fairs. The Changs owned several of the biggest businesses in Kiakhta, the border town where China's trade with Russia was conducted, and had made money since the eighteenth century trading tea, horses, and silver. The business had boomed in the early nineteenth century, when Russians of all classes began to drink tea. Then in 1862 Russia won the right to have its merchants trade directly in China and at lower tax rates than those charged to the Shanxi merchants. The Russian firms began to make their own brick tea in Hankou and ship it directly to Tianjin and on to Russia, rather than using the land route north through Shanxi. On top of this the great famine of 1877 meant that for more than a year no trade could pass through Shanxi since there was no fodder for the pack animals. More and more of the trade fell into Russian hands, but even so when Liu first went to Chewang, the Chang family remained impressively wealthy, with businesses in Shanghai, Hankou, and Suzhou, and even a branch in Moscow.[41]

The Russian trade was declining, but it was not the only source of the area's wealth. Since the 1850s many of the big Shanxi merchant networks had turned to banking and this was one of the banking centers. On a visit to the county town not long after he arrived in Nanxi, Liu wrote:

> Taigu is the wealthiest county in Shanxi and all the silver in our province is concentrated here. Now I am staying here I see a ceaseless stream of travel-ing merchants coming and going in the market streets with large ingots of silver suspended from poles over their shoulders or carrying silver bullion in their hands. When I asked the city people why there were so many people loaded down with silver, they said that today was the 25th of the month, which is the winter date for clearing fixed-term notes. The period for clear-ing the notes began today and lasts for three days. After the 25th the bills are invalid. The term "fixed-term note" refers to money lent and borrowed by businessmen.[42]

At first the Shanxi banks had been primarily concerned with funding the province's trading networks, but during the course of the Taiping rebellion the transport of tax payments in silver from the south of the county to Bei-jing became dangerous, and several provincial governments began to remit their taxes to Beijing through the Shanxi banks. Transmitting these huge sums was immensely profitable and the banks boomed. They had always done a lot of their business in Hankou, where tea grown in Fujian on the southeast coast was made into bricks for the Russian market. Then as foreign trade along the Yangzi river expanded during the 1870s and 80s, they set up branches in Shanghai, which specialized in handling the finances of the foreign traders. The period of the 1890s and 1900s, when Liu was teaching in Nanxi, was the height of their prosperity: the Yangzi trade was booming and with it the number and size of remittances the Shanxi bankers handled; they had branches in cities all over China; many provinces continued to remit taxes through them and also on occasion to borrow large sums from them; and finally the central government, too, was borrowing from them and had begun to deposit treasury reserves with them on interest.[43]

The Shanxi banks were entirely staffed by Shanxi men and all senior staff held personal shares in the business.[44] Frequent social contacts convinced Liu that "the merchants are all fine, except for the bankers, who are excessively arrogant."[45] He observed that "the millionaires live in huge mansions, ride horses or use carriages when they go out, wear embroidered clothes, and eat delicacies. They get titles without studying, win honors without having any achievements, and are hugely admired throughout the district."[46] The central government, which was endlessly short of money, sold official ranks to these men as a way of raising funds. Liu complained that everywhere he went, he met men dressed in the insignia of government office, wearing hat decorations of gold, precious stones, or crystal, who cared so little about it that they did not even know which rank it was they had purchased. One particularly galling example of the power of wealth came when a member of one of the great families in the county purchased first the position of circuit intendant and then a job in one of the central government ministries in Beijing.[47] None of Liu's own friends who engaged in the examination system ever achieved such high office. There were also highly educated men who had chosen to become merchants since, as Liu noticed, "those with sons think that it is an honor for them to go and work for a bank."[48] Liu commented that he had met several merchants who were ten times more learned than he was.[49] Sometimes, Liu admitted, he hated the fact that he himself could not be "the richest man in the district."[50]

Although Liu himself was quite well-paid for his teaching job, many other teachers were not. He met one man teaching in a village school who earned less than 20 taels a year, one-fifth of his own salary. Liu concluded that this man was not earning enough to feed himself let alone support his family.[51] One of Liu's visitors in his schoolhouse in Nanxi made the point strongly:

> It is certainly high-minded of you, sir, to have a school here and teach your pupils about the sages and proper behavior, but these days this is really a literary man sweeping up the dirt, and there are many scholars who live in poverty eating vegetable soup and wearing cotton gowns and coarse woolen jackets. Look at the rich food and fine clothes of the merchants! I once worked out the numbers and found that although study can make a man prosperous and even wealthy, only two or three percent become wealthy and seven or eight out of ten don't.[52]

Given the poverty of teachers and of scholars in general, it is not surprising that students from wealthy families did not always respect their teachers. The diary is full of complaints about the arrogance of rich young men who are coddled by their parents and flattered by those around them. Wealthy families were sometimes aware that this could be a problem for their children's education and tried to behave in ways that would demonstrate respect for their teachers. The Wu family was certainly both punctilious and generous in their treatment of Liu: the elder men of the family paid formal visits after any absence, while his pupils were sent to greet him when he returned from a visit to his parents, brought him gifts of books from Beijing, and invited him to meals.[53]

Despite the efforts of his employers, Liu remained constantly aware of the huge differences in status. In a society in which business was family-based, the tutor, like most other employees, was a subordinate in someone else's family rather than the head of his own. Loss of the freedom to come and go was an important part of Liu's poem on the hardships of teaching. He particularly resented it when it prevented him from fulfilling his duties to his own family. Not being able to visit his mother when she was sick made him feel depressed and low. Similarly, the annual Qingming festival, when his pupils went to sacrifice at their ancestral graves but he was unable to return to his own in Chiqiao, made him compose homesick poems about his loneliness.[54] As he put it, "Teaching is a real bind; you can't do what you want, and whenever you have something else you need to do, it causes you a lot of trouble."[55] He felt, he said, that his life as a teacher was like that of a tenant farmer who had lost his land.[56]

Working as a tutor exacerbated the emotional pressures Liu was under. His father had sent him to school in the hope that he would bring honor to the family by succeeding in the exams, and Liu Dapeng, too, as a child was "determined to be appointed to govern a vast area."[57] Against this his teachers had emphasized that the purpose of education was moral self-improvement, albeit with the ultimate goal of preparing oneself for government. For years in the village school Liu Wuyang urged him to study the classics for their true meaning and not to concentrate on skills needed to pass the examinations. Then, in the academy social pressures had encouraged him to invest unusually heavily in the content of the Confucian morality he was learning. By the time he arrived in Nanxi, he had failed the examinations so often that he had all but given up hope of passing them. With all this behind him he came to work in Taigu county, where a degree counted for little beside the wealth of the great merchant families and he felt himself despised for his poverty. No wonder he saw Confucian morality not so much as a dominant orthodoxy, but as a kind of embattled, minority position.[58]

Then in 1893 he had the dream of a divine figure who told him that the only important thing was to be sincere and respectful. In the dream he reconceptualized his failure as a matter of choice: from now on all he needed to do was to seek to be sincere and respectful—nothing else was important. After this Liu determined to look at passing the examinations as a matter of fate and to concentrate on living out the Confucian values he had learned. He took the name The Man Awakened from Dreams and wrote an autobiography of himself structured round this dream because it was a pivotal experience in forming an identity for himself that would allow him to make sense of his years of education and his sense of failure. After this Liu's sense of his own identity and values was set: he was and would continue to be the Man Awakened from Dreams, the man who had rejected the institutions and structures of the education system as a world of dreams and had placed himself in a real, if unrecognized, world of Confucian values.

This powerful conversion experience made sense of Liu's internal conflict, but only at the cost of alienating him still further from most of his peers. Liu's brand of committed personal Confucianism was certainly not shared by most men of his social class or educational qualifications. Indeed, believing in moral self-improvement as the purpose of the education system seemed both foolish and pretentious to most of these men. Liu did occasionally meet people

who agreed with him, but not often. On one such occasion Liu was sitting
and chatting to a man called Cui at the end of an exam. They were discussing
the test, but went on from there to talk about study generally. Cui said that
he emphasized moral quality in study, and Liu was delighted to have found
someone who agreed with him and told Cui he was "a true man of learning."[59] Some friends of Liu's from his home area overheard the conversation
and laughed. Liu was upset and hurt. He could see that it might not be
appropriate to discuss the exam in the examination hall, but he could not
understand why his friends should laugh at him and Cui for speaking of the
importance of self-improvement. But for many of Liu's friends, Confucian
commitment was a rhetoric required by the examinations, not a way of life.

Then the year after the dream, on his sixth attempt, Liu finally passed the
provincial examinations. His efforts and his Confucian commitment had
paid off, and he was bringing honor to his family at last. He went round
Chiqiao visiting each household in turn and then spent days going round
twenty neighboring villages and the county town to pay calls and receive
congratulations.[60] But passing the exams at this stage only strengthened his
new sense of identity. In fact, given his own sense of himself, being a provincial degree holder laid even heavier demands on him to behave as a model
Confucian gentleman. Having now proved that moral commitment could
after all bring success, he went on to attempt the national examinations, seeing the way now open to power beyond the dreams of even the richest of
bankers.

In 1895 Liu and a friend Hao Jiqing, who had also just won his degree,
traveled to Beijing for the national exams. The brief biography of Liu inscribed on his tombstone in the 1940s treats this as the high point of his entire life: simply attending the examinations in the capital was an experience
that made one a member of the national elite. This was the first time Liu,
and in all probability Hao, had left Shanxi province. The journey took two
weeks and involved crossing the mountains that lie between Shanxi and the
north China plain. Liu described the men who walked all day behind their
cart to collect the horse dung and the beggars who came out into the road
despite the extreme cold. In contrast to this poverty, he and Hao Jiqing were
treated as persons of great importance all along the way and were not required to pay transit taxes as other travelers were. Even before he arrived in
Beijing, Liu felt that his importance as a scholar was being recognized by the

government. When the two men arrived in Beijing they were impressed by its huge size and grandeur, and by the great crowds of people. The city was so large that there were carts and donkeys to ride just to get from one street to another. Entering the examination halls was even more exciting, with many officials of the highest rank gathered at the gates to inspect the candidates. Here at last Liu's lifetime of struggle and effort was being publicly recognized and honored.[61]

But Beijing was also a disappointment. If one judged the world in terms of a division between the morality of the classical texts and the contest for fame and fortune exemplified in the examination system, Beijing seemed to belong to the latter category. The heart of the Chinese empire did not seem to Liu to be a place of high moral standards. In fact, three days after arriving there, he declared that "looking at the customs here, they are all just a matter of empty show, every single action is just a matter of adopting the correct form."[62] By the time he had been there for nearly two months, he had come to the conclusion that the city was so extravagant and dissolute that it would surely soon receive some terrifying punishment from Heaven. He was particularly shocked by a temple fair he visited that was attended by women as well as men with no attempt to separate the two.[63] But Liu's disappointment was not confined to the city; he was also shocked by attitudes toward the examinations. In the provincial examinations the scripts were transcribed to prevent the examiners favoring candidates whose writing they recognized. Although this was also done for the national examinations it was not done for the final palace examination in which the placing of the candidates was decided. This meant that there was a huge emphasis on calligraphy. He wrote in disgust:

> In Beijing people place the highest value on calligraphy: everyone respects people with good calligraphy and looks down on people whose writing is ugly. So calligraphy is the most important thing for scholars, after that come studying exam essays and poetry. As for reading the classics and histories, that is just an extra.[64]

Calligraphy was only one of the reasons Liu and Hao Jiqing had little hope of passing the national examinations. Back in Nanxi afterward, Liu asked one of his former pupils who was visiting Beijing to buy him a copy of the most recent edition of the standard compilation of Qing dynasty statecraft texts, which he then spent the next year studying. These texts grew out of the same tradition of practical learning that had inspired Liu at the Taiyuan academy, but they took that tradition much further than he had done. As he studied the statecraft texts he regretted that he had forgotten (and indeed had never been much good with) Euclid's *Elements of Geometry*, which he had studied at the academy. He also saw that his friend Hu Ying, who was good at mathematics, had new opportunities and had been entered for a new national examination in the subject. Liu realized that familiarity with statecraft texts and at least a smattering of Western learning was no longer merely a matter of personal interest but would be essential for passing the examinations. The trouble was that it was already too late in life for Liu to acquire the skills he now realized were essential: both Western learning and calligraphy required years of study. In addition, the system was changing rapidly. When he and Hao Jiqing went together to Liulichang, which was famous for its bookshops, Liu marveled at the mountains of books of all types, including many he had never seen before, flicked through them, and regretted that he could not afford to buy much. One purchase of books was never going to be enough, and Liu in Nanxi had little hope of keeping up with the scholars of the great east-coast cities and those living closer to the centers of power. When one of the other Shanxi men taking the examinations commented enthusiastically that Beijing was just the best place because people everywhere admired it and so many talented people were gathered together, Liu replied gloomily that it was a place that had large numbers of people competing for fame and fortune. That year, of the 280 men who had come from Shanxi to take the examinations, only ten passed, and neither Liu nor Hao Jiqing were among them. They returned to Shanxi. Three years later, in 1898, they both came back to try again, and failed again.[65]

The years when Liu traveled to Beijing, 1895 and 1898, were years of high drama in national politics. In 1895 China had just been defeated in a war with Japan for control over Korea, and Li Hongzhang was in the process of negotiating a disastrous settlement, which gave up Qing influence over Korea and entirely ceded the island of Taiwan to the Japanese. Liu was concerned. His diary records many discussions and reports about the negotiations: he praises an official who had bravely called for the execution of Li Hongzhang and a local Beijing strongman who had offered to protect the

official. He also records the famous submission of protests against the negotiations by groups of examination candidates, though he himself did not take
part in them and his emphasis is on the loyalty of the official who received the
petitions.[66] Liu continued to follow the negotiations after his return to Shanxi
and to discuss them with other Chiqiao villagers. Then in the spring of 1898
he returned to Beijing shortly before the period now known as the Hundred
Days reforms, when the young Guangxu emperor briefly took over the reins
of power from the Dowager Empress Cixi and attempted to implement a series of radical modernizing reforms. Liu's former teacher Yang Shenxiu was
heavily involved in this reform movement, calling among other things for the
abolition of the strict eight-section format required for examination essays.
Afterward he was to be executed. For him and for others like him in Beijing
that spring must have been a period of intense excitement.

On both occasions Liu was present at a time and a place that is generally
supposed to have changed the thinking of many Chinese about reform and
Westernization. Liu observed the political events with interest, but they affected him in ways that were structured by his former experiences and present concerns. He was interested in the changes mainly because he knew they
would affect his own prospects. He took a train trip to Tianjin, where he
spent six days, so that when he came back to Shanxi he had seen not only the
glories of the capital but also the sights of one of the most Westernized
treaty ports for himself. He thought the train to Tianjin was "very convenient," but it did not change his vision of how the world should be. This attitude was presumably reinforced by the story of Shanxi's recently appointed
governor, who had won a reputation as a reformer. He established spinning
and weaving mills, a match factory, and an arsenal. In the villages people
talked about the opening of mines and railways, and there was even a dramatic rumor that all the schools would be replaced by new language colleges
and technical schools headed by foreign engineers.[67] Liu claimed that "all
the people now are worried that China will become barbarian," but in fact
there was little actual change.[68] The governor was widely disliked, and when
he lost his job his new projects quickly collapsed.

Liu was aware of the currents of change, especially where they affected
the all-important examination system, but his patterns of thought continued
to be structured by his life in Shanxi: his village origins, his education with
its heavy emphasis on moral values, his experience of famine, his time at the

academy in Taiyuan city, and his experience of the examination system. Indeed when he traveled to Beijing for the examinations, he does not seem even to have spoken to anyone who was not from Shanxi province. Instead, he formed what was to be a lifelong friendship with Hao Jiqing, who came from a very similar village background in Taiyuan county.[69] The experience of traveling to Beijing brought Liu together not with those from distant places with radically different ideas, but with someone who shared his background and many of his attitudes. After Liu returned from Beijing, he may have studied differently for the examinations, but he still defined himself as the Man Awakened from Dreams who had committed himself to living out the Confucian ethical code of the classical texts.

THREE

The Filial Son

When Liu Dapeng was in Beijing for the examinations in 1895 he and his friends visited the magnificent Dongyue temple, where they saw vivid depictions of hell, with statues of gods and demons that made his flesh turn cold, and one of a famous traitor, which made onlookers hang their heads and weep. It was, he explained to his Shanxi readers, "roughly like a city god temple with such a forest of hideous demons and ferocious judges that it was frightening to look at them."[1] Liu was evidently impressed by the Dongyue temple in Beijing, but he was particularly interested because there was also a Dongyue temple in Jinci, near his home. "When people go into this temple and look around, they see the awe-inspiring statue of the god with really terrifying demon soldiers arranged in rows on either side, and on the altar are arrest warrants, bamboo canes for beating criminals, and writing brushes, just as in a magistrate's court when he is interrogating a criminal."[2] As a Confucian himself Liu claims not to believe in the idea of hell, only in the idea of rewards and punishments imposed by Heaven in this life. Even so he is pleased that when people enter the Dongyue temple they are terrified, fear that there may be a hell after all, and are encouraged to change their evil ways.

In Liu's mind Heaven would reward virtue and punish vice, and filial piety, the moral duty that requires all children to repay the love and affection shown to them by their parents, was the virtue with which Heaven was most concerned. As he often said, nothing was more important than moral principles and filial piety was the most important moral principle of all.[3] When the wife of his next-door neighbor, the shoemaker Cao Dinghai, was suddenly taken ill and died in an epidemic, Liu explained: "It was because Dinghai and his wife were not filial to his mother. The *Classic of Filial Piety* says that of the three thousand crimes that are punishable by death, banishment, detention, or fines, not one is greater than not being filial. Cao Dinghai's wife was not filial to her mother-in-law. Her sin was great, so it is no wonder she was executed by Heaven."[4] But Liu did not just use filial piety to judge the behavior of others, it was also the moral quality he was most concerned about in himself. He used to begin his day by sitting quietly and meditating before he wrote in his diary, so the first section of each diary entry often reflects the subject of his meditations. In a typical entry he begins by commenting that his parents' love for him is so great that he will never be able to repay it, then writes, "My honorable father has exhausted himself doing business away from home for many years, and my honorable mother has spent all her energies in managing the household. They have done this to pay for my studies, hoping that I would act properly and make my name, but I do not have the ability."[5]

Liu had learned the importance of filial piety from the texts he had studied for the state examinations, beginning with the first book he memorized, *The Classic of Filial Piety*, which states bluntly that "filial piety is the root of all virtue and the source of all teachings."[6] In these texts and the commentaries on them, filial piety is linked to the state and the maintenance of order: governing the family is a basis for governing the empire and filial piety is the twin virtue of loyalty. In other words, the behavior of a filial son toward his parents provides a model for the behavior of a minister toward the emperor. As the basis for the well-governed state, filial piety was embedded in the structures of government. In the bureaucracy men were expected to go home and take three years' leave to mourn if either of their parents died while they were in office. Powerful officials could find ways round this custom, but they could also earn respect and prestige by their willingness to conform to it. Zeng Guofan, who was one of Liu's heroes, was widely admired for going into retirement at the height of his political career following the death of his father.

For similar reasons governments had long supported lineages, formal organizations that created social, ritual, and often economic links between relatives. Liu Dapeng's wife came from the Wu family of nearby Beidasi village, who were organized into a lineage with their own ancestral hall; every year at Qingming, when ancestors were worshiped, they would hang the great silk cloth that recorded the whole lineage on the back wall of the hall and gather together to worship in front of it. The Wu lineage also controlled the distribution of positions of authority in the village, with different branches taking turns to oversee the irrigation system. But Chiqiao was a village of much more recent migrants than Beidasi, and it had no large lineages or ancestral halls. Liu's family did own a silk cloth with the family tree written on it, which was taken out for New Year, when Liu would record the year's births or deaths. On New Year's Day it was hung up in the courtyard and Liu Ming and his wife would sit in front of it, while Liu Dapeng, his wife, and children knelt before them and bowed to their ancestors both living and dead. Twice a year in the spring and autumn, Liu took his sons to make offerings at the ancestral graves. But unlike the Wus, who gathered the whole lineage for these occasions, only Liu's immediate family were present, and the family graveyard only contained the graves of the three generations of the family that had lived in Chiqiao.[7]

The emphasis on the close family on these occasions is related to the limited nature of Liu Dapeng's relationships with other members of his lineage. There does not seem to have been any relationship at all with the mountain village of Wayao, from which the family's ancestors had come. There were some connections with other members of the lineage living in the village: Liu records how his father paid for the funeral of one of his aunts as an example of his generosity. But it is not clear that this gesture was appreciated by other members of the lineage, and after Liu Ming's death the relationship seems to have diminished. Otherwise the only time Liu refers to someone as a lineage member in his diary comes in the 1920s when Liu Duanwu, a young man who worked as a carter, came to live in the house for a time. Even though powerful lineages existed in several local villages and even though Lui himself wrote a genealogy, the lineage does not seem to have been particularly important in Liu's everyday life. At New Year he and his family honored their ancestors, but Liu was far more concerned about his parents. He would prepare gifts of clothes, shoes, hats, and fine food to present to them. In later years he would always commemorate the anniversaries of his parents' births and deaths with fasting and offerings to their spirits. Judging from the length of the entries in his diary, this personal calendar of remembrance seems to have had greater personal value than the ceremonies in honor of the ancestors.[8]

The classical texts, and indeed the twelfth-century philosophical movement that led to the construction of lineages, placed formal obedience to ritual obligations at the heart of filial piety. There were rules for the correct behavior of filial children and a heavy emphasis on the correct performance of funeral ritual and ancestor worship. Indeed, filial piety can be seen as an attempt to overcome through rules the natural inclination of children to move away from their parents. Seen from this point of view, filial piety helps to create the traditional inequalities of power within the Chinese family. But filial piety was also an expression of the natural affection between parent and child. There had long been a tension between understandings of filial piety that emphasized ritual obligation and those that emphasized affection and emotion. The sixteenth and seventeenth centuries saw great literary and philosophical interest in emotion and an emphasis on the expression of moral values, including filial piety, through intimate domestic relations. Before this time family rituals were seen as giving rise to appropriate emotion, whereas afterward which rituals should be performed was often judged by whether they were emotionally appropriate. The tension between emotion and ritual obligation continued to exist, but the new emphasis on emotion made relationships within the family seem natural as well as proper and was the origin of the kind of filial piety that we see in Liu's diary. For Liu filial piety was something that he saw above all in relationships between close family members. In his gazetteer he tells the story of a local man known for his filial piety in the eighteenth century who always called in on his mother and chatted with her when he came home. This is filial piety expressed above all in the commonplace actions of everyday life.[9]

Liu's diary depicts a similar sense of everyday affection and companionship between himself and his parents. He describes one occasion on which he returned home for the Mid-Autumn festival when his father was still away:

> My honorable mother was at home and when she saw me she was quite delighted, so she put meat and wine on the table and set out vegetable dishes and fruit. She told me and my wife to sit on either side of the table with our two sons, while she rinsed the cups and poured the wine. It was one of those happy moments when the family comes together. We chatted about what a prosperous year it had been and mother looked as if she was enjoying herself. When the sun had set in the west and the moon risen in the east, we laid out the offerings in the courtyard and put a table and benches in the moonlight so we could look up and see the moon and ponder it in our hearts.[10]

Liu's mother expressed her affection and her pleasure at Liu's return with the food she prepared: meat and wine mark a celebration appropriate to the holiday. Liu does not speak of his own happiness at his return from his rather lonely schoolhouse to his family, but rather depicts himself as taking pleasure purely in his mother's delight. Nevertheless, his account expresses his affection just as much as it describes hers.

With his father, Liu writes about outings to the Jinci temples and walks up into the mountains behind the village for picnics. One year he and his father went to a temple fair in a village a few miles to the south. The harvest had been good that year, so the villagers were thanking the Dragon God, who had brought them rain, before taking his statue back to the mountains for the winter. Liu Ming ordered a cart, took a jug of wine and five strings of copper coins, and set off with Liu Dapeng for the fair. When they got there the opera had already started. Liu Dapeng admired the selection of plays that had been chosen, which he felt illustrated "loyalty, filial piety, chastity and righteousness, and were all suitable to motivate people to do good and to drive away any bad thoughts"; but the crowd round the stage was packed so tight that there was nowhere to stand. So Liu and his father stopped the cart in a rocky spot on the edge of the plain, where a group of children were playing and they could see the birds circling the mountain peaks above. Liu's father gave him the money they had brought and sent him to buy some cooked meats to eat. Then they sat on the rocks, ate the meat, drank the wine they had brought with them, and chatted about the view. Liu Ming commented that they were enjoying the same pleasures as people did in the ancient golden age. Then he got back into the cart while Liu Dapeng wandered off and met some friends who had come out from Taiyuan city for the festival. They chatted for a while till the sun was beginning to set and Liu's father sent someone to fetch him. As Liu and his father traveled back in the cart, the moon came up and Liu Ming commented on how convenient it was for people returning home from the fair. Liu Dapeng replied that it would be good if people's hearts shone as brightly. When his father agreed with this, Liu Dapeng said "I respectfully accept your teaching."[11]

Liu Dapeng's description of this outing suggests the pleasure that father and son took in each other's company, but it also produces an image of filial behavior. Liu Ming is always dominant: he suggests they go to the fair, orders the cart, decides when they will leave. The problems with this image can be seen when Liu Dapeng suggests that a moral can be drawn from the brightness of the moon, then replies to his father's agreement as if his father had made the original suggestion. The affection and apparent simplicity of the outing is constructed out of a complicated situation in which Liu Dapeng's education and degrees set him apart from his father, while the filial piety he has learned forces him to subordinate himself. The social and educational difference between father and son is very apparent in the preface Liu asked his father to write a few years later for the *Jinci Gazetteer*. Liu Ming writes in a much simpler, rougher style than his son, complains that he does not have the energy to read the whole gazetteer, comments that the sections on education and irrigation are the most important, and comes to an abrupt end.[12] As a degree-holder Liu Dapeng confirmed his status by writing and was in a position to suggest morals, but as a filial son he described his enjoyment of occasions in which he acted in complete submission to his much less educated father.

The complexity of Liu's relationship with his father seems to have thrown an even greater emphasis on emotion as a component of the relationship. Certainly after his father died Liu was completely overcome by grief. He was aware of his ritual duties: providing proper funerals for one's parents was depicted in the classical texts as one of the most important expressions of filial piety. He even worried that mishandling the rituals would be a sin that would anger Heaven, and when he had a bad attack of diarrhea afterwards, he was sure that it was Heaven punishing him; but even so, Liu placed a higher value on emotion than on his ritual obligations: he eventually declared that he was too distraught to organize the funeral and handed it over entirely to his sons. His diary records the grief that overwhelms him: he wept and wailed so much that the whole family became fearful and tried to distract him. More than a month later he was still weeping in the morning when he woke up and every time he walked into the house and realized that his father was not there. He returned to work in Nanxi but found himself bursting into tears in front of complete strangers and his tears prevented him from sleeping at night. One night the sound of rain falling at night set him off so that the whole schoolhouse was full of the sound and his servant was wakened and startled.[13] When he wept while he was teaching "the pupils just stared, not knowing what words to use to comfort or encourage."[14] Eventually, after three months of this overwhelming grief, his friend Hao Jiqing came to visit. Hao shared the education and training that enabled him to understand, sympathize, and console. He took Liu away on a sightseeing trip for several days, then stayed with him in Nanxi for a while. By the time Hao Jiqing left, the emotional force of Liu's grief was spent.[15]

Liu's commitment to filial piety and in particular his emphasis on affection and emotion meant that during his parents' lifetime, his relationship with them dominated all his other family relationships. This was particularly true of his relation with his wife, who remained at home in Chiqiao even when Liu himself was living in Nanxi. When Liu came home from Nanxi, the description he wrote in his diary was almost entirely about his mother's happiness at seeing him; his wife plays a very minor role. This was quite conventional, but it also reflected the importance of filial piety in other family relationships. The author Mu Xiang, who edited Liu's *Jinci Gazetteer* for publication and lived in Taiyuan county in the 1930s and 40s, wrote a novel set in the area during that period. In it he has a scene where the hero, a Communist Party soldier, returns home to his village after many years absence but must spend all day talking to his fellow villagers and then to his parents before he can finally speak to his wife (with whom he is very much in love).[16] The incident parallels Liu's experience: his relationship with his first two wives (he was widowed twice) was dominated by his relationship with his parents.

His first marriage was to a woman from the Wu family of Beidasi. It probably took place when he was about fifteen years old and would have been arranged by his parents. Socially, Liu's new wife came from a very similar social background to her husband: some members of her family farmed in Beidasi, while others went away to trade in northern Shanxi, Mongolia, and Russia. Although this produced a reasonable income, the family was not particularly wealthy and most of the men were uneducated; Liu Dapeng's new brothers-in-law probably could not read. She died much younger than her husband, and after her death Liu married a woman named Guo Jing. Since he was now in his 40s it is likely that he had a much greater role in the selection of his new wife (though again the couple would not have actually met before the wedding day). Liu Dapeng's affection for Guo Jing can be gleaned from a few stray disclosures in his diary. In 1902, when she was ill, he spent the large sum of twenty taels on medicine for her. This was a fifth of his annual salary and was one of a series of heavy expenditures that put the family into debt. She recovered but her ill health continued. In 1908 Liu recorded waking in a fright after a dream in which she was seriously ill. Later that year she died, and he held an impressive funeral for her with about 200 guests, at least 60 of whom took part in the funeral procession. During Guo Jing's lifetime, Liu occasionally wrote in a worried kind of way of the importance of loving one's parents more than one's wife. He even commented on one occasion that if people could turn their feelings for their wives into love for their parents, they would be better examples of filial piety.[17]

After Guo Jing's death Liu, then 52, married a young woman named Shi Zhulou, a former servant girl who was given to him as a gift by his employers, the Wu family of Nanxi. This was a different kind of relationship from that with his two previous wives, since they had both come from established families with whom Liu developed close ties. Shi Zhulou had left her family when she had been sold into service as a child, and her marriage to Liu marked his employer's generous patronage of him rather than a relationship with his new wife's family. There is no sign that Liu felt the kind of affection for Shi Zhulou that he had felt for Guo Jing, but he did come to respect and admire her. She seems to have been a competent, practical person. He depicts her sewing his winter trousers for him, and caring for her children and for Liu's grandchildren (who were about the same age). Liu's grandson remembers that Shi Zhulou taught herself to read by listening to the children learning their lessons and went on to read the famous novel *Journey to the*

West. Shi Zhulou develops a much stronger personality in Liu's diary than Guo Jing, and this seems to be at least partly due to the fact that her marriage to Liu took place after the death of his parents. If he worried about loving Guo Jing more than he loved his parents, he had no need to do so when he thought of Shi Zhulou.

Liu's filial piety also affected his relationships with his children and grandchildren. One of the things Liu most admired in Shi Zhulou was her willingness to breastfeed his grandchildren. On one occasion he records her caring for the infant daughter of his third son, Xiang:

> Yesterday Xiang's wife gave birth to a daughter. At dawn she was crying loudly because she wanted to be fed. Shi Zhulou heard her and went just as it was getting light to breastfeed her granddaughter, because Xiang's wife has only just given birth and her milk has not yet come. The depth of love and tenderness children receive when they are newly born sets the pattern for the generosity of parents to their children, which is as vast as the boundless heavens. If children once they are grown are not filial to their parents, their sin is great.[18]

The emphasis on parental love during infancy had since ancient times been one of the standard justifications for filial piety. But this version of filial piety affected expectations of how parents should behave toward their children as well as how children should treat their parents. In particular it tended to generate a heavy emotional investment in very young children despite the high chance that they would die of infectious diseases. When Liu's daughter Hongxi died in 1901, she had been ill for only three days. She had a high fever and from the first day of her illness, Liu had known that the illnesses of small children were particularly hard to cure. As her fever burned he gave her a patent medicine called "Nine Dismissals," which was widely used for children's illnesses, but it had little effect. Then on the second day she developed acute diarrhea. On the third day she died. Liu wrote in his diary,

> Last night my second daughter, Hongxi, who was formally three years old (though actually she had not yet completed her second year and was only 20 months), reached a crisis in her illness. Just before dawn it got worse. The man we had asked to come and examine the child also said it was hard

to cure. In the early morning she was still breathing heavily. Then suddenly her appearance changed and in a short while she died. How great is my lack of virtue. How can Heaven seize such a very little girl and not let her live?[19]

Then, expressing his emotions but also following a convention of poetry on the death of infant daughters, he wrote a series of four short poems mourning his daughter's death.[20] In them he laments the brief span of her life and the sudden illness that took her from it, comparing her in one to a rare jade and in another to a flower destroyed by wind and rain just as it opens. He ends with the streaming tears he wipes away as he goes to tell his parents what has happened.

Liu had nine surviving children by his three wives: five sons and four daughters born over a span of fifty years. His oldest sons, Jie and Xuan were born in the 1870s, while his youngest daughter, Biyu, was not born until 1925. His first grandchild was born in 1896. He eventually had seven surviving grandchildren by his five sons. All these children were brought up in the family home in Chiqiao, so from the time when his own first children were born there were always young children in the house. Apart from occasional worries about the cost of having so many mouths to feed, Liu enjoyed having children around. Many diary entries describe his pleasure at being wakened by the sounds of his children playing around him. Later, when the children were a bit older he used to take them with him when he went to watch the opera or to visit the temples at Jinci. There he always told them, just as his own father had told him, to lean on the stone balustrade of the spring at the heart of the temple complex and see how the water falling from the mouth of the stone dragon looked like pearls on the surface of the pool. On his eldest daughter's seventh birthday, in 1901, he took her to watch the opera at Jinci along with his father, his four sons Jie, Xuan, Xiang, and Jin, and his granddaughter Xiyan, who was five years old. His grandson Liu Zuoqing, who was brought up by his grandfather after the death of both his parents when he was still an infant, remembers going with Liu Dapeng on business trips to Taigu county and to the great temple up in the mountains. Talking to Liu Zuoqing today, it is quite evident that he adored his grandfather, and that these feelings grew out of his grandfather's affection for him as a child. This affection was an important part of the emotional content of filial piety, for the ethics of filial piety demanded that the child repay with respect and love the boundless affection bestowed by the parents, as Liu Zuoqing evidently still does.[21]

The emphasis on acting out filial piety through intimate and affectionate relations with one's parents tended to undermine ideas of what precise behavior constituted filial piety and meant that the virtue became increasingly flexible compared to the rigid ritual codes prescribed in the classical texts. This is particularly obvious in Liu's expectations of his daughters and daughters-in-law. In a context where filial piety was seen as a natural response by children to their parents' affection, daughters were expected to have a strong and continuing relationship with their parents. Indeed, women were often seen as having stronger emotions and affections than men. Liu's daughters visited him regularly after they were married, making a particular effort to come for village festivals and for his birthday. He was disappointed if one of them could not come or, having come, could not stay with the family for a few days. He expected his daughters-in-law to have the same kind of relationship with their parents: he tells of how he woke one of his daughters-in-law on the day she was supposed to be going home to visit her parents so that she would make the earliest possible start and then wept at the thought that his own parents were dead and he would never see them again. He does talk about the need for married women not to spend too long with their own parents, but by too long he means visits of more than a month at a time.[22]

These kinds of close relations between daughters and their parents that continued after marriage were part of local culture. A version of a well-known folktale collected in the Taiyuan area in the 1890s tells of how an ill-treated younger brother went to the edge of the world and stole the clothes of one of the daughters of the Royal Mother, who had come down from the stars to bathe. He married her, and after bearing a son his wife asked for her original clothes back so she could visit her mother, but the Royal Mother was angry that her daughter had been away so long and decreed that she and her husband must live on either side of the silver river of stars and meet only once a year on the seventh of the seventh month. The tears shed by the loving couple as they tell of their separation were said to fall as a gentle rain on that day. This is a story of the proper affection of a woman for her own mother, which should have been expressed in regular visiting, but has been disrupted by the woman's love for her husband. Liu Dapeng tells another story of the educated daughter of a local official who dreamed that she entered a temple where three women sat and told her they would help her father who needed to arrest a monk who had escaped from prison. When she awoke she told her father and found out that while she was asleep, the monk had been captured by villagers in a local temple that was sacred to three chaste women. The daughter's love for her father meant that she could help him even in the world of the supernatural.[23]

A daughter's close and continuing relation with her parents meant that families had strong ties with those to whom they were related by marriage. Genealogies and lineages structured families through the male line (wives were included only by their surnames and daughters not at all), reflecting the ideal household, which, like Liu Dapeng's, consisted of married sons and their children living together with their parents and possibly grandparents. But in actual fact households often included the wife's relatives as well. A survey of a village in Taigu county found households that included the household head's married daughter or niece, wife's parents or grandparents, mother's parents, wife's brother, and a variety of other relations by marriage. Although this survey was conducted in the 1930s, there is no sense in the report that this is a new phenomenon. Indeed, given the insecurity of life it was all but inevitable that some women would have to rely on their natal families or provide support for their own parents. An emphasis on the emotional content of filial piety merely provided justification. In Chiqiao the keeper of the largest village store lived with his wife, their children, a servant, and his wife's mother. Liu's own household at one point included Jie's wife's younger brother, who was studying at the local school. But this was only part of the close relationships Liu kept up with his wives' relatives. In 1926 when several family members were ill, his brother-in-law Guo Gengwu came to stay for over a month to care for the sick. This was nearly twenty years after the death of Guo's sister, who had been Liu's wife.[24]

The same thinking seems to have justified ancestral sacrifices by daughters or to one's mother's family. Every year at Qingming, Liu and his sons sacrificed not only to three generations of his paternal ancestors, but also to his mother's parents and brother, since her brother had died without children. Later in his life Liu lamented many of the changes that were taking place, but seems to have seen no problem in his daughters and granddaughters performing family sacrifices. When Jie died in 1926, his daughter performed the sacrifices for the hundred-day anniversary of the death, even though there was a son who could have done this.[25] And on the Zhongyuan festival in 1939, Liu records casually, "After breakfast I took my six or seven grandsons and granddaughters to pay respects at the tombs of our ancestors."[26] A vision of filial piety built on ties of affection was evidently flexible enough to incorporate women taking part in ancestral sacrifices.

But the flexibility created by the emphasis on affection also led to difficulties. Most of the time there were no simple rules: the filial son was expected to be motivated by a natural affection for his parents into actions that would please them. Moreover, the relations of filial piety had to be acted out within a very confined space. In 1905 the Liu family home in Chiqiao, which consisted of two large rooms, two smaller rooms, and several storage sheds round a single courtyard, was occupied by four married couples (Liu Dapeng, his three eldest sons and their wives), four children under the age of ten, and his father, Liu Ming. Liu Dapeng and his father were both away from home working for much of the year, but all the other members of the family were in residence. The adult women, whose feet had been bound according to the Shanxi custom—which was so severe that women put out their arms or used a stick for balance when walking—seldom left the house.[27] In such a household the intense relationships demanded by filial piety were likely to be of huge importance and always under scrutiny.

A prolonged dispute with Lui Dapeng's mother, which took place in the spring of 1901, gives some idea of the kind of problems that occurred despite Liu's intense efforts to be filial. This dispute was in fact sparked by the national political situation: Shanxi was threatened by French and German troops massing on its border in response to the massacre of a large number of foreign missionaries and their families in the provincial capital during the anti-foreign Boxer movement the previous year. As reports of imminent invasion came in, Liu left his schoolhouse and returned to Chiqiao to take care of his mother in the absence of his father, who, characteristically, remained at his shop in Limanzhuang. Liu's diary records his anxiety for his parents and his wife, and his frustration at his father's refusal to return home. Then comes a distraught entry in which he reports that since he returned home, he has not done as his mother wished and he is the most unfilial son in the world. It seems that all the other villagers were leaving their homes to hide in the mountains and Liu's mother wished to go too, but he would not agree. A few days later he says explicitly that his mother is upset because he had given the servants a lecture. Exactly what had happened is unclear, but it looks as if Liu had been usurping his mother's authority in the home. For most of the year Liu's mother would have managed the household since both her husband and her son were away working. This was very common in an area where many men left home to work as merchants for long periods of time. Songs telling of wives left behind by husbands who had gone away to work as merchants were popular local New Year entertainments. Such women, especially as they got older, could have considerable authority. Liu Dapeng was forty-four years old in 1901, and he clearly wanted to make family decisions; but filial piety meant that he must defer to his mother, and the emotional component of filial piety meant that he must also accept the guilt for the dispute.[28]

Because filial piety was expressed in relationships between individuals, it could never be perfect and disputes like this generated in Liu intense feelings of sin and guilt. This is a constant preoccupation of his diary. He writes of the difficulties of being filial and berates himself as "the most unfilial son in the world."[29] Central to this sense of guilt was his failure to live up to his parents' expectations: he was aware that for years he had been financially supported by his parents, yet he had failed either to make money or to obtain government office by passing the civil service examinations. He finished one of his frequent laments on this subject with the words "How can I escape from these crimes?"[30] On one occasion the inner conflict grew to such a point that he had a dream, which he interpreted as Heaven warning him about his inadequate filial piety, in which he was sitting on a pile of grass and found that he was crushing to death two snakes.[31] Even his most positive and affectionate moments with his parents were interwoven with these feelings of guilt. The occasion when he returns home for the Mid-Autumn festival and his mother is so delighted to see him is one of the happiest scenes in the diary, but it is followed by a poem he recited that evening that expresses his feelings of guilt and his inability to repay his mother's love:

As we sit in the courtyard to enjoy the full moon my thoughts are sublime.
The moonlight is bright as we gaze from afar on the palace of the moon-toad.
The scenery of the ten thousand ranges of the Western Hills towers above us,
And smoke rises peacefully over thousands of acres of fields to the east.
A crow caws suddenly in the night as it flies south;

The Jin river babbles as it flows north.
I think of how the love of my parents is as great as heaven and earth
And remorse for my lack of filial feelings fills me with shame.
I have read the classics but have not learned their essence;
When I face the sages of old I feel regret for my lack of achievements.
I think anxiously of how to comfort my loving parents.[32]

Later that year Liu prepared a prayer for his mother's birthday, which he offered silently to the gods with incense at dawn. In it he praises his mother's generosity to the poor, then regrets that he has been unable to repay one ten-thousandth of her devotion to him. He is overwhelmed by the sense of his own sin and ends by beseeching the god to take years from his life and add them to hers.[33]

Taken together these attitudes and beliefs meant that when disasters struck the family, Liu was convinced that he was being punished by Heaven for his lack of filial piety, and he held to this in a world where suffering was widespread and life insecure. In Limanzhuang, where Liu Ming had his shop, a missionary clinic reported many cases like that of a laborer who had been reduced to life as a professional beggar when he developed cataracts. Although even the respectable could be reduced to beggary by ill fortune, families like Liu's suffered mainly from the loss of their women and children. Liu married three times, his son Jie four times, and Xiang twice, in each case because their wives died. Xuan's wife also died, but he was unable to remarry. Women died in childbirth, but they also suffered from worse nutrition than men: in all but the very poorest families, the parents-in-law ate first, then working men, and the daughters-in-law last of all. In addition, it was customary for women to eat nothing but millet gruel after giving birth, sometimes for several weeks. Bound feet meant that women took little exercise and spent much time indoors in dark and smoky rooms. Many suffered from anemia, rickets, and lung diseases. Death statistics for Taiyuan county show that far fewer women than men died of old age.[34] Children could easily be killed by infectious diseases: in 1926 an epidemic that hit the village resulted in the death of three of Liu's grandchildren within a few days. Gengzhong, aged six, died early in the morning despite all his family's efforts to find a doctor who could treat him, and his sister Ximei, aged five, died that evening. A few days later their younger sister Xiling, who was "three with a lame leg and one finger that could not hold a needle," died as well.[35] Crowded housing meant that illness spread rapidly: Gengzhong, Ximei, and Xiling slept in a single room with their parents, both of whom also became ill but survived. Everyday life was repeatedly cut through by such violent epidemics. In 1913 fifty children died after an outbreak of diphtheria in another village a few miles away. Accounts by Western-trained doctors record outbreaks of cholera, diphtheria, typhoid, scarlet fever, influenza, measles, dysentery, and smallpox—all of which killed large numbers of children.[36]

Liu nearly always wrote of sickness and death as Heaven's punishment of him. This was an orthodox Confucian belief, but it was not uncommon particularly with certain types of illnesses: missionary doctors noticed that their patients saw blindness as a punishment for some sort of crime and were thus more amenable to Christian teaching. As the head of the family Liu also saw himself as morally responsible for the illnesses of other family members, just as local officials and even the Emperor took upon themselves responsibility for drought and other natural disasters. However, the wide variety of the methods Liu used to treat illness suggests that divine punishment was only one of the interpretations available. In the early spring of 1901, he became sick with a headache and a pain in his neck and spent much of the New Year holiday resting in bed. His first thought was that his illness must be a divine warning.[37] When the pain continued he put a poultice on his neck and then scraped the sore with the sharp edge of a copper coin. He also tried using vinegar and spirits to wash the sore. At the same time he meditated on the importance of filial piety and brotherly love in preventing illness, "for harmony between family members brings not only the respect of one's neighbors, but also the submission of gods and ghosts."[38] The pain continued, and a few days later a doctor, who had been invited to treat Liu's mother, pierced his neck twice with a needle and left a prescription.[39] An old woman from the village also came and massaged the neck and then applied a poultice of husks, mud, spit, and flour. Liu was still attributing his illness to his lack of filial piety, and that night when he felt better he wrote hopefully, that perhaps "Heaven has punished me enough for my sins and will now begin to be merciful, for physical illnesses are all caused by an accumulation of sin which brings down the wrath of Heaven."[40] The cure seemed to be working and the old woman was invited again. Yellow pus flowed from the place where she had applied the poultice. Liu explained that this was the wind which had caused the illness and had now turned into a poison. Although the sore was still painful, Liu left Chiqiao and returned to his schoolhouse in Nanxi. There his educated friends analyzed the problem, decided that the sore was caused by his catching cold from the wind, and suggested another poultice. Liu got his son Xuan to massage his shoulders with alcohol and then apply the poultice. When that did not work and the pain in fact increased, he attributed the problem to his sinfulness, which was still bringing down divine punishment. He tried the common remedy of applying a small bowl in which a vacuum had been created by burning a little paper, then a friend's remedy of fried spring onions applied to the neck, and then a poultice of tiger bones and bear fat sent by his employer. By this time he had been ill for about six weeks, and his parents asked a friend of Liu's who was expert at writing in a divinely inspired trance to provide a diagnosis and prescription. The diagnosis was written in the terms of the classical textual tradition of Chinese medicine and explained that the problem was caused by tiredness and a deficiency of the blood in the liver and lungs. Liu was pleased with this medicine, but it used many ingredients from the classical pharmacopeia and was expensive, so after eight doses he gave up and reverted to his own devices. He went to the baths in Taigu county town to try and sweat the evil wind out and took a laxative drug called Ten Thousand Gold pills, which his family sent. By this time nearly four months had passed and Liu was still ill; he began to attribute his problems to fate. In the three more months before he eventually recovered, he developed a fever; saw another doctor, who suggested a medicine that would expel the wind and poison; attributed an epidemic to the killing of hundreds of Catholics the previous year during the Boxer uprising; and received a prescription from his employer, which required a young girl to rub a towel up and down a heated pestle 7,749 times.[41]

When we look at his description of his illness, we see that Liu continues to understand it as a divine punishment and to associate that punishment mainly with his lack of filial piety. Moreover, many of the treatments were suggested or applied by members of the family, thus reinforcing proper family relationships. But these Confucian approaches coexisted with a number of other interpretations, which Liu found more or less convincing. Several of the treatments were intended to expel some evil from the body: the various poultices and the vacuum bowl were supposed to cause pus to flow out of the sore, the doctor's prescription was intended to drive out an evil wind, and the laxative drugs acted as purges. While the idea of evil that must be driven out of the body is readily compatible with Liu's sense of his own sinfulness, it is also different in that the poisonous pus is a physical substance that can be seen when it emerges. The prescription obtained from Liu's spirit-writing friend shares the diagnosis of an evil wind, but by using a spiritual professional and seeking divine assistance in obtaining the prescription Liu's parents were expressing a quite different faith in the efficacy of particular deities in the popular pantheon to deal with particular problems. Liu himself writes elsewhere of the efficacy of prescriptions obtained from the temple of the Daoist immortal Lu Dongbin at Jinci. Liu's fever, which he understood as part of the same illness, was also part of an epidemic that took place in Chiqiao and would almost certainly have been accompanied by village sacrifices to the plague god.[42] Finally the idea of asking a young girl to rub a heated pestle seems to be based on a mixture of sympathetic magic and belief in the special powers of prepubescent girls. The various remedies are socially distinguished in that those provided or suggested by Liu's wealthy employer (the tiger-bone and bear-fat poultice and the rubbing of the heated pestle) are more expensive or difficult to provide than those provided, for example, by the old village woman in Chiqiao (a poultice of spittle, mud, husks, and flour). But there does not seem to be any correlation between social class and the classical medical orthodoxy of the remedies suggested. Instead the variety of different treatments suggests the extent to which Liu Dapeng's Confucian understanding of the world was compatible with several quite different worldviews that existed in the society around him.

On this occasion Liu's vision of filial piety could easily be integrated with a variety of medical remedies, but at other times his beliefs clashed with the attitudes of those around him. Funeral ceremonies followed long-standing ritual prescriptions and were the subject of a large written literature, and yet even here Liu was torn between local practice, which emphasized affection for the deceased, and the ritual requirements of the classical Confucian texts. It was hard enough for him to justify his decisions to himself, let alone to defend them against his neighbors' criticisms. One issue which arose was what to do about Buddhist ceremonies at the funeral. As he observed,

> According to Shanxi custom, one must have monks to recite the scriptures
> at funerals. It is called "delivering the dead to rebirth." It is absolutely

impossible to put an end to this custom because if anyone does not invite the monks, people think he is acting wrongly and even say that he is not filial because he does not cleanse his parent's sins.[43]

And yet when his mother died in 1903, Liu refused to invite monks to read the Buddhist scriptures at her funeral. (He claims that this was his father's suggestion, but elsewhere he describes his father sitting apart talking to his friends during the ritual because "he does not know about funerals.")[44] On this occasion Liu was taking the orthodox Confucian line in a dispute that existed across the country and had continued for centuries. It is in fact one of the classic examples of the difference between state orthodoxy and popular culture. But a few years later, in 1908, after his father's funeral Liu records that he went to the county town to return the calls of those who had come earlier to pay their condolences and sent his two older sons, Jie and Xuan, to Nanxi to do the same there. Local custom decreed that bereaved sons should go, dressed in their mourning clothes and leaning on a staff as if prostrated by grief, to each of the households with which the family had close ties and kneel at the door to pay their respects. This contradicted the orthodox Confucian idea that a filial son should be so distressed by his parent's death that he should be in a daze and only able to rest at home, and the custom had actually been banned by a Taigu county magistrate in the 1830s.[45] In both these cases Liu negotiated a fine balance between the ritual prescriptions of the classical texts, his own interpretation of filial piety which emphasized emotion and personal relationships, and local custom which tended even more strongly toward the expression of emotion and affection at the expense of the classical prescriptions.

Liu himself was always relatively successful in keeping this balance between local opinion and Confucian practice, but in his *Jinci Gazetteer* he recorded the life of Zhang Zhen, one of his classmates in the Chiqiao village school, who caused a huge storm by divorcing his wife for Confucian reasons. Like Liu, Zhang Zhen had developed a strong personal commitment to Confucianism in the course of his studies. Initially, however, he followed a more common career path: when he was fifteen his father took him out of the school and sent him to work in a business in Taigu. But Zhang Zhen was desperate to go on with his schooling. Despite a great deal of mockery from his fellow apprentices, he continued to study the classics in his spare time and eventually succeeded in persuading his family to allow him to return to the school. At the age of thirty he finally passed the lowest level of the examinations and became a degree-holder. When his father died shortly afterward, Zhang Zhen refused to eat or drink for several days until his mother begged him to take a sip of water. He also sold land to pay for the funeral, so that afterward he had to open a school in Jinci and earn his living as a teacher. In refusing food and selling land, Zhang Zhen was following the excesses of classical models of filial piety and laying claim to a reputation as a truly filial son. But most of Liu's biography of Zhang Zhen is dedicated to a single incident:

> Zhang Zhen was filial in serving his mother and even succeeded in that most difficult aspect of always adopting an appropriate expression; but his wife, Yang, was not good at serving her mother-in-law and often went against her wishes. At first his mother glossed over his wife's faults and did not let her son know, but eventually he saw that his mother was not happy and quietly urged his wife to serve his mother well, but she still could not do what his mother wanted so he thought about divorcing her.
>
> His mother said, "We can send her back to her mother's family for a short time to reform herself." He did as she suggested, but his wife's mother's family not only failed to reprove their daughter for her lack of filial piety, but actually accused Zhang's mother of being unkind.
>
> Zhang Zhen prepared himself for a fight saying, "Long ago Zengzi divorced his wife because of how she steamed a pear for his mother. Bao Yong angrily divorced his wife because she scolded the dog in front of his mother. This, on the other hand, is the first of the seven reasons for divorcing a wife."
>
> So he divorced his wife. People approached him pointing out that she had gone through the three years of mourning for his father, but he was defiant and paid no attention.
>
> In the provincial examinations of 1888, he was recognized by the literary chancellor Gao Lichen and received a government stipend. In the annual tests for lower degree-holders the next year, 1889, he was again recognized, this time by the chief literary chancellor Guan Tinge, and he was rewarded and praised as a talented man who would succeed. In the examinations by imperial grace in the autumn of that year, he finally attained the rank of provincial degree-holder, coming in thirty-eighth place so that he was widely talked about. He was then forty-two years old. The chief examiner, Xie Junhang (courtesy name Luncai), wrote on his script,

"It shows a great sense of the ultimate principles. When one reads carefully one sees that the words are sincere and the emotions genuine. One cannot read the section on the ode in which a filial son thinks of his dead parents without being moved."

The associate examiner Xu Qi wrote,

"He has grasped the meaning of 'close to the people.' When he speaks his words are very fine and his writing is deep. When I read this gentleman's script I thought of my own home and parents far away and was so moved that I shut the script book up for hours."

The assistant examiner Wang Shuofu wrote,

"Grand and deep, respectful and well structured. The moral content is serious. The intendants at the examination halls decided that this script actually comes from a man of true filial piety. Only when he came to the examination halls did we know that he had served his mother alone for many years. I agree with the perception of the intendants and it makes me sigh with admiration that this student's life can be in accordance with his essays and I hope that he will urge himself on and thus console his mother still further with announcements of his success in the national exams."[46]

Shortly after these events Zhang Zhen died, telling Liu Dapeng tearfully on his deathbed that the only thing he was sad about was that he would no longer be able to care for his mother. Liu ends his biography with a brief eulogy that sums up the difference between his own reaction to the case and the general opinion in Chiqiao:

Few people are filial these days. There are many daughters-in-law who cannot serve their parents-in-law. The *Book of Rites* says, "If a son gets on well with his wife but his parents do not like her, he should divorce her." The reason why it is unheard of to divorce one's wife these days is that sons do not reprimand their wives for serving their parents poorly but actually blame their parents for not being kind to their wives. People at the time all thought Zhang Zhen was wrong to divorce his wife because his mother did not like her so there was a lot of criticism. Only when he passed the provincial exams and the examination intendants praised his filial behavior did people finally understand that he was right to divorce his wife so the gossip stopped.[47]

Liu Dapeng was close to Zhang Zhen, and his text, which is headed "Biography of Zhang Zhen, a filial son," is intended to justify Zhang Zhen's position on the divorce by depicting him as a model of filial piety at every point in his life from his commitment to it in his childhood studies to his deathbed, where his only thought is for his mother. But we also see that this passionate orthodoxy is something Zhang Zhen has to fight for from the time when his father removes him from school and he braves the mockery of the other apprentices to continue his studies to the moment when he decides to divorce his wife and prepares himself for a battle with his neighbors.

Filial piety was not an easy virtue. There were few rules to follow and those rules that could be found in the classical texts were much disputed. The rule that the filial son should divorce his wife if she displeased his parents was quite explicit and found in the *Family Sayings of Confucius*, which Liu quotes in his commentary. According to this text, Confucius said that there were seven reasons for a husband to divorce his wife and three reasons for not divorcing her. The first of the seven reasons for divorce was if the wife did not obey her husband's parents. The other reasons were if she did not have children, committed adultery, caused arguments, suffered from ill health, talked too much, or stole property. The husband was not to divorce his wife if she had nowhere to go, if the couple had gone through the three-year mourning period for one of his parents together, or if he came from a humble background and had become rich since his marriage. Zhang Zhen's wife had in fact gone through the three year mourning period for his father, which should have prevented the divorce, but even though this was pointed out to him, he apparently considered the failure of his wife to obey his mother to be of greater importance. Liu approved, but Zhang Zhen's decision was entirely unacceptable to most of his neighbors. The Chiqiao villagers who criticized Zhang Zhen were not rejecting the value of filial piety, after all they criticized anyone who did not invite monks to take part in a parent's funeral precisely because they felt that this demonstrated a lack of filial piety. But their interpretation of filial piety was not the same as Zhang Zhen's, until, that is, the state intervened in the form of the examiner's comments on Zhang Zhen's essays. Here we see the Qing government's continued role in promoting a vision of filial piety that was based on rules and ritual obligations. Through the examination system the government was able to legitimate unpopular positions even at this village level. But even though it was possible for the state to provide legitimation for a rigid version of

Confucianism, most of the time village opinion, which emphasized the importance of affection, was a far more powerful arbiter. An essay Liu wrote in 1892 suggests the difficulty he found in coping with the conflict between his neighbors' opinions and his Confucian commitment:

Customs have a great influence on people. For example, if the words and behavior of someone living in the countryside are no different from those of the locals, then naturally nothing is said; but if one person [here Liu has crossed out the word "I"] does not do this, then there are bound to be locals who say he is arrogant and pretentious. Some of them ridicule him as ignorant, others laugh at him for fishing for compliments, others berate him for being unreasonable. Everyone talks about it and they all criticize him, pressuring him to go along with them putting himself second so that everyone gets dirty together. Even if he has something to say, it is difficult for him to get a word in edgeways. It hardly needs stating that villagers and country folk behave like this, but it is quite unacceptable for a degree-holder who has read the works of the sages not to discriminate right from wrong or find out whether or not something is in accord with the principles of reason but just agree with whatever is said. And why does he do this? Because he is constrained by custom. If he were a high-minded man his actions would be principled and his speech proper. He would restrain himself in his contacts with others and not be limited by custom or affected by thoughts of what is normally done, nor would he pay any attention to the criticism or praise of the country folk. After a long time living among them he would not only not have been changed by them, but would also have transformed their bad customs. There are not many people like this, so how can I surpass the common herd and disperse the fog of custom, improve my way of thinking, and transform the bad customs of the district?[48]

Like the Confucians we often tend to think of elite models of behavior influencing the lower levels of society, but Liu's essay suggests that in some ways that image should be reversed. It gives a sense of the intense pressure that a small community could place on members who did not conform to commonly held interpretations of shared values. Liu might attempt to live as a filial son, but he saw cases where brothers divided the family property even before their parents died, gave their parents a room to live in, and paid them no further attention.[49] Indeed, he was probably more likely to be influenced by village opinion and local custom himself than to persuade others to act up to his model of filial piety.

Despite all this, when Liu acted as a Confucian gentleman he was performing a role that was known and respected, even if his neighbors might not agree with the results. And Liu's performance as a Confucian gentleman does seem to have earned him respect in the village. In 1892 Liu Ming received two compliments on his son that Liu Dapeng recorded in his diary. On the first occasion Liu Ming was having his head shaved and queue trimmed by the village barber when he overheard a group of village men refer to Liu Dapeng being "honest and peaceable." Then a few days later Liu Ming went into one of the temples at Jinci, where a group of men were sitting chatting in one of the long verandas. A couple of them got up to greet him and one of the others asked, "Who is this old gentleman?" One of the men who had got up to greet him replied, "He's the father of Liu of Chiqiao village." Liu Ming was delighted when they all complimented him on his son saying, "Oh, we all know Liu. He's a decent fellow and makes us all really admire him."[50]

Liu Dapeng's behavior was admired because it was related to shared values. Liu writes about weeding the crops with his sons one summer and listening to the people chatting as they too weeded in nearby patches. They were gossiping about their neighbors, talking about how one family was managed or how another treated people. Liu was impressed by how correct their judgments were. On another occasion he described crowds watching the operas shown at temple fairs, who sigh when a loyal minister is treated unjustly, and abuse the actor who plays the traitor and want to beat him up.[51] But although Liu's behavior related to these kinds of shared values and was admired, that did not mean that people imitated him.

When one's parents were alive, filial piety was inevitably a problematic and disputed virtue because it had to be constructed in relation to another person; after their death, its meaning was transformed. The summer after Liu's father's death, he and Hao Jiqing were staying at the schoolhouse of Li Xianzhou (who had been with them at the examinations in Beijing). Liu dreamed of the belongings his mother left when she died and woke his friends in the night with his sobbing. The following morning his tears flowed freely when he thought of the night's dream.[52] But as time went on, the content of his dreams of his parents began to change. Several years after Liu Ming's death,

> I dreamed my late father was still doing business exactly as he always did and was chatting with his closest friends. I spoke but they did not respond, and when my father saw that I had come he went away and did not make a single inquiry about me. I desperately wanted to tell him about things, but I could not. All I could do was ask desperately where my father had gone to. Just as I was in the middle of this anxiety, the cock crowed and I woke up. I could not help grieving and wept.[53]

Here we see the nightmarish sense of abandonment which was the product of Liu's deeply emotional filial piety and continued throughout his life. It came, however, to justify a quite new aspect of his filial piety, which is seen in the other dream he had around that time:

> Last night I dreamed I saw my father send someone to buy medicine to give to someone in need. The medicine was made of pearls, jade, and other expensive ingredients, and I found out that he had spent several thousand copper coins. This was characteristic of my father. When my father and mother were alive, they put their energy into doing good, only regretting that they did not have enough time. As they grew old their good intentions were firm and as a result even when they were both very old they were in good health until they died. Today I still think of their good words and deeds, which are always before me, and my feelings of great admiration press me on.[54]

In this dream we see the transformation of Liu's filial piety into a general justification for doing good. As he says elsewhere, his parents were respected because they were good and charitable, so filial piety demands that he, too, should be good and charitable. He can still berate himself for not being as good as his parents, but he is now free to decide the content of his values for himself.[55] In other words, filial piety can be used to justify his own wishes. After his parents' deaths, filial piety was still an inspiring ideal for Liu but much of its complexity was gone.

But the filial piety that was part of Liu's presentation of himself as a Confucian gentleman had costs for other members of his family, too. The emotional intensity of family relationships meant that Liu's sons had little hope of resisting the huge pressure to succeed that grew out of his sense of failure. We meet Jie and Xuan, his two eldest sons, for the first time in the diary in 1892, when they are going with their father and his close friend Hu Ying round the temples at Jinci. The group climb up the seven stories of the pagoda and lean on the railing at the top, looking out over the flat green plain with the streams of the Jin and Fen rivers flowing across it, and the golden evening light falling on the hills behind them. Hu suggests that they compose a poem on the beautiful scene, and they agree that Hu will start the poem off and Liu will cap his rhyme. Hu begins his poem with the vanishing beauty of the setting sun, but it is Xuan not Liu who adds the final line of the quatrain.[56] Liu must have been pleased with Xuan for he recorded the incident at length. Xuan comes across as a bright boy and eager to please.

Unlike his elder brother Jie, who remained in Chiqiao for his studies, Xuan went to live in Nanxi to study with his father. When Liu was ill with the infection on his neck in 1901, it was Xuan who cared for him. Meanwhile, like his father and elder brother, Xuan prepared for the civil service examinations. Liu realized that he himself no longer had much hope of acquiring the necessary skills and began to invest his energies in preparing his sons. He employed a special tutor to teach them the techniques of writing examination essays, even though this was a skill he himself despised. The tutor was an expert in essays on the subject of filial piety, and when he talked about it his pupils stared at him in amazement, but to Liu's disgust the tutor regarded this entirely as a form of rhetoric to be mastered for the examinations rather than a model for everyday life. If asked, he would say that only the ancient sages could actually behave in the ways he had been describing. Having realized the importance of calligraphy in Beijing, Liu made his sons practice that, too, so that in the end Jie's handwriting became much better than his father's. He was also prepared to help them acquire the kind of modern education that he hated even more than essays and calligraphy. He had noted in his diary with approval that some of the staff of the province's most prestigious academy resigned when it was transformed into a Western-style university, because they were not prepared to teach alongside foreign barbarians. But when Liu heard that the new university was offering scholarships, he immediately sent Xuan to take the entrance examinations. As Liu realized that he himself would never be able to hold an official position, he put more and more pressure on his sons to do so whatever the cost.[57]

Xuan passed the licentiate degree, and in 1903 he traveled to Shaanxi (where the examinations were being held in the aftermath of the Boxer uprising) to attempt the provincial examinations. This was just a year after his elder brother Jie had passed, but Xuan failed. He had been betrothed in his teens, and in 1907 his wife gave birth to a son, Maoling, who was Liu's first grandson. But after being ill for a whole winter, Maoling died at the age of eight months. After his son's death Xuan himself became ill, but he recovered and was well enough to correspond with Liu, who had returned to Nanxi. But by 1910 he had descended into a serious mental illness from which he was never to recover. Liu describes Xuan's condition by saying that his madness makes him stupid like an idiot, and he cannot deal with things, all he does is eat and drink. The family remember his illness as a disease, but they also say that it was caused by his failure to win a provincial degree. Xuan lived on into the 1950s, and people remember him wandering round the village, his long dirty queue hanging down his back, talking incoherently, and writing every day on the floor and walls and all over the courtyard of his father's house. Although he was mad you could always tell, they say, that he was the son of an educated family.[58] It is, of course, a ghastly parody of his father's life as a scholar: walking through the village, reciting poetry, talking to his neighbors, and always, always writing. Liu Dapeng's own comment that "he only knows how to eat and drink" reinforces this, for when Liu berated himself as an unfilial son it was always at the front of his mind that he only ate and drank and did not contribute to the household. Xuan failed; he failed to succeed in the examination system and his son died; in the end he lived out his life in insanity as a model of an unfilial son who had failed to repay his father's love and affection.

Jie, the eldest son, succeeded, at least at first. When he passed the provincial examinations there was huge rejoicing in Chiqiao: crowds of people came to congratulate the family and the county magistrate sent musicians to play in front of the house. Later the village presented the family with a board to hang over their door saying "Father and Son are both Provincial Degree-Holders." The next year Jie and his father traveled to Kaifeng, where the national examinations were being held because of the destruction of the examination

the change of content in exam

halls in Beijing by foreign armies during the Boxer crisis. New "policy essays" had been introduced, essays in which the candidates were expected to discuss recent issues affecting the state, so the bookshops were full of books on current affairs and all the candidates were buying them. By 1904 Liu had given up hope for himself and sent Jie alone to take the examinations. That year candidates were asked to discuss whether schools should aim to mold citizens, train officials, or develop industry. Other questions concerned the combination of land, capital, and labor; the foreign policies of Western countries; a comparison of Japan's and Egypt's policies toward the employment of foreign specialists; and America's ban on Chinese immigration. Jie, who was little better prepared than his father to answer such questions, failed. But afterward Liu found money for his son to do what he himself had never been able to do: Jie was sent to the great port city of Tianjin to await appointment to a minor government post on the basis of his provincial degree.[59]

For at least two years Jie lived in Tianjin. He wrote to his father regularly with news of his progress toward an appointment and items of interest from the Tianjin newspapers. Tianjin in 1907 was a very different world from Shanxi. The city was a treaty port, with large areas under foreign rule. Jie would have seen the effects of foreign power: huge stone-clad buildings in Western styles, glass-fronted shops, telegraph wires, paved streets crowded with trams and rickshaws, as well as the old-fashioned carts and sedans, foreigners dressed in their strange costumes going about their daily business, and if he roamed farther afield factories where hundreds of workers were employed. Not only was Tianjin a center of foreign power, it was also a base for modernizing reformers in the government. Yuan Shikai, later to become President of the Republic, was based in Tianjin as Governor-General of the province at the time Jie arrived. A new railway was being constructed, and near the station were new model factories and schools, a municipal park, a library, and a mint. A whole range of new government institutions had also been set up: Jie sought employment in a new-style court of justice (previously judicial decisions had been handed down by county magistrates) and the Mongolian Research Institute (part of the Qing government's attempts to tie in its outlying territories), and he saw some of the many new anti-opium offices.[60] In Shanxi Jie would already have heard about and perhaps seen a few of the new Western-style primary schools, but here in Tianjin he

New modern institutes of government

must have begun to realize the true impact of the government's new modernizing policies.

Tianjin was also full of new ideas. The city had been a center for efforts to promote the new education.[61] Central to these was the criticism of what were now seen as the excessively hierarchical values of filial piety and loyalty to the Emperor. In opposition to them Western ideals of freedom and equality were taught in the new schools, from textbooks many of which were written by men who supported the idea of revolution. Indeed, ever since the first Western-style schools had been established, it had been said that their students would deny both father and Emperor. A few years earlier Liu Dapeng, visiting a member of the wealthy Chang trading family, had heard a horror story about a Beijing official who sent his son to study abroad. A few days after he returned, the son ordered a banquet. When his father asked who the guests would be, his son knelt down and said that he would only get up if his father agreed to something. The official asked what it was and the son replied, "What I ask today is that from now on our relationship will no longer be that between father and son but instead we will be equals."[62] To Liu this was a rejection not only of the natural affection between parent and child, but also of the whole moral order of the state, which he saw as structured around those natural bonds. As he said, "If it is really like this, the force of moral obligation will be totally destroyed and the whole country will fall into disorder."[63] A couple of years later, he heard another similar story, only now the young man concerned had not even gone abroad but had merely studied at a Western-style school in Taiyuan city.[64] These stories may well not have been true, but they pointed to a very real process that was going on in the new schools where the parallel ties that bound together filial piety and loyalty were being undermined by new ideas coming in from the West and promoted in the cause of nationalism.

Waiting for an official appointment in Tianjin, Jie must have met the students of the new schools, read the newspapers, and seen the changes that were taking place in the government. He was in his thirties, probably older than the young man Liu heard of whose filial piety had been so dreadfully affected by his studies in Taiyuan city, but Tianjin was surely even more different than Taiyuan. Indeed, the modern urban culture that was changing Taiyuan and making it so different from the village had its roots in Tianjin and the other great coastal cities. Jie was influenced by some of the new ideas. His second daughter, Xiluan, who was born in 1900, was never sent to school or even taught to read, but she was the first woman in the family not to have bound feet. The decision must have been made about the time that Jie was in Tianjin, since footbinding usually began at the age of six or seven. This would have made her one of the very first generation of Shanxi women not to have bound feet, since before 1906 natural feet were almost entirely restricted to servants and Protestant converts. Jie never obtained an official appointment, and in the end his hopes were destroyed by the revolution of 1911. He came home to Shanxi and found employment as a teacher in the county's higher primary school. Then after several years he went away to Dai county, a center of modern education, in the mountains on the other side of the central Shanxi plain, to a slightly better position in a women's teacher-training school.[65]

Since he evidently concealed much of his life from his father, it is impossible to tell how Jie felt about returning from Tianjin with its modern ideas to village life in Shanxi, but it was certainly not an easy transition. During the 1910s and 20s the intellectual attack on Confucian morality and in particular its core value of filial piety intensified. Filial piety was condemned as feudal by modernizers determined to transform Chinese society. The modernizers were based in the great cities of the east coast, but Jie, teaching in a women's school in a town with a large number of other modern schools, can hardly have been unaware of their ideas. But in Chiqiao and the villages around it family structures changed little, while at the same time the modernizing state gradually withdrew from the Qing dynasty's sponsorship of Confucian morality. Thus the state no longer provided the emphasis on ritual obligation that had served to balance the trend to intensify the emotional content of filial piety. The result was to increase the demands for an emotional expression of filial piety in the villages, even at a time when in the great cities on the east coast the whole system of Confucian morality was under attack. Thus even as Confucian morality was detached from the state and condemned as feudal, it came to be associated with rural areas. Modernizers worked to create a more egalitarian political order where men and women would have a direct relationship to the nation-state, rather than one mediated through the family or Emperor; but their actions had the potential to develop the rural family as a refuge from the state and even a place of resistance to it. For Jie, who understood the new ideas but whose family was dominated by a father who was still utterly committed to Confucian morality, the emotional demands of filial piety must have been deeply problematic.

Liu Dapeng's affection for his eldest son continued, and he wrote of his delight when Jie came home from Dai county on visits. Jie must have succeeded in preserving the behavior of a filial son in front of his father, but that performance was only for his father. In fact it must have been a relief for Jie to get away from Taiyuan county to distant Daizhou. Liu knew that Jie drank heavily, but after all he himself enjoyed drinking. But Jie, who smoked two packs of cigarettes a day, never dared to smoke in his father's presence. In later years Jie also began to smoke opium. The rest of the family all knew this, but Liu never did. In 1928 Jie died. He was buried in the fine clothes and expensive coffin that Liu had bought for himself. A few days later Jie's young wife took an overdose of opium, leaving their two-year-old son Zuoqing to be brought up by his grandparents. Like Liu's other daughters-in-law, she came from a wealthy family and found life in Chiqiao hard. Without Jie to support her, she must have felt that she could no longer cope. Liu understood her death in terms of a wife's proper loyalty to her husband, but other villagers criticized the family, and the young woman's own family was furious and broke off all relations.[66] Spending most of his time away from home, Jie had managed to act out filial piety for his father, but his filial piety was a performance that covered both unhappiness and fear. The intense emotional nature of the Confucian family relations that Liu sought was never easy, but it was particularly difficult after they began to clash with quite new ideas that the younger generation were absorbing. Xuan and Jie both sought escape in ways that illustrate the emotional power of the system as well as its destructiveness.

When Liu Dapeng committed himself to acting out the values he had learned through the education system, he was committing himself to filial piety above all. But his vision of filial piety was created not only by the classical texts he read, but by an interpretation of them that required huge emotional investment in the relations between parents and children. This meant that Liu's relations with his parents dominated every other relationship in his family. It also created an intensity of emotional involvement and parental expectation that was very hard both for Liu himself and later for his two elder sons. Although acting out the role of a Confucian gentleman had its costs, it also had its rewards. Other villagers did not imitate Liu, they did not always even agree with his values, but they respected his behavior, and it was that respect which provided him with opportunities to make a living when the modernizing state declared his classical education irrelevant.

FOUR

The Representative of the People

In the autumn of 1901 Liu Dapeng had a dream that he had passed the highest levels of the examinations and was being received in an imperial audience:

> The other officials were silent and had nothing to say, so I alone stood forth to speak, presenting detailed proposals that the present abuses such as the selling of government offices should be stopped, taxes in money and grain should be reduced, suitable and well-qualified candidates should be appointed to positions in the government, but dishonorable men should be dismissed, schools should be rebuilt, agriculture and sericulture should be valued, the common people's feelings for the dynasty should be confirmed, and the basis of the state strengthened. I also put forward policies for the restoration of the dynasty and proposals on suppressing disorder. The general outline of these was to find good officials who would be able to strengthen the people's determination, employ generals to reinforce the borders and drive out the Western and Japanese barbarians, and to convert the Christians into law-abiding subjects. I made my proposals boldly and the whole room was shaken

by my words. The Emperor bent his head and listened attentively. He did not dislike the new proposals, indeed there was delight on the imperial countenance and I hoped to be honorably rewarded. Only the two grand secretaries at his side glared angrily. I could not help suddenly pointing them out as traitors who would prey upon the country and harm the people. I did not even know what their names were, but just begged the Emperor to execute them to delight the hearts of all people.[1]

That, after all, had been what he was hoping for through all those years of study: to win government office and real influence. How unrealistic, and yet how easy to understand. But the warm reception Liu imagined for his deeply conservative proposals was even more of a dream than the hope that he might pass the examinations, for the conservatives at court had been overthrown and the reformers were in the ascendant.

The reason for the conservatives' collapse was the disastrous Boxer uprising, which also directly affected Liu in Chiqiao. In 1900 the conservatives had finally succeeded in persuading the court to declare war on the foreign powers. Shanxi's new, conservative governor sponsored village militias that had been forming and had arrested all the foreigners in the province. Chinese Christians were also considered to be enemies, because they were members of a heterodox sect and were seen as being allied with the foreigners. But many of the men in these militias (known in English as Boxers) were inspired by ideas of spirit possession that would normally have been considered just as heterodox as Christianity. They were, moreover, extremely violent. One group was started up in a village near Chiqiao under the leadership of a strong young man who earned his living wheeling barrows of coal down from the mountains. Their first act was to murder the village butcher, who was a Catholic. After that the members began to train in the temples at Jinci, where Liu saw them invoking the gods and going into trances in which they performed a kind of dance with knives and spears. When people asked what they were doing, they replied that Heaven was angry and had sent them as soldiers. It was, as Liu said, all very strange. Later Liu stood at his door to watch a Boxer army marching out from Jinci to attack the Catholic communities in nearby villages. In one village that he knew well the Boxers killed one hundred people and burned down many houses as well as the church. The Boxer militias were strange, violent, often unruly, but in Liu's mind and in the opinion of most of his neighbors, they were also members of officially sponsored groups helping to resist a foreign invasion that was to be spearheaded by the Catholics. Other men with backgrounds and opinions similar to Liu's even became involved in organizing the movement: a provincial degree holder, who like Liu had been employed as a tutor in Nanxi, organized a Boxer troop in his home village. In response to the violence against foreigners and Christians, the foreign powers sent a force that sacked Beijing and then demanded a huge indemnity and a range of measures intended to punish those who had supported the Boxers. Some leading officials were executed and many were dismissed. The war was a political disaster for the conservative faction at court, and from 1901 on the government was effectively dominated by those committed to political change and modernization. The modernizers' first move was to reverse the policies of 1900: Boxer groups and particularly their leaders were to be punished, while Christians were to be compensated for their losses. Taxes had to be raised to pay for the indemnity, and part of the money was distributed to the Christians.[2]

Liu and many other people were horrified. Stories were eagerly passed round about places where people had resisted the new policies. Liu heard that people in the mountains that bordered Shanxi to the east had rebelled and attacked the foreign barbarians who were forcing officials to extort the indemnity. As Liu said, "although it is a rumor, it is what people are thinking about."[3] Later he read about the uprising in the metropolitan gazette (a record of recent government edicts transcribed by publishing houses and circulated to the provinces). Liu copied the edict he had read into his diary and commented,

Liu's comment about Boxer

The uprisings are all caused by the foreigners and Christians tyrannizing the common people, and the fact that the officials cannot protect them. If the common people oppose the priests of the foreign religion, they are accused of being rebels and soldiers are used to put them down. The people cannot accept this so I suspect that incidents of murders of officials, and killing of soldiers, will occur in more than one place. I fear there will be revolts in all the provinces under the Emperor's rule. When the people have security there is peace; when they do not have security they rise up. It is both inevitable and reasonable. At the present moment the indemnity is huge and the people can scarcely survive. On top of that the Christians rampage through the villages preying on the people, while the officials actually protect the Christians and oppress the people. How can there be an end to the uprisings?[4]

For some time afterward there was a great deal of talk about this uprising, and the predominant feeling was anger with the government.[5]

People were angry because they were suffering from the tax increases, but also because they felt that the government had betrayed them by abandoning its own principles. Someone watching the political scene in Beijing might have seen some years earlier that the government was moving away from its traditional, Confucian values. Indeed, when Liu Dapeng went to Beijing for the examinations in 1895 and 1898, he sensed the emphasis that was already being placed on new forms of knowledge in appointing officials. But for most Shanxi villagers, the state had continued to be identified with Confucian orthodoxy, and they expected to be rewarded or punished accordingly: filial sons and chaste widows were honored, sons who struck their fathers were severely punished by the law. Heterodox groups, like the Christians, might be ignored if they did not cause trouble, but if they did they were bound to be suppressed. Liu, like many people, had seen the Boxers as "good folk," that is to say law-abiding subjects, and the Christians as heterodox sectarians who were collaborating with an invading army. When the Christians were rewarded and the Boxers punished, he felt betrayed.

The confusing sense that the state was abandoning the very principles that justified its existence intensified when the government began to raise taxes further to pay for modernizing policies that quite obviously worked against its Confucian values. These new policies began with a further shift away from the classics in the examination system, so that, as Liu put it, the country was selecting as officials people who were good at Western learning rather than those who studied the way of Confucius and Mencius. Then in 1905, the examination system itself was abolished. Liu woke up a few days later "with a heart like ashes" as he realized that his hopes for an official career had now completely vanished. When the sun came up he went out into the village street and found that everyone he met was talking about the end of the examinations. He talked with them about what a disaster it would be for the country, especially since no one knew what the graduates of the modern schools would be like. Together they wondered about what other changes there would be in the next few years.[6] People realized that the ending of the examination system would transform channels for social mobility and that many other changes would inevitably follow. They also knew that those families, like Liu's, which had invested heavily in education would be the first to suffer.

Liu and many of his friends lost all hope of holding government office, but they also faced a more immediate problem: with the end of the examinations, education was transformed and many of them lost their jobs as teachers. Liu disliked teaching, but it had given him respectable employment, good living conditions, and a reasonable salary. Some wealthy families had already laid off their tutors: Liu's friend Hao Jiqing lost his position in 1902, when his employer decided to send his sons to study the new Western learning. But with the end of the examinations villages, too, realized that education as they knew it had lost its value: in 1906, all the villages in a large area to the south of Chiqiao closed their schools. Even where schools were not closed, parents withdrew bright pupils in the belief that they would now be better off in commercial apprenticeships.[7] Many village schoolteachers had been scraping by on low salaries in any case, and there was little chance of other employment for them. Usually their only option was to return to their families and help farm. The sense of personal catastrophe is vividly depicted in Liu's account of Qu Yuwen, a lower degree-holder who had hung onto his job for a few more years and was threatened with losing it in 1913:

> Student Qu Yuwen, an old licentiate of this county, sought me out. He is poor with no other means of making a living and supports himself by teaching for which he earns just two or three thousand cash a year. He looked very down at the heels and his elbows were poking through his sleeves. He said that an official from the education office had just ordered him to go to the county town to take an examination on the 22nd of this month, and if he does not pass he will not be permitted to have a school and then he would have nothing to live on. He asked me to protect him, crying and with tears pouring down his face. I have agreed to mediate for him. Alas! The harm the new policies do to people can really be said to be severe.[8]

Liu Dapeng himself kept his job for a few years after the end of the examination system, but his pupils lost interest in their studies and his position became increasingly insecure.

Liu disliked the changes to the education system not only because they destroyed his prospects and left many of his friends unemployed, but also because the new education denied his values. He hated the schools' discussions of current affairs: "It is all about wealth and power and they do not speak of the proper relationships or principles at all. The whole aim of the system is to glorify the state and harm the people, and every aspect involves using the barbarian learning and changing China. It is terrible."[9] Here he comes to the heart of the problem: the aim of government had been transformed from reproducing a Confucian society to mobilizing wealth for the state to compete internationally.[10] It is important to realize quite how shocking this was, not only to Liu but to many others of his generation. Liu had always thought of most ordinary people as being motivated by the desire for money and respect, but the rhetoric of the government had been opposed to this. Instead, officials were supposed to be driven by the desire to act rightly and to work for the benefit of the people. Liu had learned from his education that "no disaster is worse for the country than when benevolence and righteousness are set aside and talk is of money and profit."[11]

The addition of mathematics to the elementary curriculum was emblematic of this change since it appeared to be primarily concerned with questions of commercial profit and loss. As Liu put it later, "Today's teachers use mathematics to teach people and the learning of the foreigners to instruct them. Will they really be able to get many good men? The foreigners' learning specializes in profit which is the exact opposite of our learning. It is most regrettable to rush toward it like ducks to water, not knowing that it is wrong."[12] The main skills acquired in elementary education continued to be reading and writing. The difference was that they were no longer taught through the memorization of the Confucian classics, but rather through the memorization of textbooks written in Shanghai that promoted the new ideas of the time. The skills learned were roughly the same, but the moral content of education was completely transformed. Undoubtedly most people were not as articulate as Liu in their criticism of the changes, but they could see that those who had come through the new system no longer shared their ideas and attitudes. Liu went on a visit to Taigu county town, where everyone was talking about a young man who had been awarded one of the new-style degrees after studying three years with the English and had recently returned from Shanghai dressed entirely in foreign clothes. "Everyone stares at him as a foreign barbarian and even the members of his extended family treat him as a member of a different species."[13]

The new style of education also required a significant increase in resources. Most villages could afford the old schools because they required only a simple schoolhouse and a teacher. Boys brought their own benches to sit on, and their few textbooks had been in use for centuries and were readily available in cheap copies. Taxes had to be raised to pay for the new schools, which were far more expensive than the old.[14] In some cases new Western-style buildings were constructed to house them. Teachers who knew something about the new Western learning had to be employed, and since they were harder to find, had to be paid more than the pittances received by men like Qu Yuwen. Textbooks had to be bought in Shanghai, and pupils needed new textbooks for each class each year. In theory a really good school also needed facilities for students to study science, which required expensive imported equipment. Given the costs involved it is not surprising that some of the earliest Western-style schools in Shanxi were established by great merchant families. The immensely wealthy Chang family of Chewang village near Nanxi set up a new elementary school in 1903 and a girls' school in 1905. Liu also visited another new school set up by the Qiao banking family. He was bemused by the importance of physical education classes ("which are really just children's games") and dismayed by the informal style of the teachers. But the Qiao family had also realized that even with this fine new school, Western-style education could not be delivered entirely in the village. In the past the family had banned its young men from studying except in the family school; now they were sent on to the American mission school in Taigu county town and then far away to Tianjin. The Chang family sent several of their sons to Japan. Modern education provided access to new forms of social mobility, but unlike the old-style education it demanded resources that even the wealthiest Shanxi merchants could not provide in their villages. Indeed, in sending their children to Tianjin and Japan wealthy families implied that, at the highest levels, a successful modern education could not be provided in Shanxi at all.[15]

For most villages even establishing an elementary school was prohibitively expensive. Liu reported that one town had set up a modern school at the huge cost of 2,000 taels, with the money assessed on the town population, a move that was deeply unpopular, while six or seven local schoolteachers were left unemployed. A few years later Liu would have attended a debate in the provincial assembly on the cost of new schools. The proposal put to the assembly was to radically reduce the cost of the new schools. School expenses were to be limited to 110 cash per year, plus the cost of textbooks and the teacher's salary. The school would only need a room with a blackboard and benches, plus somewhere for the teacher to live. There would only be one set of textbooks and all the teaching could be done by a single teacher. It is clear from the record of the final decision that the assembly members thought that all this was hopelessly unrealistic. They pointed out that it cost approximately 1,000 taels to establish a school and that many schools employed managers as well as teachers. Liu himself was particularly critical of the fashion for making the new schools look foreign, which involved spending large sums of money on decoration. Of course cheaper schools were set up: Taiyuan county raised a tax of just 40 taels to establish a new school in the town. In Jinci the new school was set up in a temple that had traditionally been used by the district's scholars. It was funded by a tax on the area's water mills, but this did not provide enough money for running expenses and the school also had to charge student fees. The result was that the school was both unpopular and endlessly short of money. Nor did it have access to particularly modern teaching: Liu Dapeng was employed there in 1913 to teach Chinese and ethics, which he insisted on doing in the old style. He ended up resigning after six months because his salary had not been paid. Schools like this provided a cheaper version of modern education, but the lack of resources meant that they were never able to compete successfully with schools funded by the provincial government, which were almost exclusively in urban areas.[16]

The new schools were also less accessible than the old. In 1908 Taiyuan county had nearly 8,000 children of school age (7–15). Of these, 1,359 were said to have attended traditional schools, 132 had attended one of the new schools, and a mere 20 had attended the new higher primary school in the county town. Numbers attending the new-style schools rose in the years that followed, but even so education, and especially education beyond the elementary level, remained the prerogative of the few. In fact the new higher primary schools were significantly less accessible to boys from poorer backgrounds than the academies they replaced, since the county government had provided a stipend to students attending the academies whereas the new schools charged fees and provided no stipend. In Chiqiao so few boys completed higher primary school that one man born in the 1920s remembered that he was appointed for a job as accountant in the village office simply because he was the only higher primary graduate in the village. This was not quite true: Liu's fourth and fifth sons, Jin and Hongqing, as well as at least two of his grandsons, had also graduated from the Jinci higher primary school, and Jin had actually gone on to study at a middle school in the provincial capital. Even so the old man's recollection gives a sense of how difficult it felt for Chiqiao villagers to succeed in the new system. Hongqing would have liked to go on to middle school too, but the family could no longer afford it. Some traditional-style schools continued, but they provided what was quickly recognized to be a second-class education with few prospects. Most villages were no longer able to provide schools that would allow pupils to compete on a provincial level, and the cost to the family of education above elementary level had increased significantly. All this signaled the beginning of a shift of resources, and more especially opportunities from rural to urban areas, which accompanied the government's abandonment of Confucian ideology.[17]

The central government did also aim to promote industry and commerce, but this brought little benefit to the towns and villages of central Shanxi. Chambers of commerce were set up in county towns, but the main effect the new policies seemed to have on local commerce was to harm it by increasing taxation. When Liu read in the newspapers that a new exhibition hall set up in Beijing to display Chinese products had been burned down, he interpreted it as Heaven's warning against the new policies. The few provincial government policies that promoted modern industrial development were seen as a threat. Liu particularly objected to the establishment of the Baojin (Protect Shanxi) Mining Company. This was set up in response to student-led demonstrations in the provincial capital against the sale of mining rights to a British-dominated consortium. But these nationalist feelings were not enough to make the new company popular with investors, so eventually the capital was raised by requiring each county to sell a certain quantity of shares. Taiyuan county had to provide 15,000 taels, a huge sum. Since it seemed highly unlikely that the new company would ever achieve profits to match this vast capital investment, the arrangement was extremely unpopular. Moreover, the company's mines would inevitably compete for business with existing coal mines. In practice, as far as Liu was concerned, the new policies mostly appeared to consist of the government extorting money so that it could invest in railways and mines and become rich. Of course government spending also had benefits, but on the whole these were experienced in the cities where the new offices, government-funded schools, exhibition halls, and occasionally factories were located rather than in country villages.[18]

The first stages of government-sponsored modernization in Shanxi were expensive, provided little in return, and were introduced at the same time as money was being raised to pay off the Boxer indemnity. It was inevitable that the new policies were experienced above all as an increase in taxation. Liu's first proposal to the Emperor in his dream was for the reduction of taxes. Before this time Liu had shown little interest in taxes, probably because his family paid little. Liu Ming had used the money he and Liu Dapeng earned to buy property so the family now also received rent from some shops and farmed a few fields, but as a degree-holder Liu Dapeng would have received a discount on the surcharges that made up most of the land tax. Liu Ming's furniture store might have been subject to occasional exactions by the county government and would have been affected by some transit taxes, but Liu Dapeng's teaching salary would not have been taxed at all. Then, in 1901 existing taxes were increased and several new taxes were introduced. The family would have been affected by the new surcharge on the land tax, but it is unlikely that this did much more than keep pace with inflation, which was also increasing crop prices. Liu's main concern was the fact that transit taxes now made a real difference in the price of everyday goods. Liu blamed the new wine tax for the fact that several local distilleries had gone out of business that year, while the county government tried to make up the sums lost by pursuing the wine shops. The cost of winter heating (and the fuel expenses for the Chiqiao paper-making businesses) rose when an entirely new tax was levied on the pack animals used to bring coal down from the hills. The villagers also had to pay a levy based on the number of rooms in each house. Liu complained that the government offices were constantly full of the sound of people being beaten for not paying their taxes. The Boxer indemnity had been carefully structured to penalize counties like those in central Shanxi which had been centers of violence against Christians and foreigners. The extractions needed to pay the indemnity lasted for many years, but were particularly intense in the years immediately following the uprising. When the cost of the government's reforms was added to this, it was inevitable that there would be complaints.[19]

Government policies promoting modernization were deeply unpopular, but this unpalatable fact could be ignored by those in power because by the late 1900s the government had so completely abandoned its Confucian past that there was hardly even a language left in which to criticize them. Officials who did attempt to oppose the reforms were simply labeled "conservatives" or, more commonly, "reactionaries."[20] According to Liu, "No one dares say that the new policies are uncharitable. Anyone who speaks of it is immediately accused of being a member of the reactionary faction. In serious cases he is accused of a crime, loses his post and is not reemployed, and at the very least his faults are pointed out and he is censured."[21] Liu saw himself as a lone voice crying in the wilderness. After the revolution of 1911, he wrote, "I am completely at odds with the current situation. Everyone is for the reforms, and I alone hold to the old ways. Everyone is destroying the bonds of relationships, and I alone hold to principles. Everyone wants an official job, and I alone am willing to remain loyal."[22] But this comes in the context of a diary entry describing a rumor about an uprising against tax increases. It is clear from Liu's accounts of local gossip that although the potential government officials Liu saw as his peers might support the reforms, in fact his opposition to the building of new government institutions was widely shared. People grumbled and talked of outrageous taxes in other places: a tax on brothels in Guangdong, a tax on gambling in Guangxi. In 1906, when the building of new schools was at its height, Liu reported stories of tax resistance in the mountains to the east, where several thousand people were said to have attacked government offices and burned down the hated new schools when officials tried to use the police to collect taxes by force. The enthusiasm with which people discussed these events suggests the sympathy many felt.[23] Unfortunately for them, this kind of resistance to the new policies weakened the government and played into the hands of the most radical of the modernizers, who had begun to plan the overthrow of the dynasty and the establishment of a Republic.

The revolution, when it finally took place, looked more like a military coup than a popular uprising. Along with other provinces, Shanxi had been building up a new Western-style army, staffed by officers who had received military training in Japan. By 1911 there were two brigades, commanded by Yan Xishan and Huang Guoliang, both of whom were committed to the need for radical modernization. Yan Xishan and many of the other officers were also members of secret revolutionary groups. That autumn news came through of a major army mutiny in Wuchang, and then that several provinces had removed their governors and declared themselves independent. The nervous Shanxi governor ordered Huang Guoliang to take his forces to the far south of the province. Huang went a short distance south and waited, while Yan Xishan and other revolutionaries led their troops to attack first the offices of the provincial government, where they murdered the governor and his family, and then the city's Manchu quarter, which fell after some fighting. The next day disorder broke out in the city: soldiers set fire to and looted the provincial treasury, the city's banks and pawnshops, and many of the homes of the wealthy.[24]

Taiyuan county shared in the general lawlessness that followed these events. The frightened magistrate created a defense troop and managed to hang onto his position for several months. But in the end the people of the county town were so harassed by these soldiers that they sent two men to the provincial capital to ask the new leaders there to remove the magistrate. The county town was walled and gated so although the defense forces were troublesome, passing troops could be kept out without much difficulty. Jinci, on the other hand, suffered from the fact that one of the province's main north-south routes ran directly through the town center. Mostly this was an asset for trade, but in the chaotic situation that followed the revolution, it was a disaster and the town was constantly harassed by passing soldiers. Hu Ying, Liu's friend who was an expert in mathematics and had been teaching at the new Shanxi University, put up a notice in the temples explaining that the revolution was necessary to resist the foreign powers who sought to divide China and calling on people to be peaceful. But one notice in Jinci can have done little to redeem the images of disorder. Liu Dapeng suffered personally when he was grabbed in the street and his queue was forcibly cut off. He retired home in disgust, and despite considerable pressure, refused to head the new county assembly that was being set up until his hair had grown back.[25]

Attitudes toward the revolution were not improved by the fact that it was a disaster for the local economy. In Taiyuan banks and pawnshops were burned and looted, and the rich Shanxi banks were natural targets in many other cities across the country. At the same time the looting of the Shanxi provincial treasury had left the new military government with no cash to pay its troops. In the long term this meant higher taxes, but in the short term revolutionary leaders extorted large amounts of money from the big banking and trading houses to meet the new government's immediate needs. At the same time across the country the destruction of property meant that many loans the Shanxi banks had made would now never be repaid. This was an especially serious problem in the Yangzi port cities of Wuchang and Hankou, which were both centers of the brick tea trade with Russia and Mongolia and the site of the mutiny that started the revolution. Moreover, much of the bankers' most profitable business had involved remitting and investing Qing government funds. In the last few years before the fall of the dynasty, this business had come under threat from new Western-style banks set up by various government bureaus, and some Shanxi banks had collapsed as a result. But the Western-style banks had never managed to achieve a monopoly, and several of the largest Shanxi banks continued to make huge profits from government business. When the Qing government was overthrown, not only did the banks lose a great deal of money in loans to various government bodies, but the changes also affected the Shanxi bankers' credit more generally. It was soon clear that any new government would be more committed to modernization than the Qing and therefore likely to give the Western-style banks a monopoly over government business. The first branches of the Shanxi banks to collapse probably did so because of the immediate destruction and losses of the revolution, but the reduction of their creditworthiness because of the new political situation did not help. With each new bank failure, others were implicated. The city of Kaifeng in Henan had had thirteen branches of Shanxi banks before the revolution; by 1915 only five were left. A handful of Shanxi banks survived for a few more years, but by 1920 almost all were closed. In their boom years, during the 1890s and 1900s money from these banks had poured into the towns and villages of central Shanxi; after the revolution, the profits ended and the banks' former employees came home to their villages, where large numbers of unemployed merchants now joined the unemployed schoolteachers in farming.[26]

The revolution also affected the Shanxi trading houses, though less dramatically. Their business had been declining for some time, as more and more of the Russian trade was shipped by sea to Tianjin, and from 1905 overland via the new trans-Siberian railway.[27] The revolution disrupted commercial activities for several months and the destruction of Hankou in the fighting caused serious losses. Many businesses also suffered because they had invested in the banks that were now collapsing. Liu's employers, the Wu family of Nanxi, had been suffering financially for some time. Shortly after the revolution, Liu's former pupil Wu Renhe went to Shandong on business for his father but was so intensely pressed to repay the family's debts that he began to spit blood and died. His wife committed suicide five days later. The revolution also affected the Mongolian trade. The Mongols had never seen themselves as part of a Chinese state and had been growing increasingly opposed to Chinese political and economic dominance (a situation for which the exploitative practices of the Shanxi merchants were to no small degree responsible). In 1912, in response to the revolution, northern Mongolia declared its independence, enacted laws discriminating against Chinese residents, and instituted free trade with Russia. Five years later, in 1917, the Russian revolution effectively ended the overland trade between China and Russia. The Chang family of Chewang village near Nanxi, who had a shop in Moscow, lost 1.4 million taels in Moscow debts, and many others lost large sums when the rouble collapsed.[28]

Like many people Liu Dapeng was affected by the downturn in the local economy. In fact his family began its own financial decline about this time. With the death of Liu Ming in 1908, the timber and carpentry business had been taken over by a manager. The worsening economy of Taigu county, which had been at the center of the banking industry, meant that the furniture trade there inevitably suffered and profits declined. Limanzhuang, the formerly wealthy village where the business was based, turned into a ghost town as residents sold their possessions and then the timber from their houses.[29] Liu Dapeng himself had finally lost his teaching job. He had always disliked teaching and maybe his father's death simply made it possible for him to resign, but the irrelevance of the education he could provide and his employer's financial troubles must also have played a part. Like many men at the time who lost jobs which had kept them away from home, he came back to his home village and spent much of his time in the fields; he was effectively unemployed.

Popular antipathy to the Qing dynasty's modernizing reforms, social disorder, and economic decline may have been the outstanding features of the events of 1911 in central Shanxi, but the revolution was nevertheless a major victory for the modernizers. A new provincial government was set up in Taiyuan led by Yan Xishan, who was to remain the sole ruler of Shanxi until the Japanese invasion of 1937. From Liu Dapeng's perspective the new government was most certainly not legitimate. Looking back on the revolution a couple of years later he wrote, "The treacherous official Yuan Shikai overthrew the dynasty's government, concealed the Emperor in the depths of the palace, and took the position of president. More than a year ago he gave an order that the country should henceforth be known as the Republic."[30] Looked at in this light, the revolution amounted to little more than the usurpation of the throne by a disloyal official. The economic ill-effects of the modernizing policies, which the new government continued, and of the revolution itself meant that negative assessments were inevitable.

In the face of these problems, the new republican government based its legitimacy on its commitment to modernity and democracy, ideals that were closely intertwined and profoundly in conflict with Liu's Confucian values. The changes that accompanied this commitment at village level were largely symbolic, but no less unpopular for that reason. The magistrate made considerable efforts to enforce the use of the new solar calendar, and one of Liu's friends resigned from his position as headmaster of the county's higher primary school when he was rebuked for allowing the students to go home to celebrate the lunar New Year holiday.[31] Liu himself continued to keep his diary according to the lunar calendar and began nearly every new volume with an attack on the solar calendar. In the spring of 1915 he wrote:

> The 4th year of the Republic began on the 16th November of 1914, but none of the people respect it. They still follow the old calendar and regard today as New Year's Day. Every household is celebrating the New Year, and everywhere there is nothing the magistrates can do except let the people celebrate as before. The 18th of last month was February 1 by the solar calendar, and today is February 14th. The ordinary villagers only know that today is New Year's Day, how can they know it is February 14th by the solar calendar? The change to the calendar is not in accordance with the people's wishes, so although they say they have, they have not really changed.[32]

As both these examples suggest, the new calendar was confusing and just about everyone wished to continue celebrating the New Year holidays, which were the biggest in the year, on the lunar date. Liu himself wore his degree-holder's skull cap for the New Year celebrations, "not following the rebels' etiquette," which would have suggested a fashionable felt hat.[33]

The new state also claimed legitimacy as a republic. The idea of a republic was more familiar than other terms the modernizers used; it drew on ancient ideas emphasizing the importance of the people to the state. But in Liu's mind, "If you create a people's state but go against the people's wishes, then you lose the point of it's being a people's state."[34] In other words, the legitimacy of the government depended on how popular its actions were, not the mechanism by which it was appointed. This completely contradicted the new state's emphasis on elections, another expensive new policy with which it tried to confirm its legitimacy. Local elections had begun in Shanxi in 1909 as part of the Qing's preparation for constitutional government, and Liu himself had been elected to the new provincial consultative assembly. After the revolution, elections became even more important. Each county had an assembly, whose members elected a provincial assembly, which in turn elected a national assembly in Beijing. In 1912 and again in 1913, Liu was elected to head the county assembly. The first year he refused to serve because of his shorn queue, but the next year he reluctantly agreed despite fearing that the unpopularity of its modernizing activities would affect his reputation. Elections also became quite a common way to select people for other posts. In 1913 Liu was so worried about being elected to head a new Jinci district council that he got up before the voting began to announce that he would refuse to take the post.[35]

Elections were so important to the new republic that when President Yuan Shikai wanted to become Emperor, he decided to hold a referendum to change the constitution at the same time that a new National Assembly was being elected. Liu participated in every stage of these elections from the establishment of the voter registration committee to the balloting in Taiyuan city that finally elected the new National Assembly members. As one of the county's representatives to the former provincial consultative assembly, he was naturally appointed to the voter-registration committee. This was charged with the task of identifying voters who met the voting qualifications of having either a middle school education or a sufficient amount of property. Liu was provided with meals when he attended meetings, paid $15 (a considerable sum of money, equivalent to half a year's wages for a farm laborer), and sent off around the villages to find qualified voters. This was not a particularly easy task. No one was likely to want to declare a large amount of property and there were no middle schools in the county. So Liu walked from village to village asking for holders of the upper-level examination degrees, which were regarded as equivalent to a new middle-school qualification. He also found at least one man willing to declare property holdings that made him eligible to vote.[36] Presumably he already knew most of these people at least by reputation, but nevertheless he went diligently from village to village "investigating." The task was not easy. On one particularly depressing day in which he went to the villages of Xiaozhan and Xiaozhanying and failed to identify a single voter, he wrote in his diary that it was a very exhausting task and "after many days I have hardly found any people, which is because the requirements for voters to qualify are too strict. I fear there will be bad people among them."[37] This suggests that he thought, not unreasonably, that elections were designed to select upright and worthy men for government office, just as the examination system was. This attitude was reinforced by the fact that the voters he was registering were precisely examination degree-holders.

Given that the voters in 1915 were a small group of men many of whom knew each other, it was likely that those who were elected would be men who got on well with their peers. The first round of voting took place in the city god temple in the county town. Liu himself was elected, presumably at least in part because he had just visited many of the voters to register them. One of the other two men who were elected was a member of one of the county's oldest and wealthiest families. Many years later, when he was arrested as a counter revolutionary by the Communists, hundreds of people from his village went to rescue him because he had distributed food to the people in his village during the Japanese occupation (he had also sent grain to Liu Dapeng's family).[38] Presumably he was both generous and popular. The emphasis on personal relations continued for the second round of voting in the provincial capital. When Liu arrived there he found that most of the men who had come for the election were old friends, that is to say men he knew through the education and examination system. Liu was elected and became one of the 120 representatives from across the province who would elect members to the new National Assembly.

Liu responded to his election with the comment, "The whole country has selected 120 citizens' representatives. The balloting was yesterday. In the end I was one of the representatives, but I don't know what a representative is."[39] When Liu had been elected to the provincial consultative assembly before the revolution, his position was that of "assembly member," which clearly meant some kind of paid government employee. The term "representative" was new and much harder to understand. Up until this point, as far as Liu knew, the process had been to elect a national assembly. His confusion grew when the representatives were unexpectedly required to vote on whether a constitutional monarchy should be established, in other words whether Yuan Shikai would become Emperor. Liu described the events that followed in his diary:

> This morning all 120 provincial representatives went to the military governor's administrative offices, which are the offices of the former provincial governor. The civil governor also came. The representatives voted to decide on a constitution. The ballot papers said "Establish a constitutional monarchy," and below that we wrote the word "Agree." Everyone did the same, no one wrote any other words. This was what those in the government instructed the representatives to write. Everyone was confused and I too was muddled.[40]

Liu knew perfectly well that Yuan Shikai wanted to be Emperor. He had read about it a few days earlier in the *Shenbao* newspaper and commented then, "In the present circumstances considering who is in charge of the Republic and who the constitutional monarch could be, then the only person is that man Yuan."[41] However, he had also read in the newspaper that General Zhao Xun had praised the idea of constitutional monarchy but wanted to restore the Qing Emperor.[42] Under pressure to conform, Liu managed to convince himself that by voting for a constitutional monarchy he was voting for the restoration of the Qing dynasty, but in truth he knew that he was voting for Yuan Shikai. When he got back to Chiqiao he had a nightmare about what he had done:

> Last night I dreamed that President Yuan Shikai was declared Emperor and took the throne in Shanxi's former Chongxiu Academy. Those who were performing obeisance to him were wearing peacock-feather caps and court

robes and jackets. Several dozen men forced me to follow the group to per-
form an obeisance. I did not want to but was forced. I wanted to die but
could not. I wanted to hide but there was no way out. I secretly planned not
to accept a position from him and to take any opportunity to get away. But
Yuan sat in the hall looking very stern, his face was white as snow. Just as he
took up his pen to write down the names of those to be awarded positions
and honors for their ancestors, I woke up. When I was in the provincial
capital and agreed with constitutional monarchy, I meant that the Xuantong
Emperor should be restored to the throne and Yuan should return to his
position as a minister so that the correct relationship between monarch and
minister would shine over the world and rebels and traitors would tremble
in fear. To dream of Yuan being declared Emperor is quite the opposite of
what I originally wanted. If Yuan really is declared Emperor, then where is
the proper behavior between monarch and minister?[43]

A couple of days later Liu was still trying to convince himself that the Qing
Emperor would be restored. But as the nightmare suggests, he knew that
under pressure he had voted for something of which he hugely disapproved.
The constraints of elections as he experienced them meant that they were
not even a situation in which it was easy to express an honest opinion.

None of this presented elections in a very good light, but even so the final round of voting for the members of the National Assembly was a shock.
Liu was horrified by what he saw as the candidates' degrading behavior. He
wrote a poem titled "Campaigning to be an assembly member":

Who says that elections are a fair method?
All I see is people campaigning:
They have little sense of modesty and are not bashful,
When they beg for your vote they treat you like a god.

Just because they plan to become assembly members
They invite a great crowd and set out a banquet.
They all forget to avoid the scorn of onlookers,
But just appeal for sympathy to the others like them.

They don't know about current affairs and have no sense of shame,
They just wag their tails and beg to become assembly members.
They beseech the onlookers to do their best to speak for them,
And every day at their offices they set forth fine banquets.[44]

The overthrow of the Emperor and the ending of the examination system had destroyed the only legitimate routes to political power. The country's highest officers, like Yuan Shikai and Yan Xishan, had come to power as the result of their military connections, but for other people elections seemed to provide access to government office and hence an important new form of social mobility. But they were also quite new and strange. In the examination system appointments were supposed to be based on objectively assessed merit. Of course there were officials who tried to get themselves selected or promoted, but they had to do it by indirect means and the whole activity was highly dubious. An election campaign, on the other hand, inevitably involves the candidates persuading the voters that they are the best people to hold office. At the county level it was possible to be elected, as Liu presumably had been, given his aversion to any form of campaigning, simply on the basis of a good reputation and previously existing connections; but with the larger electorate at the provincial level few candidates were likely to have this sort of reputation. Since both political parties and self-promotion were morally dubious, it was not surprising that some candidates tried to create rapid personal connections by offering banquets and flattering their guests. To Liu, though, these activities appeared to be an intrinsic part of the election process, and they cast it in a very dubious light.[45]

But this was only the beginning of the campaigning. Things got even worse when the candidates moved on to straight bribery. The night before the final ballot, a shocked Liu was offered money to switch his vote and refused.[46] In 1901, Liu had complained in his dream about the sale of ranks and offices by the Qing, but that practice was clearly enough defined not to undermine the legitimacy of examinations as such. Elections seemed to provide similar opportunities, but the boundaries were quite unclear. The concept was new, the system had little inherent legitimacy, and there had been almost no discussion of the role that money would play. The buying of votes seemed to Liu a natural extension of the moral depravity of campaigning and thus an intrinsic part of the whole new system. When the ballots were counted the next day, the candidates elected were those who had campaigned most vigorously "and had absolutely no sense of shame. How can we look forward to their being of benefit to national finances or the people's standard of living?"[47]

The importance of appointing upright men as officials was central to Confucian thought. As Liu had told the Emperor in his dream, the role of government was to appoint suitable and well-qualified candidates to office and dismiss dishonorable men. After the election was over, Liu wrote a report to the county magistrate in which he stated that "It has become common to buy votes and to campaign to become an assembly member. This is the worst fault of the selection policy. From now on upright gentlemen will not be able to be assembly members."[48] He ended by pointing out that only those who were both wealthy and powerful could get enough votes to win elections. This was not just a reaction to Yuan Shikai's admittedly corrupt election, but rather a more general problem with the whole system of choosing representatives. Three years later Liu commented on recent elections for the provincial assembly: "They are still using the method of election by ballot, so all the rogues and villains intrigue for office by campaigning and the ones who have most money win. How can we possibly get decent officials from a selection process like this?"[49]

Liu backed up his judgments of the new Republic by observing a series of signs that Heaven condemned it. In the spring and summer of 1914, he recorded a long list of meteorological events: a strange sound in the night, which people said was Heaven crying out; a triple aurora round the sun; a shower of sleet in midsummer; white clouds stretched across the sky at night; and a red arch in the night sky. He added to these local phenomena a report that he read in the newspaper about a shower of red rain far away in Jiangsu province. At first he interpreted these events merely as a sign that disaster would surely follow the stealing of the throne. Later he was clearer about exactly what the disasters were: war had broken out in Europe, the Japanese had occupied Qingdao, and Sun Yatsen and his band were using this as an opportunity to cause disorder. The portents were undoubtedly widely discussed. Indeed, the strange sound at night and the red arch in the night sky would not have been valid omens if popular opinion had not interpreted them as "Heaven crying out" and a warning of fighting, respectively. On one occasion Liu writes about how he and the Jinci town head, Niu Yujian, chatted about a dark arch Niu had seen in the night sky and decided that it was a portent of war. Niu Yujian, like Liu, was very much opposed to the revolution. It is impossible to gauge how many people shared their views, but Liu was probably not the only person to think that Japan's invasion of Chinese territory was a form of divine punishment for the revolution that overthrew the Qing.[50]

Interpreting the political events of the Republic through the lens of the previous moral order was not confined to the discussion of omens. Ten years later, when Shanxi was threatened with attack by warlord troops, Liu went to the temple of the Daoist immortal Lu Dongbin at Jinci to find out what would happen. He drew lots to determine the answer to his question, "Is the Jinyang river area in danger or not?" and received as an answer a slip printed with a hexagram and the interpretation:

> The five unbroken lines lie above the one broken line in accordance with Heaven's will.
> The upper position of the strong unbroken lines is an auspicious omen.
> Although it is much shaken, it changes little and is not destroyed in the end.
> The benefit is seen in the midst of a time of peace.[51]

Further, simpler advice followed, but Liu would scarcely have needed the interpretation since the hexagram was drawn from the *Classic of Changes* which he had studied as a young man. As he commented in his diary "It is a very positive sentence, so we can expect that the rebels will not come and harass us."[52] In the event the deity was proved right, Shanxi was spared, and Liu kept the slip he had received hidden between the leaves of his diary. Forecasting the future through the *Classic of Changes* threw political events of the Republic back into the world of the Confucian classics with its familiar moral order. A true prediction by the Daoist immortal using the Confucian texts also underlined the universal and eternal value of the classics in a situation where many were rejecting them. Liu's interpretations of Republican politics mixing Confucian texts, heavenly portents, and the efficacy of a Daoist immortal may not have been so alien to the village men who squatted with their bowls in the shade of the big tree by the stream below his house, chatting over their dinner.[53] After all it is unlikely that the moral structures people had grown up with would be overturned in a few years, especially since there had been relatively little social change and the few boys who had received a modern education were still too young to influence the opinions of their elders.

Had the new government succeeded in generating economic prosperity and driving the foreign powers out of China, Liu might have felt differently about its modernizing policies. After all, that was what he had called for in his dream. But it showed no sign of doing either of those things. Instead, economic collapse was rapidly followed by news of renewed foreign incursions. In 1914 Liu read in the *Shenbao* newspaper of the Japanese attack on Qingdao. As the details became clear, he noted in his diary that Qingdao was a German concession in Shandong, and that Japan had joined an alliance of foreign powers that were at war with Germany.[54] But he believed that "Japan's aim is not Qingdao but to swallow up China."[55] In 1919, when the Versailles Peace Treaty was being negotiated and it became apparent that China would not regain Qingdao, he heard reports of student protests in the provincial capital and in other cities. He also discussed the boycott of Japanese goods with his son-in-law who was a student at Shanxi University and had himself been on strike. Then in 1925 there was the storm of protest against the killing of Shanghai demonstrators by British police, which Liu read about in the newspapers. This was experienced in Shanxi primarily as a student campaign against excessive taxation, and particularly a new tax on rooms that had been introduced by the government. Liu was delighted when huge student protests in the provincial capital forced the government to withdraw the new tax. This was also the first time school pupils in Jinci were organized to demonstrate, and Liu heard them shouting slogans. He could not hear exactly what they were saying, but he wrote about their desire to make China strong enough to fight the foreigners and win. Like the modernizers, Liu cared greatly about preserving China's sovereignty from foreign incursions; he disagreed with them only on how this should be achieved.[56]

Liu read about all these events in the newspapers, which were mostly published in the treaty ports and supported the modernizers. At different times he read the *Shenbao*, a major national daily published in Shanghai, the *Shuntian Times* and *Tianjin Yishibao*, which circulated throughout north China, as well as the various Shanxi provincial newspapers that succeeded one another over the years.[57] Those who wrote for the newspapers used the new terminology of reforms, freedom, equality, the nation, the foreign powers. But Liu read the newspapers each morning after he finished his meditation, at the time of day when he had previously studied the dynastic histories. Inevitably he thought about national events in the language of Confucian morality. He condemned the leaders of the new Republic for their lack of loyalty, referring to Sun Yatsen as "the chief rebel" and Yuan Shikai as "the rebel minister."[58] Similarly, he insisted on talking about the countries taking part in the 1914–18 European war, which the newspapers referred to by their names, as foreign barbarians. Where he does use the modernizers' language, it is ironic. A few years before the revolution he had commented that although the modernizers talk about "self-strengthening," their reforms are actually "self-weakening."[59] After the revolution he wrote mockingly: "The dates have been converted to the Republic, but I still refer to the years according to the reign of the Xuantong Emperor because I am a man of the Qing and not of the Republic. Everyone makes his own decisions and cannot be forced; this is what the reformers call freedom."[60]

Liu hated the republican system and believed it to be immoral, but despite everything he still wanted to be an official. So he tried to adapt, making speeches, taking part in elections, and seeking appointment to some of the institutions created by the reforms. In 1912 he was elected to head the county assembly and accepted the appointment. Like so many of the new institutions, the assembly was expensive to run and it was far from clear what it was supposed to achieve. In particular, how were its responsibilities to be divided from those of the county magistrate? The idea of the separation of legislative and executive powers must have been hard for anyone brought up in the Qing system even to imagine, especially at the county level. The position of the county assembly was correspondingly problematic, torn between the traditional executive and policy-making functions of government and some unexplained new role. Thinking this problem through, Liu came to the conclusion that the assembly should oversee the county's finances to increase profit for the government and eliminate corruption. This fit with his understanding of the new policies as a whole, and also drew from his experience in the provincial assembly, which had been actively involved in a campaign to put local government finances in order. He hoped that this would make the assembly popular and would reduce the potential for extortionate taxation. But when he began to investigate, the county's finances turned out to be in total confusion with no clear budgets, and both income and expenditure carried over from the previous year. His efforts to sort things out met with considerable resistance from both the magistrate and other members of the assembly, but were supported by the chamber of commerce, since commercial taxpayers had borne the brunt of the new taxes. Indeed, the members of the chamber of commerce threatened to resign en masse if Liu left. Matters came to a head at a stormy meeting when Liu himself threatened to resign and was supported only by a small group of the younger assembly members. Eventually he did resign because he finally realized that there was corruption as well as mismanagement and became afraid of getting into trouble. He tried again four years later, in 1917, during a provincial government campaign to put county budgets in order, but again he resigned in the face of the magistrate's indifference and opposition from other quarters. Given that his family was not wealthy, Liu's prestige as a degree-holder and his carefully cultivated reputation for Confucian commitment were his only political assets. Since the reforms of the 1900s the value of both had declined drastically, and after the revolution it became obvious that they were no longer even enough to allow him to operate locally in the face of entrenched interests.[61]

The declining political value of Liu's moral capital becomes even more apparent when we look at his participation in a series of repairs to the Jinci temples that were made between 1915 and 1918. Liu was one of a committee of local dignitaries in charge of the repairs. He claims that his Confucian reputation was an asset when the committee went from door to door urging people to donate. But when there was a dispute over how much should be contributed by a certain group of villages, Liu allowed it to go to arbitration, which meant that both sides would have to make concessions. He became even less popular with the other managers when he made a speech accusing them, and particularly the Jinci town head Niu Yujian, of accepting bribes from the contractors and wasting money on meals. Public speaking was still quite a new practice and very closely tied to the ideas of the new Republic, but ironically Liu was trying to use it to reinforce his own position, which was heavily based on his Confucian reputation. His opening sentences were almost entirely constructed from classical quotations (very different from his usual workaday style). These brought to the fore the strict Confucian morality on which his reputation was based, since providing meals for the managers of public projects was not usually considered to be a form of corruption. But Liu was worried that his reputation as an upright man, his only real asset, would be compromised by the rumors that were circulating about the committee. At the same time he was reminding an audience largely composed of lower degree-holders that as an upper degree-holder he outranked them. Sadly for Liu, the value of his reputation and degree had declined to the point where it was easy for the committee to ignore him.[62]

Then that summer Huang Guoliang visited Jinci. The town, with its beautiful ancient temples and clear fast-flowing streams, was a popular destination for visitors from the provincial capital. Huang had avoided taking a major government position after the revolution, but he still commanded the second brigade of the new army and was one of the two or three most powerful men in the province. All of Liu's descendants remember him as the one genuinely powerful and famous person their family ever had contact with. After Huang's visit Liu, Niu Yujian, and three of the other managers traveled to the provincial capital to ask Huang for a donation. Liu stayed on in the capital for the elections and received a large donation from Huang, which he paid into a bank in Jinci without informing the rest of the committee. Liu claimed that that summer, while he was away, the other managers had invited Huang for what turned out to be a disastrous dinner at which Niu Yujian got drunk and started cursing the revolution. They then compounded their folly by charging the meal to the repairs, so that when Huang returned the next summer, he saw the cost displayed in the accounts, which were posted on the temple wall. As a result, Huang handed complete control over his original donation to Liu. He then announced his plan to collect money for further repairs and decided that "the old gentleman Liu" should manage this sum, too. Niu Yujian and the other Jinci leaders were naturally angry at being excluded from the project. This cannot have been helped by the use of some of Huang Guoliang's money for a project that blatantly benefitted Chiqiao. Liu had a pretty little pavilion built over the steps that the Chiqiao villagers used to get down to the main spring of water in the temple to wash their paper pulp twice a year when the river was dammed so the irrigation ditches could be cleared. Chiqiao laborers washing pulp hardly fit with the elegant surroundings and the practice had been a thorn in the side of the Jinci townsfolk for decades, with several attempts being made to close the steps. Legal disputes had always ended with magistrates allowing the Chiqiao villagers to continue washing their pulp, but their actions were hardly something the Jinci townsfolk wanted to celebrate.[63]

Liu's political weakness without Huang Guoliang's support became obvious the next year, when Yan Xishan finally managed to oust Huang from power and attempts at mediation between Liu and Niu Yujian failed.[64] As the pavilion project was about to finish, Niu told the craftsmen to stop work. By this time Liu was getting nervous. He described how in Chiqiao everyone was angry, "and a crowd of them were pushing me to go to Jinci and stand up to him. They all said, 'Niu Yujian doesn't have three heads or six arms and legs to kill you, and he's not a ferocious tiger or horrible beast that can bite you. Why do you need to be afraid of him? Why don't you go and discuss it with him?'" The crowd grew and stayed till it was dark pressing Liu to go and telling him how much he would lose face if he did not, but he still refused to go, arguing that this was a matter for his own conscience and Niu would die and be punished in the end. But the next day when he was describing the incident he added, "They meant that Niu Yujian was behaving outrageously, but the Jinci people are all terrified of him, so why should I be the only person who isn't?"[65] In the end he sent mediators with an apology to Niu, but Niu was not yet finished. He accused Liu of embezzling Huang Guoliang's donation. Liu was convinced he could clear himself if only the case could be brought to court, but the magistrate, who could see trouble coming, refused to hear it. Liu continued appealing to the authorities, but without effect. He put much of the decline of his reputation down to this episode, and his hatred of Niu Yujian lasted till 1935, when Niu was burned to death in a domestic fire. Liu then added a delighted note to the end of his account, pointing out that Niu had after all been punished.[66]

Niu Yujian's prosecution ended Liu's participation in local government. Local projects no doubt always involved infighting, and part of Liu's problem was that he was simply not very good at this, but his inability to operate was also the result of the change in government. He was not wealthy and what authority he had came from his education and behaving as a Confucian gentleman, both of which had been seriously undermined by the new values of the republican state. He had learned to speak and believe the rhetoric of Confucian values, but that rhetoric no longer had the power to move government officials. Moreover, Liu's Confucianism was by its very nature rigid and more than a little self-righteous, which made it difficult for him to build alliances with his peers. In this way, as in many other aspects, Confucian values expressed the deeply hierarchical nature of the state that had fostered them. At a more practical level, the abandonment of traditional education and the examinations had undermined the value of Liu's degree. In the past he would have significantly outranked Niu Yujian, a mere licentiate, and that in itself would have increased his influence. Now, the position of town head was becoming more and more powerful as local government expanded its power and the number of personnel it employed. With the support of the state gone and his status undermined, Liu became fatally dependent on his personal reputation. At first this seemed like an asset because it encouraged people to donate money to the project, but in the end it became a liability, for it meant that Niu's slander had the power to destroy him as a political actor.

Liu Dapeng never again became seriously involved in local politics, but his education did still give him the confidence to complain when things went wrong. As a result he became a kind of resource for Chiqiao villagers and other local people, though this was hardly the high government office he had once hoped for, nor was he particularly effective. In 1926, when the taxes being levied on the county seemed almost unbearable, he agreed to go and speak to Huang Guoliang, who was then in charge of some aspect of military provisioning. When Liu arrived Huang refused to see him, saying he was ill; Liu returned several times but the visit was not a success. Later that year some of his neighbors asked him to intervene in a dispute with the Chiqiao village head who had been unable to provide an adequate set of accounts. Liu's speeches blaming himself for the failure of his virtue to transform the village did not work, and the village head was thrown out of office by an angry crowd shortly afterward. Over the years Liu sent streams of complaints to the provincial government. A collection of drafts for these from the year 1933 survives. Many return to the same themes that had concerned him since the 1900s: taxes, the expansion of government institutions, the unsatisfactory nature of elections, and local corruption. He complains that the village office adds its own surcharge to the grain tax and several other charges, and that the village head, his deputy, the neighborhood heads, the village secretary, and their friends all get free meals in the village office while the taxes are being collected. Taxes had once been handled by five or six people in the county office, but now 167 villages all have ten people, all eating at public expense. Just occasionally Liu succeeded: he once managed to persuade the county magistrate to reduce the tax on wedding certificates from one dollar to 40 cents, and many years later, when there was an epidemic in the county prison, he got a much less sympathetic magistrate to agree to release all the people who had been arrested for failure to pay taxes.[67]

As time went on and his own circumstances declined, Liu began to identify more with his neighbors than with the officials and local leaders who were in some sense his peers. He became increasingly concerned that the rich should pay their fair share of taxes. In the summer of 1926 he attended a meeting of the county gentry called by the magistrate to discuss how the grain tax should be allocated. He had already had a bad morning since a gong had been rung in Chiqiao to announce that every household must provide 20 lbs of straw and pay 10 cents by noon or be fined. When he got to the meeting he found that everyone else wanted the county to borrow the money to pay the grain tax and then to divide the cost up by household. Liu proposed making the wealthiest households pay the full sum so that the poor need not be troubled. Liu's proposal made sense from his own point of view since his family was certainly not wealthy, but it was hardly surprising that the other people at the meeting did not take it up. In fact no one supported him and he was reduced to making an angry speech accusing the magistrate of allowing the wealthy households to make money at the expense of the poor.[68] That winter he threatened that "in the future as soon as there is disorder, the poor will hate the rich households for taking advantage of them, and they will be sure to rise up in a crowd and rob the rich households."[69] In 1932 he actually recorded a dream "that I was leading a great crowd of people to force the wealthy households to pay in full this year's spring grain taxes in order to alleviate the suffering of the poor."[70]

Liu came to identify with his neighbors in large part because he shared their troubles. As his hopes for political appointment vanished and his family gradually lost money, his economic situation was little different from that of his neighbors. He suffered from the economic and political consequences of the revolution, and his voice, like theirs, was not heard when he protested. He was popular in the village and admired for his courage even though the villagers laugh today when they remember his refusal to admit defeat. A story is recorded on the inscription set up when he died of how he appealed to the Nanjing government against the harsh taxation in Shanxi. The villagers remember and tell this story as his attempt to bring a legal case against Yan

Xishan in Nanjing. They remember a letter, a very large letter, which arrived in reply from the Nanjing government, ordering the Shanxi provincial government to reduce taxes. Everyone was impressed by the letter and by Liu's audacity, but the old men laugh when I ask them whether Yan Xishan was concerned about this, and they tell me that of course he was not when he learned who had made the complaint.[71]

FIVE

The Merchant

In 1913 Liu Dapeng resigned from his teaching job at the new school in Jinci, because he had not been paid, and was left unemployed at home with a family of eight adults and six children to support. The only family members with any income were his eldest son Jie, who was teaching at the county higher primary school, and his third son Xiang, who was a village schoolteacher. The family did own some land, and that summer Liu spent a lot of time working in the fields. But as the wheat and millet harvests came in, he calculated how long it would feed the family, and knew that it would not last to the end of the year. The family's finances had been drained by Jie's wedding and that of Liu's daughter Hongyu that year, and plans were already under way for the wedding of his fourth son Jin and his eldest granddaughter Xiyan the next year. Four weddings in two years would have been a heavy burden on any family, let alone one that had practically no income and was supporting another son who was studying at the middle school in the provincial capital. The family did still get some money from Liu Ming's carpentry shop, which was being run by one of the former clerks, and Liu Dapeng was soon involved in an attempt to expand it by opening a new store in the town of Yangyi. The family also received rent from some shops in Chiqiao that Liu Ming had purchased. The idea of a family supporting itself by agriculture and teaching was a commonplace of the classical literature that Liu had studied, and he sometimes described his own family in that way; but in fact a large part of the family's income had always come from Liu's father's business, and it was not surprising that Liu now turned to business to try and make a living.[1]

The business he entered was coal mining. Shanxi is rich in coal, and the Fen river and the streams that flow into it have cut through the rocks, leaving seams of coal exposed in the mountains that ring the plain. The coal had been mined for centuries, and a popular rhyme described the mines of Taiyuan county as being as many as the stars in the sky. More prosaically, there were said to be 120 mines in the county in 1918. In fact it was almost impossible to count the number of mines because many of the mountain villagers farmed millet and potatoes in the summer and supported themselves through the winter by literally digging holes in the ground to get at the coal. After a few months when the hole got too deep, they would move to another site and dig there. Government reports described the men who operated these small mines as coolies who made barely enough money to feed themselves, while Liu noted that many of them could not afford to marry, leaving the mountain villages chronically short of women. The county's larger mines were much more profitable, but in other ways shared many of the characteristics of these ephemeral enterprises. Like the small mines they operated only in the winter months when labor was readily available, coal was needed for heating, and the mountain roads were frozen hard.[2] Moreover, even large mines were frequently abandoned if the mines struck water or there was insufficient natural ventilation. As the common saying went, "If water floods the mine or the lamps don't shine, the coal is left to future generations."[3] Nevertheless, where large seams of high-quality coal were readily accessible there were mines of considerable size and indeed antiquity.

Liu Dapeng found his visits to these large mines exciting. In one of his gazetteers he describes the scene at Shimen mine, which he managed for many years. Shimen, like most of the large mines, was a drift mine with a horizontal shaft leading directly into the hillside. Liu describes the coal yards and workers' housing that clustered around the entrance to the mine. The miners slept during the day and worked at night, so all night there were coal fires burning amidst the shouts of the ox-cart drivers who hauled the coal out of the mine, the sound of the hewers cutting the coal, and the hustle and bustle of the carters preparing their loads so that at first light they could set off for the valley. Occasionally, Liu went down into the mines to inspect the coal faces. He carried an oil lamp, but it was still very dark and the uneven surface made it difficult to walk. He described the shadows cast by the little oil lamp flickering on the jagged walls from which water slowly dripped. Down in the mine he saw the hewers cutting the coal face. This was skilled work and most of those who did it had many years' experience: they chipped away the coal above and below the chosen block and then used levers to make it fall. Large blocks were particularly valuable, and these men were well-paid and sought after. In the autumn when the mines were about to open for the winter, owners would try to poach skilled laborers from their competitors. Some laborers even managed to become mine owners themselves. But the work was hard and dangerous: flooding, fire, and collapsing roofs were ever-present risks. Liu thought that the miners' life was like that of a rat in a hole.[4]

The work of the hewers was better than that of the laborers and the porters who brought the coal out of the mine. In Shimen mine, the coal was shifted from the rockface onto ox carts, which hauled it out of the mine. Oxen were a major part of the mine's capital expenditure and driving them was a responsible job, but even so, in his poem Liu emphasizes the hardship of the work:

The Miner

He goes home in the morning and comes to the mine in the
   middle of the night.
Although his body is worn with labor his mind wanders,
With an oil lamp strapped to his head he yells at the load,
With a whip in his hand he urges the oxen on.

The sound of his voice is easy to distinguish
But his face is always hard to make out.
Making a living beneath the mountain ranges,
All year he must hurry bent double at the waist.[5]

In many other mines the entrance was too steep for oxen, and men struggled along the low passages carrying the coal out in sacks or leather backpacks. These jobs were tough, dangerous, unskilled, and poorly paid. The workers grumbled that a man who entered the mine with shoes and socks would be washing his bare legs when he came out. The population of the mountain villages was tiny compared with the needs of the mines, and impoverished migrant laborers employed on piece rates provided a large part of the workforce. Some mines that needed large numbers of porters also made extensive use of bonded laborers bought for the winter at the late autumn temple fair at Jinci, which also sold second-hand clothes for the winter months. One of these men described how he had been working as a shepherd in the south of the province, was laid off over the winter, and heard that it was possible to make a living in the mines. But when he arrived at Jinci, he was tricked by a dealer and sold as a contract laborer to one of the mines. After working the whole winter and being beaten if he did not carry enough coal, he was finally released with two pounds of millet and a new pair of trousers. Not all contract laborers were tricked, but it is scarcely surprising that mining suffered when military campaigns gave laborers the alternative of joining the army.[6]

When the coal reached the surface, it was sorted into lumps of different sizes and sold to carters and porters who would transport it down to the plain and sell it there. Ox carts, mule carts, camels, donkeys, wheelbarrows, and men with carrying poles all gathered at the mine entrance during the night ready to set off at crack of dawn. Some of the carts came from considerable distances and would have stayed the previous night in Taiyuan county town, which had many inns that specialized in the coal business. Transporting coal was profitable, and many young men from Chiqiao and other plains villages went up to the mines with wheelbarrows (and sometimes a donkey to help pull) and made enough to support their families over the winter. A strong young man could push well over a thousand pounds of coal at a time, but it needed skill to keep the load balanced, the mountain roads were narrow and dangerous, and there were many accidents and deaths. When the carters reached the plain, they sold some of the coal for heating and the remainder for local industries.[7]

Because transporting coal across the plain was expensive and inconvenient, many industrial enterprises gathered in the villages at the foot of the mountains. Chiqiao was one of these villages and was primarily an industrial community: more than 80 percent of the village's population made their living primarily as paper makers.[8] By the 1930s it felt to the locals as if half the people in the village were migrant laborers, mostly from the paper-making district of Xinyang in Henan province. The paper makers bought straw from local farmers, soaked it in lime, and boiled it into pulp in great vats over coal fires, then washed the pulp in the river, and molded it into sheets that were pasted up to dry. The resulting paper was coarse and used mainly to strengthen mortar for building. Some was also sold for wrapping and toilet paper. During Liu's lifetime no one in his family made paper, but the industry formed the backdrop to their daily lives. For most of the year the village was surrounded by great heaps of straw waiting to be pulped. The sound of the treadles beating the pulp filled the village all day and late into the night, and sheets of paper were pasted to dry not only on special drying walls at the foot of the hills, but also all over the walls of houses. Paper making structured roles within the family: men stood in the river washing the pulp, worked the treadles, and did the heavy, skilled work of drawing the mold through the pulp to make the sheets, while women, children and the elderly pasted the sheets on the wall to dry. Paper was also used as a kind of currency with the village shops accepting bundles of paper in return for goods. This meant that wet weather, which prevented the paper from drying, could be a disaster for the poor. One man tells of his grandmother desperately drying a few sheets on a griddle over the stove, and Liu records the theft of heads of maize from his fields when the paper makers could not afford to buy food because of the rain. Paper making even structured the calendar. In the autumn cheerful chatter filled the village as the paper making families helped one another replaster the drying walls. In the spring even those who did not make paper were involved when married daughters came home and friends visited for the village's main temple festival which was held in honor of the paper-makers' god and paid for by a tax on each of the pulp vats in the village.[9]

Chiqiao also had an alum works. Alum is a chemical that was used in mortar, as a mordant to set dyes, and also in cooking. Seams of shale that could be used to produce alum were found alongside some seams of coal and were often mined at the same time. A 1919 survey found that all the villages along the edge of the plain made alum. Chiqiao's alum works was founded in 1851, but the industry dated back to at least the sixteenth century. The production of alum required large quantities of coal and water as well as the alum-bearing

shale. Two different methods were used to produce alum of different quali-
ties, but both involved boiling the shale in water, adding saltpeter, then
draining off the solution and allowing it to crystallize. The crystals were
then repeatedly removed, dissolved in fresh water, boiled, and allowed to
crystallize again. The whole process took several months, but the shale was
cheap to buy and the end product was valuable. Indeed it was so valuable
that a wheelbarrow load was usually followed by a man whose only job was
to keep passers-by from stealing handfuls. Alum prices soared with the dis-
appearance of imported dyes as a result of the 1914–18 European War. Before the war German aniline dyes, which produced brilliant reds, blues, and
greens, had been sold in every village in pedlars' packs. When these disappeared with the outbreak of war, indigo farming revived, shops sold Shanxi
homespun, and alum sales boomed. Prices continued to be good for some
time after the war ended, but the industry was hard hit by Yan Xishan's entry into the Chinese warlord wars in 1925, which pushed up the price of saltpeter. Saltpeter, which was also used in the manufacture of gunpowder, was
manufactured in another district on the edge of the mountains just a few
miles south. Paper, alum, and saltpeter were only a few of the wide range of
products manufactured in villages in this area. Chiqiao was unusual in the
very high proportion of villagers exclusively employed in paper making, but
specialized village industries were typical.[10]

Liu Dapeng's business activities began as a result of his reputation. In
1914 as a respected but currently unemployed member of the local community, he was called in to sort out the finances of Shimen mine. The mine
owner had died two years earlier, leaving a widow and young child who were
unable to take control of the enterprise effectively, and the mine had been
losing money ever since. Shimen was the largest mine in the valley that lay
directly behind Chiqiao. It was said to have been founded in the sixteenth
century, and by the time Liu became involved twenty to thirty oxen were
used hauling coal in the mine. Its annual production two years later was
7,000 tons of coal. Liu arranged the payment of the mine's debts and was
then offered the job of managing the mine for an annual salary of 176 taels,
which was considerably more than he had earned as a tutor. His advanced
education, interest in accounts, and reputation for moral integrity made him
a popular mediator in these kinds of situations. As his grandson put it, people called him in because he was warm-hearted and fair, and because they

were afraid of him. On this occasion he convinced himself that he was taking on the job in order to protect the previous owner's widow and child, and he did indeed ensure that they received a share of the mine's profits. The next year, however, he decided to enter into a partnership with the mine's owner, presumably in the expectation that he would make more money than he was receiving as wages. He did not have enough capital to do this so he and one of the mine's head clerks, a Chiqiao man Liu had recommended for the job, put the capital together from a series of small investments by others. Since Liu could not have repaid this sum, the investors who trusted him with their money were inevitably relying on his reputation for moral integrity. The final arrangement was that Liu provided two-thirds of the capital while the owner's family would provide the oxen and tools, which would be considered to be equal to the remaining third, and the profits would be split accordingly. The day-to-day management of the mine continued to be undertaken by the two head clerks, Liu's friend from Chiqiao and a blind man from one of the mountain villages who did the accounts. Liu became, in effect, the investors' representative. For the next fourteen years he went to the mine roughly twice a month over the winter mining season, usually for a couple of days, but sometimes for longer, especially during the run-up to New Year when all business debts had to be cleared. In 1919 his friend the head clerk became ill, and Liu stayed at the mine, undertaking the day-to-day management. He probably also did other odd jobs from time to time: on one occasion his diary records that he was driving a sick ox down from the mountains when it fell over and died. But mostly his work seems to have consisted of talking things over with the clerks, and inspecting the books and occasionally the mine workings.[11]

Shimen mine was profitable. Years later, after he had lost the contract, Liu claimed that the capital invested in the mine was considerable, "but as everyone knows the profits are very great."[12] Liu had also been lucky in entering the industry at the start of a very profitable period. New modern industries, such as machine-making, flour-milling, and electric power plants were being founded and provided additional markets for coal. One of the Taiyuan county mines sold much of its coal to the new electric light plant in the provincial capital. But most Taiyuan county coal was unsuitable for modern industry and was used for heating and for traditional industries. These markets boomed when the outbreak of war in Europe in 1914 removed many imported products from the market: as mentioned earlier, German dyes disappeared and alum production rose; imported matches vanished and the province's only match factory suddenly became so profitable that two more were founded. These kinds of small-scale local industries never made profits on the scale of the great banking and trading houses, but they did provide employment for other men like Liu who had lost jobs in teaching, banking, or trade as a result of the political changes, like Liu's friend the Shimen mine clerk who had worked for a bank in Jinci until it collapsed in 1913. It took some time after the end of the Great War for European exports to recover, so the period from 1914 to 1925 when Liu was managing Shimen mine was one of almost continuous expansion and profits for the coal industry. Moreover, in 1920 there was a serious drought in Pingding, a mining county on the other side of the plain. Like the paper makers from Henan who came to Chiqiao, the coal miners of Pingding moved to areas where they could find employment that used their skills. Many arrived in the Taiyuan area, reducing the cost of labor and making the mines still more profitable. The growth of the provincial capital and the railway junction town of Yuci also increased the number of consumers. By 1921 the Taiyuan county mine owners were wealthy enough to rebuild the temple to the Mine god in the county town. They invited Liu to come and paint in the pupils of the eyes on the new statue of the god, to make it come alive. He declined, but agreed to attend the ceremony.[13]

Realizing that the coal industry could enable him to support his family, Liu made a series of further investments. The first of these was in Xiping mine, another large-scale local drift mine with high-quality coal, though the mine had become so deep that it was no longer very efficient to work. Its annual production in 1918 was said to be worth 3.2 million dollars. (By this time the silver dollar had become the standard unit of local currency. It was worth about the same as the tael.) This mine was owned by Wu Guangwen, who lived in one of the nearby mountain villages. He agreed to contract the mine to Liu and two of his friends, Yang Zhuo and Hao Liuji, for five years, with half the profits to go to the owner and half to the contractors. Again Liu had no money to invest as capital in the project; his diary records that Yang and Hao arranged the money for him. Why should they have done this? The sum involved was sizeable, and there is no indication that they expected Liu to be involved in the day-to-day management of the mine. Yang and Hao were both Jinci men who had longstanding connections with the coal industry. Yang was the owner of another large coal mine, and his family had owned coal mines for at least a hundred years. Hao appears to have been a professional mine manager. Both were close to Liu, supporting him in the dispute over the Jinci temple repairs, but they were not relations and the two of them worked together on other projects in which Liu was not involved. Bearing all this in mind, it seems likely that Yang and Hao invited Liu to take part in the project primarily because of his status and reputation. It is possible that they needed him to fix the original deal with the owner, or hoped that he might be able to influence the mine's tax payments. Alternatively he may have operated, as he did for Shimen mine, to collect small investments which he would then oversee. All of these possibilities suggests that they were hoping to make use of his reputation for Confucian commitment.[14]

In later years Liu also invested in the Huigou alum works, and in Daguan, Qiwadong, and Houwa mines. Like other alum works, Huigou went into crisis in 1925 when the price of saltpeter, which was needed to make the alum, rose to impossibly high levels. Liu, who described his position as that of manager, ended up involved in a long and bitter dispute when he refused to let the other investors withdraw capital from the business in the face of this disaster. Then, in the late 1920s, Liu lost his contract for Shimen mine when the owner's family took back full management, and when the contract for Xiping reached its term the mine was closed. After this Liu invested in Daguan mine. In this case his role was more straightforward: he was invited in by the mine manager to provide investment and protection through his status and connections. He also continued his previous partnerships by investing in Qiwadong mine, which was owned by Yang Zhuo and managed by Hao Liuji. Finally, he used a loan of 100 dollars from one of his sons-in-law to buy shares in Qiwadong mine. But by this time the local economy was in decline, and none of these ventures were as profitable as Shimen had been.

Liu Dapeng had very little capital to invest in coal mining. The money he had earned as a teacher had been used to buy land and to pay for the education of his sons. He lamented that this lack of capital limited the amount of money that he could make from his business ventures. But even though he lacked capital, he managed to support his family through his involvement in business. His continued involvement in business through the 1920s suggests that the Confucian self-presentation of businessmen continued well after such

morals had become irrelevant to local government. Trustworthiness—with
its continued relation to commercial credit—was at the heart of this link between morality and business. Trustworthiness was one of the core Confucian
virtues, and Liu's diary at the time of the disputes over the temple repairs is
full of references to the necessity of preserving people's trust.[15] One of his
entries reads,

> Zixia said "The superior man must be trusted before he can impose labors
> on his people. If he does not have their trust, they will think he is oppress-
> ing them. He must be trusted before remonstrating with them. If he has not
> won their trust, they will think he is vilifying them." Now the word trust is
> at the basis of human life. In one's contacts with the world and dealings with
> people, one must not lose it for a moment. When one loses trust, one can-
> not profit and has no sense of direction. Confucius said, "I do not know how
> a man without trust can get on. If a large cart has no cross-bars or a small
> cart no pins to attach the yoke to, how can it be made to go?" We can learn
> much from this teaching that has been handed down to us.[16]

The two passages quoted in this diary entry drawn from the *Analects* and the
standard commentary, which Liu Dapeng studied for the examinations, make
it clear that trust in this context means both being sincere and being believed
by others.[17]

The same term for trust was also used in the sense of commercial credit.
A local acquaintance of Liu Dapeng's noted that in his county, trustworthiness was the most important virtue and that this was because trade had played
such an important part in the county since the eighteenth century and there
were few legal means of ensuring payment. Trust was essential to commerce
and banking in a world where most exchanges relied on credit, with bills being settled only at the end of the financial quarter, and commercial credit
was heavily dependent on personal reputation.[18] During his dispute with Niu
Yujian over the repairs to Jinci temple, Liu had persuaded several leading
members of the town's chamber of commerce to help him administer Huang
Guoliang's donation. When Niu Yujian sued them, the members of the chamber of commerce appealed alongside Liu, explaining that "public reputation
is worth as much as our lives to us" and "when we merchants receive this slur
on our name, it not only shames us in the business community so that every-

one despises us, but also makes us unacceptable to our investors so that we are truly afraid that we will lose our positions."[19] Toward the end of the dispute Liu claimed, with some exaggeration, that the attacks on his reputation had totally destroyed his "everyday credit."[20] The importance of trust meant that a reputation for sincerity and personal integrity was an important element in raising capital for business. Liu's lack of capital diminished the amount of money he could make in the coal business, but even without capital he was able to make a living because wealth was not simply a matter of how much money one had. In Liu's case it was also a matter of his neighbors' judgments about how trustworthy he was and thus how much credit he could be given.[21]

Liu's reputation for moral integrity was based on his education, but it was built up by his constant work as a mediator for business and other disputes. The case of Zhang Zishen provides a good example of this work. Zhang Zishen lived in a village not far from Chiqiao and did business in Qingyuan county town a few miles to the south. Liu had once taught one of his sons, and his own son Jie was married to a woman from his family. So when in 1914 Zhang Zishen's grain store collapsed with huge debts and he was arrested by one of his creditors, it is not surprising that his first response was to send for Liu to come get him out of prison. Liu arranged for someone to provide bail so that Zhang Zishen could be released and was then given the task of trying to get Zhang's creditors to agree to a settlement. For several months he went regularly to Qingyuan, meeting with the creditors, dining with them, and trying to persuade them to agree to a deal. In the end he succeeded in getting them to settle for 60 percent of what was owed to them. Liu rather enjoyed the job. It was essential that a mediator should not be paid for his work, since that would have compromised his reputation for moral integrity, but he got to stay at various stores that had connections with Zhang Zishen's business. He ate at them, too, and his diary is full of comments on how well he was looked after and how comfortable he felt. When he was not meeting with the creditors he walked in the mountains, went sightseeing, and went to the opera and puppet theater. All this was a pleasant change from the heavy labor in the fields that he spent the rest of that summer grumbling about. Mediation relied on an assumption that the mediator's judgments would be predictable and based on values that were accepted by all those involved. At the same time the prestige of the mediator was crucial, since this was what made it difficult for the parties involved to refuse his proposals for concessions. Thus the process of mediation had the pleasant effect of confirming both Liu's values and his status.[22]

Liu spent much more time mediating business disputes than family disputes. Possibly by the 1920s his values were more acceptable in a business than in a family context. Certainly his account of mediating a dispute between a nephew and uncle about how to divide their family property suggests that his opinions on family matters were too rigid to be of much use. In this case he simply urged the nephew and uncle to continue living together in a joint family. But it also seems likely that Liu also mediated a lot of business disputes because he had an interest in accounting and a certain degree of financial acumen. He had been interested in local government finance since his education in the academy in Taiyuan city, and his efforts as head of the county assembly had been primarily concerned with finance and accounting. Local government and business used related accounting systems, and a large proportion of Liu's business activities were also concerned with overseeing accounts. All the businesses and other institutions Liu dealt with kept records of income and expenditure, and at the end of the year accounts had to be calculated and agreed on by all interested parties. One of the things that made Liu so angry with Niu Yujian during the repairs to the Jinci temple was that he and the other members of the management committee were not invited to be present when the accounts were calculated. He wrote to the magistrate, accusing Niu Yujian of failing to have the accounts properly audited.[23] Moreover, when the accounts were posted at Jinci and everyone could see how much money had been spent, "Everyone who saw the accounts was extremely critical of them and pointed out their errors. When I heard this I deeply regretted that I had worked with those men so that my reputation had been totally destroyed, and they were behaving as if there was nothing the matter."[24] In the same way Liu's involvement in business as a shareholders' representative meant that it was essential that he was present and understood what was being said when the annual accounts were calculated and any discrepancies had to be resolved. Any errors found later would reflect on his reputation.

A good understanding of business accounting was also essential to Liu's work as a mediator. When he wrote about his mediation in his diary, fair financial division was usually central. So, for example, when in the spring of

1926 the owner of one of the remaining banks in Jinci tried to sack its three elderly clerks and reorganize the business, Liu was called in by the clerks to act on their behalf. He spent several days at the bank negotiating the terms on which the clerks would resign, which included a payment of half the year's salary and a lump sum to reimburse them for the share in the bank's profits that was normally distributed to longstanding staff in accordance with their competence and seniority. Although he does speak of urging the clerks not to quarrel, most of his description is taken up with the negotiation of the terms. On another occasion Liu negotiated a settlement between the partners in another Jinci bank in which the cash accounts and shop fittings were to be split. That night he woke up and realized that he had miscalculated the profits and had therefore given one of the partners more than the other. He went over and over the problem in his mind. The next morning he wrote a letter explaining the problem, blaming it on himself, saying that he felt he had lost his moral authority, and asking that his name be withdrawn from the contracts. In this case it is particularly clear that correct accounting is closely linked both to his sense of moral integrity and to his reputation.[25]

Liu's value to the business community was recognized when he was first appointed to be a paid administrator by the county chamber of commerce, and then chosen by the county's mining households to be the manager of the new coal mining office. From 1915 to 1916, he was employed by the chamber of commerce as a trouble-shooter and general administrator. He arranged monthly meetings and recorded decisions on topics ranging from the fixing of new rules for the payment of stamp duty to the purchase of a clock (which would make chamber meetings among the first in Liu's experience to be held by clock time). But most of his work involved settling disputes between chamber members and between the chamber and the local government. One of the most dramatic of these came about when the magistrate, on the orders of higher authorities, decided to shut one of the Jinci banks. Liu was dining in Jinci at one of the other businesses when he saw the government clerk coming to announce this decision. Realizing that it would inevitably cause a run that would probably bring down the bank and would be a disaster for investors, Liu rushed off to the county town to persuade the magistrate to change his plans. He then went to the chamber of commerce offices and called a meeting of all the chamber's members in the county town and persuaded them not to withdraw their money.[26] Afterward, Liu grumbled that the magistrate did not understand commerce and did not bother to think through the implications of his actions. This sounds like any businessman complaining against any bureaucrat. On the other hand he also often wrote in a way that showed that he did not consider himself to be a member of the business community, complaining when he was asked to do too much work for the chamber that "all merchants have a very dependent nature."[27]

In his work for the chamber of commerce in 1915, Liu was still to some extent an outsider employed because of his status and connections with the local government, but when he worked for the coal mining office through the 1920s it was as an active member of the business community. Liu had been involved with the office since it was founded to create a group that could resist the power of the wealthiest mine owners to control the allocation of taxes. Some of the initial discussions were held in his house, several of the early members were his friends, his son Jie wrote the constitution, and Liu drafted announcements for the secretary to copy out. Before the office was founded, the allocation of taxes had been dominated by the men who were the mining heads for each of the county's nine valleys. In 1915, shortly after the founding of the office, Liu went to Liuzi valley to investigate the allocation system. A fixed sum had to be raised and was to be divided in accordance with the number of carts owned by each mine. The valley's mining head had reported the total number of carts in the valley, but there had been many complaints that he had been corrupt and the figures were incorrect. Presumably he had been taking bribes in order to keep carts off the books. Liu went to stay at one of the big mines and ordered all the small mines to bring their carts for him to inspect. He then went round the other large mines to find out how many carts each had. This type of inspection by a representative of a group recognized by the local government combined with Liu's status and known integrity to back it up meant that the magistrate could be forced to accept the coal mining office's figures and even possibly to punish the valley's mining head. In the end the office undertook to contract all the taxes on coal, collecting them and then handing them over to the government. But this became increasingly difficult as the amounts demanded by the government grew, and in 1926, when Yan Xishan's military demands imposed really impossible levels of taxation, Liu resigned. Until this time, however, his position first at the chamber of commerce and then in the coal mining office gave him a degree of power in the business community. This must have benefitted him financially: the chamber of commerce almost certainly paid him a salary, and the involvement of the coal mining office with tax division suggests another reason why he was invited to become a partner in business operations despite his lack of capital. He held these positions as a result of his presentation of himself as an upright Confucian gentleman, the reputation for integrity and financial even-handedness that this generated, and the concern with finance and accounting that went with it.[28]

Liu's experience with mining and the coal industry was so closely tied to his presentation of himself as a Confucian gentleman that he even began to write about the mining communities as an alternative world where ancient values were still respected. Before he himself had been involved in mining, there are few references to the mountains or mining in his works, and those few negative. In 1896 he wrote,

> Many people open mines in the Western mountains. They often cause loss of life, financially exploit the laborers, and other things like that. There are innumerable bad reports of all kinds about how the families of those who open mines often bring Heaven's punishment on themselves: some have died of starvation in prison, some have been beaten to death, and some of their women have had affairs. Those who mine do so only to make a profit, not considering whether it is good or bad for them, but spending their lives in the midst of it all.[29]

After Liu himself became involved in the mining industry, his images of the mountains changed. Even as he inspected mines and negotiated business deals, Liu began to depict the mountains as an isolated world whose inhabitants led a simple pastoral life reminiscent of antiquity. This is most obvious in his gazetteers of two of the mountain valleys, written in 1921 when he was heavily engaged in the mining business and regularly visiting the mountains.[30] Here Liu describes a world whose simple, subsistence economy reminds him of the golden age of antiquity. He describes how "the men farm and the women weave," a division that suggests ancient ways and the proper ordering of the sexes.[31] In another tiny mountain hamlet, the men farm the fields in summer and mine for coal in winter. Apart from paying their land tax they have no other business, so they are not worried when there are tax increases or political changes. This, he says, is "what the *Book of Odes* calls 'obeying the laws of God without need of knowledge or wisdom.'"[32] The quotation refers to the rule of King Wen in the golden age of antiquity, to which Confucians traditionally looked back in admiration.

This image of the mountains as an isolated and idyllic world is applied even to places where he had elaborate business dealings. So, for example, Liu knew Chaizhuang village well because it was the home of Wu Guang-wen, the owner of the Xiping coal mine, which Liu, Yang Zhuo, and Hao Liuji contracted to run from 1915 to 1926. Wu had established the mine in 1886 with 300 taels capital, and its annual production in 1918 was worth 3.2 million dollars.[33] Yet when Liu described Chaizhuang he wrote of how it reminded him of "Peach Blossom Spring," the famous story of a man who finds himself in an idyllic rural world whose inhabitants have become cut off from history. He writes,

> The people are simple and their customs are honest. They do not know the latest news, nor that the dynasty has ended, or the changes in the political situation. And as for the squabbles of the men who compete for power and the greedy passions of the foreigners with their covetous glances, they know none of it. This is indeed Shanxi's "Peach Blossom Spring."[34]

Isolation from the state is in fact an essential feature of this rural idyll. The mountains became a place of refuge from the policies of the modernizing state and Liu revels in the ignorance of the mountain people. He reports that they keep to the old lunar calendar and that their children do not attend modern schools. Occasionally he depicts himself bringing news of the outside world to these isolated communities, as when in the midst of a ferocious campaign against opium use in 1928, he visited a mountain village and found himself warning the people of the tough new policy.[35] In Liu's writings the mountain folk live frugal lives dominated by the changing seasons and the demands of their environment. They are unaffected by the demands and pressures of the modern state that are changing the lives of the plains villagers. The importance of nature in Liu's descriptions of the mountain villages is mirrored in his sense of the naturalness and authenticity of human relationships in the mountain villages. The mountains become a Peach Blossom Spring: a world of nature and ancient values, and a fit subject for poetry.

Liu's depiction of the mountains as an isolated pastoral world is part of the process through which he depicts himself as a Confucian hermit withdrawing from the world. In so doing he is emphasizing that in his own mind at least, he is a scholar and a gentleman, not a merchant, but he is also doing more than this, for he writes about his business affairs in considerable detail. As he goes to the mountains to check accounts and conduct his business affairs, he nevertheless writes of the mountains in his diary as a place where the selfish desires against which he constantly battled are simply wiped away and only the underlying moral principles remain.[36] An anonymous poem that he says he found inscribed on a rock in Liuzi valley and copied out depicts the mountains as a place of seclusion for men of honor:

> The new folk are happy, the old folk are sad,
> The world has become yet more dangerous,
> I look for a hidden place in the mountains and deep woods,
> Where I can stay for a while by the rocky cliffs.
>
> The officials are even more corrupt and oppressive than before,
> Eight thousand robbers and bandits fill the world,
> Only the mountains are fairly tranquil and secluded,
> The many harsh taxes are hard to remove.
>
> The reform party is spread all over China,
> They struggle for power in a tangled heap,
> Worthy and eminent men all live in seclusion,
> Choosing homes by the springs and rocks, where the clouds drift.[37]

In this poem withdrawal to the mountains is part of Liu's presentation of himself as a hermit sharing in the centuries old tradition that saw the hermit's life as the honorable alternative to government service. This was true in times of peace, when it could be argued that the hermit's closeness to nature was inherently superior to the political involvement of the official, but even more true in times of chaos and disorder. Thus the isolated and morally pure world of the mountain villages Liu visited on mining business is contrasted with the immorality and disorder of the government.

Even when Liu is writing about the coal mines themselves, his work is tinged with this imagery. In a long poem he wrote about Shimen he began by discussing the state of the coal and alum industries. Then he described smoke in the air, the lights shining and the fires blazing, but also the birds flying among the mountain peaks, the sheep and cattle grazing, the cicadas singing, and the rest of the natural scene. In a world where darkness at night was almost universal, the lamps and fires, that lit up the mines where the miners entered at dusk and the coal was collected by carters who arrived before dawn, were one of the most striking features of the area's industrialization. Yet Liu describes them as part of the natural landscape in a poem that goes on to depict the mountain scenery in luscious imagery rich with fabulous creatures, bright colors, jade and pearls. In this magical landscape Liu feels as if at any moment he may come across the hermits who withdrew from the world in the golden age of antiquity. The poem ends with the line "To visit this place over a long period is to be a butterfly dreaming of Zhuangzi."[38] This refers to the story of the philosopher Zhuangzi, who saw a butterfly and wondered whether he was dreaming of the butterfly or the butterfly was dreaming of him. The valleys and coal mines have become the world of dreams, that same world Liu had long identified as the location of authentic moral order in a time of political disorder. Liu was the man who had awakened from dreams to the world of true values; it is striking that he felt that he had found that world when he visited the coal mines on business.

But of course Shanxi's coal industry was not a pastoral idyll cut off from the modern Chinese state. Levels of taxation were a serious issue for all coal mines. Taxes on coal had begun in 1901. The carters had to collect a ticket when they bought the coal from the mine and hand it over to the government clerks who were stationed on the road just where it reached the plain. The rates depended on the size of load: 20 cash for a large cart pulled by a mule, 10 cash for a donkey or small cart and 5 cash for a barrow. Only porters carrying the coal on their shoulders were exempt. Liu's only recorded positive comment about Christians came when a group of them beat up one of these tax collectors after a Christian coal porter had been arrested. Later the actual payments were taken over by the mines, which was why in 1915 the newly founded coal office was so concerned with registering the sizes of all the carts. The rates for these taxes were regularly increased: by 1919 the rate for a large cart was 30 cash and a barrow 10 cash. By the early 1920s the tax was raising approximately 25,000 dollars each year for the county government.[39]

At the same time many other taxes increased. Overall the provincial government's tax income more than doubled between 1915 and 1920. Liu records taxes being introduced on wine, coal, contracts, official documents, wedding certificates, haircuts, opera performances, and even street doors. The stamp duty was so effective that a visiting militarist praised the fact that it was even levied on theater tickets. Liu described it as the people's blood and sweat given to officials to wine and dine on. There was even a rumor that there would be a tax on dogs. Government policies were also funded locally by fines. Fines for foot-binding were set at three to 30 dollars for binding a child's feet, but also for selling soles for shoes for women with bound feet, or acting as matchmaker for a girl with bound feet. The money provided by the fines was used to pay the expenses of the women sent to investigate. In Chiqiao a bell was rung in the village to tell the women that they must un-bind their feet, but Liu was soon complaining that even those women who had unbound their feet were being fined and imprisoned until they paid up. What happened with the campaign against queues was similar: a fine of one dollar was levied on anyone whose hair was more than an inch long. Liu himself inevitably had to remove his queue. The campaign against opium, too, was experienced as extortion and government intrusion. Liu reported a story that was circulating about how soldiers had been sent out to search households on New Year's Eve. The soldiers destroyed one family's brick bed and found a large sum of silver and an opium pipe hidden in it. But they also searched many households where they found nothing.[40] New Year's Eve was a time when the whole family was supposed to come together to eat and everything was happy and auspicious to welcome in the New Year. Soldiers bursting into the family gathering to destroy the furniture and steal money seemed to epitomize the violence of state intrusion into the local commu-nity. To Liu Dapeng these campaigns were meaningless: the people were ha-rassed for no reason and naturally hated it. Indeed it was in this context that he referred to a "government disaster"—as if taxation was in the same realm as drought, fire, or flood.[41]

Still, up to 1925 the tax burden was endurable, but then Shanxi's governor, Yan Xishan, entered national politics. Before this time Yan had made use of Shanxi's formidable natural boundaries to keep the province out of the wars that had destroyed so much of the country. Now he, too, began campaigning for power on a national level. Military expenditures shot up, and the gov-ernment had no way of meeting them. In 1926 the provincial government demanded a "loan" of 10,000 dollars from Taiyuan county, and later in the year a further loan of 22,500 dollars. The coal mines were responsible for 10 percent of the business contribution. There were also ceaseless demands for military supplies. Taiyuan county town had to provide large numbers of carts, horses, and camels, as well as fodder. While carts were being requisitioned, almost all transport came to a halt since none of the carters dared go out. The fodder had to come from the county's supply of straw, which was normally used by the people of Chiqiao as the raw material for their paper. Interruptions to local industries also reduced the demand for local coal. There were also random assessments on households: in 1926 every household in Chiqiao was required to pay 6.7 dollars, and in 1931 Liu's family was given three days to pay 2.8 dollars (then approximately two days' wages for an agricultural laborer). Farming households, too, suffered. In 1926 the entire annual grain tax, including all the surcharges, was collected in the spring and then again in the autumn. By 1932 the grain tax was so heavy that the grain shops were refusing to contract the tax since it would be impossible for them to collect the full sum. When farmers, paper makers, and others had to pay out large sums to the government, they were forced to reduce expenditure elsewhere and the market for coal for domestic heating suffered. At the end of 1926 Liu reported that no one was buying rice, alum, or paper, and the market for coal was very poor. Taxes more than doubled again between 1925 and 1928, but even so the government could not meet its expenses, which had been rising even faster. Since the revolution Yan Xishan had tried to concentrate all banking activities in his Shanxi Provincial Bank, repeatedly barring other banks from printing and circulating money. Now, as the province's deficit grew, he responded by using the Shanxi Provincial Bank to print money, inducing rapid inflation and financial crisis.[42]

As these troubles hit the mining industry in the late 1920s and early 30s, the provincial government, true to its modernist credentials, became ever more concerned with rescuing the larger modern mines at the expense of their smaller competitors. From the start policies encouraging industrialization had favored large-scale, heavily mechanized, enterprises over existing rural industry. This is particularly apparent in the case of Taiyuan county coal mining, where smaller, unmechanized mines were usually more profitable than large, heavily capitalized operations. Mine owners interested in modernization tended to open deep mines with vertical shafts rather than the commoner drift mines that entered the hill horizontally. These deep mines were interesting to these modernizers because they made it possible to reach seams of better quality coal, which might be used for modern industry and might even be exported. They were not new to the county, but were not widely used because it was known that they had trouble competing with the cheaper drift mines. Liu recounts the story of a wealthy man from one of the plains villages who foolishly opened a deep shaft mine in the 1880s. The coal was good and abundant, but the cost of driving the shafts and employing the men to operate the pulleys used to haul the coal to the surface was so great that the mine's profits were never even equal to half its capital. The same problems afflicted modernizers who tried to open deep mines in the 1900s. The Jinfeng company, which was opened by two men from eastern China, was heavily capitalized and aimed to mine very high quality coal. Ten thousand taels were spent over three years on driving two shafts into the mountain, one for coal and the other for ventilation. The coal was very hard and of good quality, but because the mine was so deep the ventilation was poor, fire broke out several times a year, and many lives were lost. It was also necessary to extract 4,000 buckets of water each day to keep the mine from flooding. The mine operated for twenty years but never made a profit and was eventually abandoned. Similar problems afflicted owners who used other forms of capital investment. When a Cantonese man took over a large coal and alum mine in the valley in 1916, he decided to replace the oxen that hauled the coal and shale to the entrance with rails and carts that could be pushed by men. Liu was impressed by the fact that the carts saved the cost of having an ox, but doubted whether the owner could ever recoup the huge investment required to buy the rails and carts from Tianjin. Heavy capitalization in the coal industry is always problematic because of the fact that any coal mine will eventually be worked out. In Taiyuan county mines were in fact often abandoned long before the coal was gone, when they became flooded or gas build-up caused explosions or fires. It seems that the Jinfeng company went on operating in this situation despite considerable loss of life precisely because of the amount of capital that had been invested in it. Highly capitalized mines are profitable in other situations; in Taiyuan county it was the geology that made it impossible for them to compete. The abundance of coal and its easy accessibility meant that they would always be competing with mines whose owners had made far smaller capital investments and could therefore charge lower prices.[43]

In this situation, government regulation was designed to encourage the reformers' dream of modernization. The government claimed that all minerals belonged to it rather than to the person who owned the land, and from 1919 on, all mines were supposed to register before they were allowed to open. Registration cost 200 dollars and involved providing detailed maps of the area to be mined and a great deal of other documentation. In addition, mines that registered were required to pay certain additional taxes. But for the time being, this regulation was not enforced against the small mines. Then in 1932, as the profits of the large mines fell dramatically, all mines large or small were required to register and owners who had failed to register their operations were dragged off to the county government. Liu wrote that registration for the small pits cost 70 dollars, and the aim was to put the small pits out of business so that the large pits could sell what they produced and gain control of the market. The immediate result was that none of the small mines opened the next year, causing widespread unemployment. The ensuing poverty was so intense that a group of county governments petitioned the province, requesting that the small mines be allowed to reopen. The provincial government's compromise suggests that Liu's accusation about the aims of the exercise was correct. It agreed that small mines should be allowed to open, but only where there were poor roads and little coal, or where no coal had yet been discovered. Moreover, the small mines were only to operate on condition that they did not prevent the large mines from making a profit.[44]

Government regulation against small mines also made it easier for others to exploit them illegally. After Liu Dapeng's resignation from the coal office in the face of what he felt were impossible tax demands, his position was filled by a very different character. This was a man called Ge Rui, who came from outside the province. According to Liu, who paints him in the blackest possible terms, Ge Rui had made a fortune dealing in morphine and had used the money to buy up three of the area's largest mines. Liu petitioned the county government, saying that Ge Rui was using his position to force the small mines to register and using the registration taxes to enrich himself. Presumably he was either accepting bribes and agreeing to overlook certain small mines or adding a surcharge to the registration fee. Such behavior was typical of those who came to power in rural areas in the 1920s and 30s, when increases in government extraction meant that respectable members of the local community were no longer prepared to be involved. But the example also suggests the way in which the process interacted with government suppression of rural industry.[45]

Liu Dapeng had managed to support his family for more than a decade by using his reputation for strict moral integrity to generate a position for himself in the local business community. By the late 1920s, however, that business community was on the verge of collapse. The closure of the Mongolian frontier as a result of the 1911 revolution and the Russian revolution of 1917 had transformed Shanxi from a major trading corridor into an isolated backwater. As Russian control over Mongolia tightened during the 1920s, Chinese businesses there, most of which were run by Shanxi people, closed one after another. According to statistics held in Shanxi there were 470 Chinese businesses in Mongolia in 1924 and only 270 in 1925. Shanxi's trade was collapsing just when the loss of Qing patronage had already destroyed the banking industry. Rural industries benefitted from the war in Europe, but suffered from a modernizing provincial government that impoverished them both through taxation and through the kind of industrial development that it sought. Nearly all the Chiqiao paper-making businesses were in debt as the financial crisis ate into their sales.

By the early 1930s much of the rural population once supported by the province's commerce and industry was sliding into poverty, and Liu's family was no exception. Their mining investments made less and less money. Jie was dead and the family was still supporting the mentally ill Xuan. The only one of Liu's sons with a good salary was Jin, who was working as a clerk for the army in the provincial capital under the patronage of Huang Guoliang. The youngest two sons, Xiang and Hongqing, were both teaching primary school. Hongqing had been denied the chance to attend a middle school since the family simply could not afford it. Of Liu's three adult grandsons, two had left the province: one as an apprentice to his maternal uncle, a Western-style doctor, and one as a driver for the army. The remaining adult grandson was a factory worker in the provincial capital. Although more members of the family were employed than had been in 1914 when Liu began mining, several of them were in jobs that paid very low wages and were therefore unable to send money home. Thus the family was reduced to surviving from the small amount of land it owned.[46]

The Farmer

As the coal mines Liu Dapeng managed became less profitable, the family's small farm became increasingly important. In the 1890s the family had owned about 1.5 acres of land, and while Liu was teaching the good salary he earned was used by his father to buy more. In 1902, when prices were low because of the drought and the near famine that followed the imposition of the Boxer indemnity, the family bought another 1.5 acres. By 1926 they owned a total of 6 acres, which included rice paddies as well as irrigated land that could be used to grow wheat and some unirrigated hill fields that could be used only for millet. But with most of the family's adult men working away from home, the potential workforce was reduced to Liu, now nearly sixty, and his grandsons Quanzhong and Jingzhong, aged 17 and 12. Most village women did not work outdoors until the autumn millet harvest, and Liu's wife and daughters-in-law did not work outside the house at all. Given the intensive nature of local agriculture, six acres was simply too much for Liu and the two boys to work efficiently, so most of the land was rented out,

leaving the family with about 1.5 acres to cultivate. The valuable rice paddies, which were particularly labor-intensive, had been rented for more than
ten years to a man named Guo from a neighboring village. When a Chiqiao
villager asked to take over the tenancy at a higher rent, Liu refused on the
grounds that Guo would not be able to support his family without those
fields. Although this implies that Guo was not well off, the wording also suggests that this was not the only land he was farming. Another reference to a
plot of one-sixth of an acre that had been left unplanted by another tenant
suggests that the other fields too were rented to farmers who owned or
rented other land as well. Liu used the land that was not rented out to grow
wheat, millet, and vegetables.[1]

All his life Liu had helped occasionally in the fields at busy times of year.
In 1895, the year he traveled to Beijing for the national examinations, he was
out in the fields at harvest time helping plough the ground for the winter
wheat alongside the hired laborers. Someone shouted out to him: "You over
there, aren't you too tired to still be working in the fields?" Liu replied, "Whoever said that doesn't understand me. Our family makes a living from farming and study. If we don't farm, we won't have enough to eat, and if we don't
study, we won't know how to behave properly."[2] The person who shouted
out was obviously surprised to see Liu in the fields, the implication of his re-
mark being that a scholar would be weak and unused to heavy agricultural
labor. Of course being thought too grand to work in the fields (even if you
have to) has its advantages over always thinking that people are despising
you for your poverty. But Liu, like his father who had passed the military examinations, was a big strong man: all his life he was proud of his physical
strength. Many years later he went with a group of local dignitaries to visit
rock carvings up in the mountains. The other elderly gentlemen all had to
be carried up the last stretches (and the hated Niu Yujian refused even to attempt them), but Liu was stronger and wrote delightedly, "Only Liu Dapeng
went up on foot using a walking stick, as if he were walking on the plain and
did not need anyone to help him. Everyone commented that Liu was already
75 and none of the others was yet 70, but none of them was as strong and
healthy as Liu."[3] He attributed this to years of walking in the mountains, but
a lifetime of farm labor no doubt also played a part. After the revolution,
when his main income came from coal mining, which took place in the winter, he was free to farm in the summer.

Work in the coal mines drew to an end as the ice thawed and the mountain tracks could no longer be used by heavy carts; the same thaw marked the start of the agricultural year. The farmer's first task was to manure the earth to make it ready for planting. Liu's family might have had access to some animal manure from the oxen that worked in the mines, but most of the manure would have been human nightsoil collected over the year in the family privy. Families whose houses, like Liu's, fronted onto the main road that ran through the village had privies beside the road both for ease of access and to attract passing custom. The tiny village of Jinsheng a few miles north of Chiqiao, had thirty privies along a short stretch of the same road. A hygiene-conscious traveler commented that in the villages all along this road when it was wet, the privies' contents overflowed, and when it was dry the stench was terrible. Carrying and spreading the manure was heavy labor, and in 1926, which was typical of his later years, Liu hired a man called Zaohuar for three days to do it. No one in the village now remembers Zaohuar, which means that he was almost certainly not a Chiqiao native. Many outside laborers seeking a day's work would gather early in the morning with their tools beside the bridge just down the road from Liu's house. Farmers from several nearby villages would come to hire them. In the peak agricultural season, there might be as many as two hundred people seeking work there. Liu liked to go out in the morning and find out what the going rates were for the day, but that spring he was really looking to hire a long-term laborer who would come and work for the family for the whole season. However, 1926 was the height of Yan Xishan's military expansion and many of those who would usually have taken such jobs had been recruited into the army. Still, apart from spreading manure, the farm work at this time of year was light, and Liu simply got his grandsons to help clear the fields in preparation for ploughing.[4]

Ploughing the fields and sowing wheat were the first major agricultural activities of the spring. Years earlier, Liu had described the scene: the ground damp with a fresh fall of rain, the sound of the plough as it turned over the heavy clods, the shouts of the farmers as they urged the oxen on, women and children struggling with heavy hoes, and the first rays of the sun rising over the plain. Since the work was too heavy for Liu and his grandsons, two neighbors came to help. They would have been paid for their work, but nevertheless they were doing Liu a favor that would become part of broader networks of exchange. (Later that year one of them reappears in Liu's diary when he comes to ask for a remedy for a woman who has taken an opium overdose.) Meanwhile Liu and the two boys helped with the work: planting small plots of beans, potatoes, yams and maize, repairing the irrigation channels, and watering the winter wheat sown the previous autumn. Liu had noted the previous year that although his old age meant that he could only do light tasks, he was still a better worker than most of those who hired themselves out for half pay.[5]

Eventually, more than a month after the farm work began, Liu managed to hire a man known familiarly as Fourth Wang. Wang had in fact worked for Liu for the previous four years but had been home to visit his brother in Leping county on the other side of the plain over the winter. Liu occasionally calls himself an "old peasant," but he called farm laborers like Fourth Wang "people who have a tough life," which was also how such men referred to themselves. Liu felt sorry for Wang because he owned no land and had to provide for himself, but most of all because he had no wife or children. Like so many of the poor, Wang had never been able to afford to marry. Wang had worked for the family for several years so he knew what to do and could be trusted to hire extra day laborers if necessary. Liu wrote happily that often he could just tell Wang what needed to be done and there were many days when he himself did not have to go to the fields at all.[6]

The main crop they were sowing was wheat. Noodles made of wheat did not form the family's staple diet, but they were what people preferred to eat. Because most of the family's fields were irrigated by the Jin river, they could be used to grow a crop of wheat followed by a crop of millet in the same year. Wheat also had the advantage that it needed relatively little labor compared to millet. In the uphill fields only a single crop of millet was possible. In addition to wheat Liu grew vegetables. This seems to have been an experiment. In the past, he had used all the land for wheat, which was easier and probably more valuable; vegetable-growing was regarded as a specialized industry and vegetables could be bought in the market. But by 1926, the instability of the province's paper money had made many farmers more concerned with self-sufficiency. Liu decided to turn over some of the family's land to vegetables. He planted beans and maize, then cucumbers, green beans, peppers, turnips, leeks, radishes, and three different types of cabbages. He also bought a pint of cotton seeds and tried growing a small patch of cotton.

The seeds had to be soaked for several days and mixed with fertilizer before planting. They would be more troublesome still after they started to grow since they needed constant care. Cotton had not traditionally been grown in this part of Shanxi, but it was being vigorously promoted by the provincial government. It was also much more profitable than other crops.[7]

As well as ploughing and sowing, Chiqiao farmers were busy watering the winter wheat they had sown the previous autumn. There had been no snow all winter, and without watering, the young plants would have died. One of the streams of the Jin river flowed through the village, and at this time of year the farmers could use the water whenever they needed it. Liu and his grandsons cleared and tidied the channels and let the water out onto the fields. Later in the year, when everyone's crops were growing, water use would be much more tightly controlled with a strict system of rotations between villages. Indeed, some unfortunate villages received water only at night: a novel about the area describes people coming down from the mountains at night and seeing lights moving in the fields as the farmers let the water out.[8]

In 1926 the maize seedlings were destroyed by frost and the cotton by bugs, but by May both plots had been replanted. The last vegetables that had been stored the previous winter had been used up, but the new ones in the fields were big enough to eat and the family could look forward to moving from a monotonous winter diet of grain, root vegetables and cabbages to more varied summer food. Liu wrote happily of bringing a couple of baskets of fresh vegetables home from the fields on his carrying pole to give to friends. Meanwhile, the winter wheat was well grown and Fourth Wang was planting millet between the rows of wheat while Liu cleared the ground for him. They were also busy with thinning and hoeing the seedlings which would continue all summer. When the farm work was busy Liu did not feel he could leave Wang to work alone without a hired day laborer so he usually helped himself. Hoeing, weeding, and thinning the seedlings was skilled work and monotonous but not particularly heavy. The men crouched down in the fields selecting the strongest seedlings to preserve, thinning the rest and hoeing out the weeds. Liu remembered his grandfather telling him that only when you have hoed in the midday sun with the sweat pouring from your body do you really appreciate the labor that has gone into bowl of food you are eating. Wang was ill with diarrhea for much of June and unable to work so Liu found himself doing all the work. He wrote in his diary that he was working as a beast of burden for his sons and grandsons, but the complaining tone was offset by the pleasure with which he noted that despite his age, he was just as strong as when he was young. When he first started farming full time, he grumbled more often about what hard work it was and that his hands were blistered after a day in the fields. Now after 12 years in the fields he was more inclined to compare his weeding to eradicating one's faults than to complain after a day's work. He enjoyed resting in the shade of a tree and chatting to the other farmers after working in the heat of the summer sun.[9] And when he was away from the fields for several days, because he too had had diarrhea, he wrote that he felt bad about not going because "I am an old farmer and my heart is in the fields."[10]

The busiest season of the year began with the harvest of the winter wheat. After that the crops came in one after the other: first the spring wheat, then the three different crops of millet. When the wheat was ripe, Liu hired several day laborers to come and harvest it, but for the millet harvest he could not find enough labor and had to contract the crop out to someone else. The harvesters worked in a group, pulling the plants up by the roots, and singing as they did so. Those like Liu who could not do such heavy labor followed behind, pulling the corn into sheaves. At this time of year, the whole family was busy since they provided food as well as money for the harvesters, and the meals were expected to be some of the year's best. The sheaves of corn were brought to the family threshing floor, a piece of ground that had been cleared and pounded solid. For the millet harvest, the heads had to be cut from the stalks, which were used for construction, a task traditionally done by women. Liu describes them hurrying down the street to their work early in the morning. For both wheat and millet a donkey with a stone roller was led over the heads until the grain had been removed. The grain was then spread to dry in the sun and winnowed with a basket in the wind. As it lay on the threshing floor, it had to be swept and raked to dry it thoroughly. Standing all day in the hot wind and blazing sun was hard work, but it was important to get the grain dried as soon as possible. As long as the grain was out in the open, there was always the possibility of rain, or pilfering at night. Liu would go out to the threshing floor in the middle of the night or early in the morning to make sure that the watchman was not asleep (which he usually was). The family also owned some date trees, which grew around the family tombs built on the edge of the hills behind the village. When the dates were ripe several people came to help and they picked for three days. Last to be harvested were the cabbages that would be eaten over the winter. Soon after the harvest was in and the winter wheat had been sown for the next year, the ground froze and the agricultural year was over till the spring.[11]

In Liu's mind farming was quite simply part of the intellectual tradition in which he had grown up. It was both a proper activity for the gentleman who was not serving as an official and a model for the ruler and his officials. He liked to quote the passage from the *Classic of History* where the virtuous Duke of Zhou teaches the young prince that the gentleman should not lead an idle life, but must "first understand the painful toil of sowing and reaping."[12] The idea was that the diligence of the farmer should be a model for the king, but the quotation was also used to remind the ruler how hard-earned was the wealth of his subjects and thus to discourage the government from excessive taxation. For Liu there was surely also the implication that the painful toil of sowing and reaping was a proper activity even for the greatest in the land. This is even more clear from his response in his diary to a letter from Jie, ever the filial son, urging him not to work so hard:

> Recently as I labor in the fields, I have felt very happy with no room for any private worries. The letter from my oldest son Jie begs me to rest and take care of my health, but this is a way of resting. In antiquity, "Yi Yin was a farmer in the lands of the Prince of Xin, delighting in the principles of Yao and Shun." I am nearly 70 this year but only when I "cultivate the channeled fields" do I finally know that Yi Yin's delight in these principles was not empty talk. Of course I do not have Yi Yin's talent, but who can say it is not a pleasure to act as Yi Yin did in every situation?[13]

After writing this he spent the day in the fields planting maize and beans. The quotations are from one of the *Four Books of Mencius*, which Liu learned as a child. The story of Yi Yin tells how he was summoned from his fields to guide the ruler and became one of the famous virtuous ministers of antiquity. Thus the story also fits with Liu's favorite image of himself as a hermit, the educated man who should rightfully be guiding the government but has withdrawn to a private life.

Liu often uses the standard contemporary division of society into four classes of scholars, farmers, workers, and merchants. He lists the classes in this traditional descending order, but this did not mean that he despised merchants. Instead it reflects this sense of agriculture as the best model and thus the most suitable activity for the Confucian gentleman. He often wrote of the value of agriculture and study as a way of life; and it was indeed the one that he practiced. Agriculture was hard work and exhausting, that is after all the point of the anecdote about the painful toil of sowing and reaping, but it was certainly not demeaning. Liu moved easily from the fields to his responsibilities as a member of the local gentry. Messengers sent to invite him to the county town to take part in official committees would find him in the fields, watering the millet. On one occasion the magistrate of neighboring Qingyuan county called to visit but missed Liu who was out in the fields, busy with the wheat harvest. When in the summer of 1926 the county's business community and gentry held a meeting and recommended Liu and five others to go to the provincial capital to request a tax reduction for the county, he refused on the grounds that he was too busy with the wheat harvest, though in the end he gave in and went. He was aware that life as a farmer was not what his parents had hoped for him, but the Confucian ideology he had accepted as part of his education provided a positive vision of agriculture that helped to balance the disappointment.[14]

Farming and the cultivation of plants was also one of the central metaphors of the neo-Confucian school in which Liu had been trained. Important concepts in this tradition were explained in terms of agriculture: fixing one's determination was like sowing the seeds, the reverential attention needed for self-cultivation was like watering the plants and constantly banking up the roots and so on. Liu himself was particularly fond of the metaphor of weeding for the cultivation of the mind. After a day spent weeding, he would regularly remind himself that, for example, hoeing a weed as soon as they saw it was how the sages of antiquity eradicated all evil things. Weeding out selfish desires was one of the most important tasks of the moral self-cultivation required of a gentleman, and it was one Liu acted out all summer in the fields.[15]

For Liu, farming was a comfortable space to act out the personal beliefs he had acquired from his education. As he did so he worked with images of diligence, determination, and personal responsibility. Farming was the ultimate example of an activity in which diligent labor brought its own reward. Some of his neighbors also saw farming in these terms some of the time.

Proverbs reminded them, "If a man works hard the land will not be lazy and both large and small vats will be full"; or in more familiar terms, "You'll eat as much as you sweat."[16] But for most people this was only part of a more complex series of myths and metaphors. Central to these understandings was the fact that agriculture was dependent not only on the farmer's labor but also on the timing and amount of rain and access to water.

When the dates were picked in the autumn of 1926, they were put out to dry on the roof of the house; a couple of days later Liu was wakened early in the morning by his wife, Shi Zhulou, in a panic, saying "It's started to rain and we haven't covered the dates drying on the roof. What are we going to do?"[17] It turned out to be just a brief shower, but rainfall and the lack of it was a constant worry. That year there had been a shortage of rain in the spring, leaving the millet seedlings in the hill fields withered and weak. A few days later the rain did fall, but at precisely the moment when the winter wheat was ready to be harvested. Liu and Fourth Wang got the wheat in safely, but Liu's worries about the weather did not end. After the wheat was harvested, no rain fell for the millet. Prices were rising and people began to get nervous. The millet in the unirrigated fields withered, and the people who lived in the mountain villages realized that they would be able to harvest less than half the crop. There was thunder but no rain; Liu remembered that this was what the weather had been like before the great famine of his youth and worried even more.[18] In the end it did rain, much of the millet recovered, and the mountain villages saved at least part of their crop. These kinds of worries happened every year. In fact Liu's diary probably has more on this subject than any other. Irrigated land provided security, but the river could never provide enough water for all those who hoped to use it, and most farmers owned at least some unirrigated land. Growing a good crop on unirrigated land depended on rain's falling at precisely the right times of year, which it seldom did, and even irrigated land could suffer from the flash floods of the mountain streams as they rolled down onto the plain. As one of Liu's local acquaintances put it, "If there is not drought there are floods, so there is a disaster almost every year."[19]

Liu was constantly worried about rainfall because, like many farmers in the area, he owned some unirrigated land. His family also ate more grain than he could grow. By the late 1920s, he was buying the cheapest sorghum and beans to feed them, but even so the price was a matter of concern, and even a few days without rain at a crucial time of year could cause prices to shoot upward. Farmers tried to ensure good crops not only by working hard in the fields, but also by placating the dragon kings, the gods who sent rain. These dragon kings were thought to live high up in the mountains, in caves and in pools of clear water that never dried up even in the harshest drought. The mountain people told strange stories about the power of these pools: when a boy who urinated into one died shortly afterward, people said that the dragon god had executed him, and after that they were even more afraid. Every year the plains villages would fetch the figures of the deities down from the mountain in the spring, worship them in village temples over the summer, and return them in the autumn after the harvest. Up until the 1850s, Jinci, Chiqiao, and several other villages had fetched the Black Dragon King from a little shrine near a spring high up in the mountains. Then one year a tiger mauled the statue of the deity and tore his cloak, so the people did not dare take the actual statue down to the village but just carried it to the great Buddhist temple complex in the mountains and asked the monks to sacrifice to it. The other rituals continued despite this, and in the autumn after the harvest was in there were sacrifices in the great offering hall at Jinci, accompanied by a fair and opera, which drew large crowds and meant that Liu's family was always busy with guests. This was followed by a joyful procession to the mountains with all sorts of entertainments and floats. In good years this was sufficient and rain fell for the crops, but sometimes these regular rituals were not enough. When the villagers needed rain they went up into the mountains to pray to the Dragon Kings. There the effectiveness of their prayer depended on the sincerity of the community as a whole as they begged the gods to have mercy on them.[20]

In 1913 Liu records that his three sons Jie, Xiang, and Jin went with the other villagers to pray for rain, but he himself did not. In his mind good weather, like good health, was a reward for virtuous behavior, not something to be begged from the gods. Thus success in agriculture was the result of diligent labor and virtuous living, not the favor of local deities. He was even dubious of official prayers for rain. Historical sources recorded how the Holy Mother, the goddess of the Jin river, had answered prayers for rain, and when drought threatened the provincial governor would send someone to make offerings at Jinci. The county magistrate, too, sometimes prayed for rain at Jinci. One of the methods the provincial government used in its prayers for rain was to execute the dragon responsible for the drought outside the south gate of the provincial capital. A foreign author describing this ritual as it was performed in 1902 says simply that the dragon was constructed on the governor's orders and was made of paper, but Liu clearly had not heard about this.[21] He wrote:

> On the 28th of last month the governor of Shanxi executed a drought dragon at the south gate of Taiyuan and sent one of his staff with the drought dragon's head to Jinci to pray for rain. (He came early yesterday.) The dragon's head was immersed in the Nanlao spring. Many of the villagers went to Jinci to look at it. They saw the dragon's head in the water bound with red rope. There was an official messenger there guarding it who would not let anyone lift it up and examine it, so they did not know if it was really a dragon's head or some other object made to represent a dragon's head to calm people's fears of drought. To conclude, it is most implausible and cannot be believed.[22]

He was even more dismissive of another provincial government effort a few years later when the governor sent a man to throw tiger bones into the spring at Jinci, in the hope that the dragon in the spring would fight with the tiger and this would bring rain. This, he felt, was completely ridiculous and he copied out a derogatory newspaper report about it. For Liu as an orthodox Confucian, prayers for rain relied on the efficacy of the virtue of the official praying. Since the officials of the Republic were by definition traitors, it was hardly likely that their prayers would work. The villagers who visited Jinci to look at the dragon's head were skeptical too; they wanted to lift it out of the water and see if it really was a dragon's head. And they, too, emphasized virtue in their prayers for rain as they went together to the temple of the dragon god and begged sincerely for rain.[23]

Prayers for rain could plausibly be integrated into orthodox Confucian thought. After all, officials prayed for rain even though they did not do so in quite the same way as Chiqiao villagers. But as well as being dependent on the gods for water, farmers were also dependent on the power structures of the irrigation system that gave some villagers more water than others. The Jin river, which provided the water for irrigation, originally flowed from a spring at the foot of the hills down across the gently sloping plain and into

the Fen, which flowed along the bottom of the valley. The river was divided
into three streams to irrigate the largest possible area, but because of the
slope of the plain the villages at the foot of the mountains naturally tended to
receive less than those lying between Jinci and the Fen, which were marshy
and liable to flood. Over the centuries an elaborate system had developed
to divide the water between the villages. There were handsome stone-faced
channels and a series of hatches that could be opened and closed allowing
the water to flow down toward the river or forcing it back to irrigate the
more distant villages. During the summer months, when the water was most
urgently needed, there was a system of rotations (inscribed on large stone
tablets in case of dispute) according to which the hatches would be opened
and closed to send the water to each village in turn. The villages appointed
hatch-keepers to oversee the rotation, and there were also channel-heads who
controlled the system as a whole. The more water a farmer knew he would
get, the more money he could expect to make from his land, but the distribution of water between the villages was by no means equal. Some of the inequalities were due to the lie of the land, others to distant historical causes
(villages that had been military colonies in the fifteenth century tended to do
well), but it was obvious to everyone that the water made some villages
wealthier and more powerful than others.[24]

People were aware of the inequalities, and there was a long history of
struggles between the villages for access to water, but the system also generated a variety of myths and metaphors that justified the existing distribution
of power. For centuries people had been passing down the story of the virtuous Miss Liu, who had married into a family in Jinci village where she was
harshly treated by her mother-in-law. This was a long time ago when there
was no water at Jinci, and Miss Liu went every day to a distant spring so that
her mother-in-law could have the best water in the district. One day as she
was walking home, she met a stranger who asked if she would let his horse
drink from the water she was carrying. She did so and as a reward he gave
her his whip and told her that if she stirred it round three times in the water
jar, it would cause the jar to fill with water and save her the journey. For some
time she secretly used the magic whip, but then one day she went home to
her mother's house, and her husband's younger sister tried to make the water flow by stirring the jar. The jar overflowed and became a stream that
flooded the house and flowed down the hill. The family called Miss Liu, who

returned and sat on the jar until the water flowed quietly, by which time she had been transformed into a divine being. This story was told about the goddess who came to be known as the Holy Mother and was worshiped in the huge and magnificent temple that stood over the spring at the source of the Jin river. In it filial piety and self-sacrifice are rewarded by the gift of an ever-flowing and controllable supply of water.[25]

In his gazetteer Liu Dapeng described how every summer the channel heads and hatch-keepers would come to make sacrifices to the Holy Mother. Each village came in turn, and when the channel heads had made their offerings, the villagers would dine together, usually after returning in procession to their village office. Chiqiao, which was subordinate to Jinci town in the system, took part in the grandest of these sacrifices which involved a feast in the temple and three days of opera. The season of sacrifices ended with a great festival in honor of the Holy Mother. This was the high point of the year for most local people: all the families in Chiqiao had visitors and there were huge crowds who came for the opera and for the fair, which lasted five days. At the center of the festivities was a great procession to take the statue of the goddess from her temple to visit the temple of the Dragon King in the county town. The procession, which passed down the main road through Chiqiao right in front of Liu's house, included musicians and groups of villagers who had prepared entertainments. The most spectacular of these were floats with boys and girls dressed up to represent figures and scenes from famous stories and operas. The children, who were usually only four or five years old, were tied tightly to the poles that supported the platform to stop them falling off, and carried high above the shoulders of the crowd— sometimes by a single man, sometimes by groups of up to eight men. It was dark by the time the procession reached the county town, so the next day it formed up again and paraded the streets. When the floats reached the government offices, the magistrate would reward the children with pieces of silver and his womenfolk would give them brightly colored flowers. The streets were always packed. The festival in honor of the Holy Mother drew crowds from as far away as the provincial capital, but it was not just entertainment. The goddess was a powerful deity, and when the hatch-keepers and channel heads took part in the annual sacrifices that led up to the procession, they were associating their power with hers. Liu claimed that the festival in honor of the Holy Mother had been held since 1369. By doing the same thing every year, the channel heads not only linked their power to that of the Holy Mother, but also made it seem permanent and unchanging. Liu was dubious about these rituals and the power structures they enshrined. Like other Confucian scholars since the seventeenth century, he told a quite different story about the Holy Mother. She was not, he said, a river goddess at all, but the mother of an ancient prince who was also worshiped at Jinci. Liu's family always had guests for the big summer festival in honor of the Holy Mother, and Liu often found himself in the county town on the day of the procession, but all the same he did not approve of educated people taking part.[26]

The second great myth concerned a young man from the village of Huata, which controlled a crucial hatch that had to be closed for water to flow to the villages farther north. This made it one of the most powerful villages in the irrigation system. Almost everyone in the village belonged to the Zhang family, and every year they would go to Jinci to make an offering to their ancestors, who, they said, had died fighting for control over the water. The story they told was that once upon a time the villages of the north and south streams of the river had fought over the water. To solve the dispute, a cauldron of boiling oil was set up beside the spring and ten copper coins were dropped into it. The water was to go to whoever picked out the coins. A young man from the Zhang family of Huata village picked out seven of the coins. He died from his injuries, but after that the north stream received seven-tenths of the water and a member of the Zhang family always held the position of north stream channel head.[27] The rituals, which were held right beside the hatch that divided the water between the north and south streams, were an annual reminder of the heroism of the ancestors of the Zhangs of Huata, which had rightfully given later generations control over the water.

The story of young Zhang's sacrifice also gives a sense of the way in which control over the water was seen as a kind of property that could be handed down from generation to generation. The channel heads kept written accounts of exactly when particular hatches were opened and closed, as well as all the events and decisions that affected the distribution of water. Local opinion regarded these volumes, known as river books, as documentation of ownership of the water. According to Liu, the villages treated the river books as "secret treasures" and would not allow outsiders to see them. There was a story of how the Zheng family of Dongzhuangying village had once controlled a part of one stream, but one of the family's daughters-in-law stole the river book and took it with her when she married into the Wu family of Beidasi. After that, the Wu family always held the position of channel head.[28] In 1927 the Wu family was involved in a legal dispute over the control of the water and erected a stone inscription recording the case. In this the family lays claim to complete control over the water and justifies this claim by saying that "the inscriptions about irrigation in the Jinci temple all say this, the county government has it on record, and the river book includes it."[29] Once owned, water could be bought, sold, or stolen. Channel heads levied charges on villagers for their use of water as part of the system of rotations, and during the winter, when the rotations were not so strictly fixed, they sold water that their own villages did not need. In a case that Chiqiao people could still remember, a Chiqiao man named Wang Liang secretly diverted part of the water flowing through the village on New Year's Eve and sold it to a relative who happened to be the channel head of Guchengying village. When the theft was discovered, Wang Liang was able to intimidate the other channel heads, and for more than twenty years Guchengying village paid several hundred taels to him each year for the water.[30] In these cases simply defining water as property, rather than a natural resource, made the unequal distribution seem normal and acceptable.

Disputes over control of the water frequently gave rise to legal cases. In these, magistrates, who were often unhappy with the idea of ownership, tended to regard water as a resource to be distributed for the benefit of all, which meant that their decisions often favored the weak. Copies of these decisions were recorded in stone inscriptions that were placed in the temple of the Holy Mother at Jinci and in the relevant villages. Every year when the Jinci channel head and his Chiqiao subordinate went to make their sacrifices to the Holy Mother, they also honored the eighteenth-century officials whose decision in a dispute with one of the south stream villages had permitted Jinci to have its own channel head.[31] Legal cases were the last resort in a whole variety of mechanisms that served to make the unequal distribution of water seem right, fair, or at least officially recognized. Stories, rituals, violent intimidation, and the law all legitimated the fact that some villages could make more money from agriculture than others. This recognition of the importance of deeply embedded local power structures was quite different from

Liu Dapeng's Confucian vision of success in agriculture depending on industrious labor.

Liu was clearly interested in prayers for rain and the irrigation system; after all he wrote about them at some length, but he did not participate in them. This attitude, combined no doubt with the small size of his landholdings, had the effect of excluding him from the local power structures that controlled agriculture. Liu never acted as the Chiqiao hatch-keeper and only attended the feasts that accompanied the annual sacrifices to the Holy Mother when extreme old age had turned him into something of a local celebrity. Instead he tried to lay claim to influence over the system by writing about it. His Jinci gazetteer includes a lengthy account of the irrigation system, and he explains that the point of the great detail is to replace the secret river books held by the channel heads with openly available knowledge. He also wrote a gazetteer of the Jin river, the only one of his books to be preserved in Chiqiao, presumably because the knowledge contained in it was truly valuable at the village level. Liu based these texts on the river books of the part of the south stream that included Chiqiao, and his own detailed observations. By compiling these records Liu was trying to shift power away from the channel heads who controlled the irrigation system. His exclusion is suggested by the fact that he was never able to see the river books controlled by the other channel heads.[32]

Liu's writings describe the irrigation system as it existed in the 1900s. The changes that took place as a result of modernization influenced how agriculture was structured in the village, but not perhaps in the ways we might imagine. Liu's family was typical in that agriculture contributed an ever-increasing portion of the family budget. This was because the family lost its other income from commerce, mining, and teaching, and even where these other forms of income continued, they became much more closely tied to the agricultural economy. Liu had been well-paid as a tutor for a family whose wealth came from trade, whereas his sons Xiang and Jin became village primary school teachers dependent for their low wages on the agricultural economy. This increasing importance of agriculture in the local economy was primarily the result of the decline in commerce. After his father's death Liu Dapeng and his father's former clerk had opened a new branch of the furniture shop in the town of Yangyi. By that time Limanzhuang village, where his father had worked, was declining, but Yangyi still seemed prosperous. Yangyi families owned shops in Vietnam and Tokyo, as well as at least 44 shops in Beijing and a variety of others across north China. They traded in wine, grain, cloth, oil, tea, soy sauce, medicine, coal (in Tokyo), leather, pearls, vinegar, antiques, carts, boxes, silk, tofu, vegetables, flour, meat, and cigarettes. Like most Shanxi traders, they had been hard hit by the civil war that engulfed the country in the 1920s. The world-wide recession, which hit China around 1929, was the last straw for many of them, and by 1935 20 percent of the town's households were unemployed. In this situation it is not surprising that the Liu family's furniture business in the town was not doing very well. The income that the family earned from the business gradually decreased until they were eventually bought out by the manager in the 1930s. As opportunities for trade declined, wealthy families moved their money into land. This trend was exacerbated by the instability of the provincial currency. Soldiers and officials who had become rich as a result of the modernization policies bought land as a safe investment. The area round Jinci was particularly badly affected because it had good-quality irrigated land, and with the construction of a new motor road it was easily accessible from the provincial capital. Jinci was also famous as a tourist site because of its beautiful temples, and many of the province's leaders began to build summer houses there. During the course of the 1920s land prices in the area roughly doubled.[33]

Increases in the price of land might have led to helpful investment in agriculture, but at the same time that land prices were rising, agriculture was becoming less profitable. The provincial government succeeded in doubling its income between 1925 and 1928, and much of that extraction had come from the rural population. When the government nevertheless ran out of money, it simply requisitioned what it needed for the military. These demands fell particularly heavily on the rural population since they were most likely to have the fodder, carts, and draft animals that the government wanted. Then the world-wide recession hit Shanxi. After years of inflation, prices suddenly dropped. This affected farmers particularly badly and was exacerbated by a series of good harvests across north China. The new railway meant that large quantities of grain could be imported into the province. As a result the price of grain collapsed: millet at harvest time cost more than 2 yuan for the standard peck in 1932 but only 1.1 yuan in 1933. Wages fell proportionately: the monthly wages of the cook employed by Liu's family during this period fell from 2 dollars in 1932 to 1.5 dollars in 1934. The consequence was a vicious cycle in which rural industries collapsed because the local population simply could not afford to buy their products. Soon the situation was so bad that no mines in the county were making money. A survey of farmers in a district slightly to the south of Taiyuan county found that cotton was the only crop still making a profit. If one took into account the cost of seed, fertilizer, labor, and taxes, then farmers were suffering a loss on all their other crops. The newspapers began using a new term "peasant bankruptcy," though as Liu commented gloomily, even if you wanted to go bankrupt it wouldn't be possible because by this time no one would buy the land.[34]

The decline of the agricultural economy explains several aspects of Liu's farming. Increased taxation on grain and the instability of the currency drove him to grow vegetables in addition to grain. In such uncertain times, subsistence agriculture developed an attraction it had not had in the past. Another strategy was to grow cotton which could be sold to the new government-sponsored textile mills, but all the cotton plants Liu started in 1926 died, and his efforts in later years were not successful. Finally, the decline of the agricultural economy explains Liu's continuing labor into old age. At the age of seventy-four, he was doing a large part of the farming along with the family's young boys, in this case his youngest son, who was twelve, and a grandson of about the same age. He wrote in his diary that he could still do half the work of a hired laborer and with the children's help he did not need to hire often, which saved money in wages and also saved food. In 1936, when he was seventy-nine, he was still struggling away and lamented that he was so exhausted from his work in the fields that he did not want to get out of bed in the morning.[35] Liu carried on working in the fields into his old age because his labor cost his family nothing and this, along with the gradual sale of their property, enabled them to just about scrape by. It is probably from this period that the village story dates that describes Liu as so poor that even if he had the county magistrate to lunch, he would feed him gruel made from sorghum, the coarsest and cheapest kind of grain.

The combination of these processes meant that agriculture, and therefore access to water, became more important to villagers even though it was also becoming less profitable. This in turn meant that the villages that dominated the irrigation system became more powerful. The underlying causes of this change were the internal and external pressures on the country to modernize, but the results in this case were quite the opposite: traditional structures became increasingly powerful. This can be seen in the increase in expenditure on the festivals of the irrigation system at a time when the farmers who paid for them were becoming poorer and poorer. In his youth Liu enjoyed these festivals and saw them as a sign of local prosperity, even if he disapproved of the religious content. But from the mid-1920s onward his comments are mainly complaints about the cost. The funds came from a charge on each acre of land that had traditionally been fixed. After 1911 the charge began to be increased, and the increases were considerably higher than the rate of inflation. Liu complained that those who raised the levy did not understand that the money involved was the sweat and blood of the farmers. In this process festivals had gone from being a symbol of prosperity to being a form of exploitation, and modernization had created the circumstances for this exploitation.[36]

Thus the decline of Shanxi's village-based commerce and industry meant that during the 1920s and 30s, the rural economy was both impoverished and refocused round agriculture and its traditional structures of power. This process led to a quite new sense of difference between the villages and the urban areas. In the nineteenth century Taiyuan, the provincial capital, was distinguished above all by its huge walls. These were 30 to 50 feet high, wide enough for two carriages to pass on the ramparts, and surrounded by a deep ditch. The city was a military fortress, and popular legend recorded a rhyme: "The iron city of Taiyuan is proof against attacks by man." The city was also a center of government: inside its walls could be found the province's government offices, examination halls, and academies. But much of the land inside the great walls was actually farmland, while the province's trade centered on the towns and villages of the central plain. As late as 1916, Liu could find the whole city full of people praying for rain. The provincial capital was a center of government, not particularly a center of industry and commerce.[37]

Government policies of the early twentieth century reshaped Shanxi's economy and in doing so turned Taiyuan into an industrial and commercial center. As happened across China, the promotion of modern industry by the government had the effect of refocusing industry and commerce around centers of government. In Taiyuan city this began with the founding of the provincial government's "machine works bureau" in 1898. The bureau, usually described as an arsenal, used imported machinery to repair guns and manufacture swords, spears, and Western-style drums. By 1911 most of its staff of 200 were employed making guns. In 1918 Yan Xishan devalued the province's copper coinage, effectively taking money from the rural poor to pay for its development. It grew to employ several thousand people, and in 1932 there were eight factories making weapons, machine tools, locomotives, railway carriages, rails, motors, steam boilers, and agricultural machinery. To these were added a huge new steel mill, a tannery, paper mill, distillery, print works, brick kilns, and cement works. These businesses were not profitable, but rather drew money from taxation into the city, where they created jobs and opportunities. The rapid expansion of government itself had very much the same effect. The result was both a huge increase in the urban population and an increase in the wealth of the provincial capital compared to other areas.[38]

Since the 1900s the city had gradually been transformed so that visitors were immediately struck by how different it was from the surrounding countryside. Iron railings replaced the brick walls around government offices, and along the main shopping streets nearly all the buildings were soon in the new foreign styles with glass shop fronts and decorations in stucco. From 1909 onward the streets were tarred and lit at night with electric street lights. These things quickly became part of the everyday life for people who lived in the city. They were accompanied by a whole new range of goods and services: kerosene, cigarettes, bicycles, rickshaws, oil lamps, flashlights, straw boaters, cars, buses, trucks, stamps, mailboxes, telephones, films, clocks, and public libraries. Many of these new modern goods did reach the countryside: young women in Taiyuan county town could be seen staring wistfully at mats spread out in the streets by hawkers selling towels, stockings, soap, and toothpaste. Schoolboys bought boiled sweets. And Liu saw a shooting star and wrote excitedly in his diary that it was brighter than an electric light.[39] But on the whole these goods, which defined their owner as a modern person, were too expensive for the increasingly impoverished rural population. Liu, who was getting on in years, seldom went to the city any more, but when he did he now went by bus. The very details of his description of the journey home give a sense of the strangeness of the experience:

> After breakfast I said goodbye and went out the new south gate to the bus station to buy a ticket. It is 17 miles to Jinci and the ticket costs 90 cents. At 12 o'clock we boarded the bus and it set off. The journey went smoothly and at 1 o'clock we arrived at Jinci.[40]

Liu had attended government meetings whose time was set by the clock, but clock time as part of everyday life was almost as unfamiliar as the bus. The ticket was expensive, costing roughly ten days' wages for a farm laborer. A survey of rural incomes in the area that year found that an average family of five needed to spend about 45 dollars a year on food, clothing, and other everyday expenses, and that most could not even afford this. Clearly 90 cents for a bus ticket was all but impossible from such a budget. Many Chiqiao people, especially women, had simply never been to the provincial capital.[41]

Thus, in his old age, Liu like many of his neighbors encountered the modern consumer culture when people came out from the city. His youngest son, Hongqing, worked for a time in the factories in the city when the family could not afford to send him on to middle school. He borrowed a friend's bicycle to come home for the weekend (another new concept). Bicycles had first been bought by wealthy young men in the late 1890s. In 1919 Yan Xishan, then aged thirty-six, staged, and himself won, a bicycle race at a sports meet in an attempt to urge local officials to use bicycles. In the 1920s bicycles and rickshaws came into widespread use when the main roads were tarred for motor traffic, as the road from the provincial capital to Jinci was in 1921. By the 1930s there were bicycles in the villages; a survey in one Taigu county village found five, as well as two rickshaws, but the same village had 118 wheelbarrows. Chiqiao got its first bicycle sometime in the 1930s, when the son of the village's wealthiest family (who ran a truck company) bought one to go to the higher primary school. Meanwhile bicycles had become so widespread in Taiyuan city that the police were making efforts to register them and force them to use lights. As a factory worker in the city, Hongqing was much more likely to have access to a bicycle than as a farmer in the village. People coming out of the city also brought with them new styles of clothing.

One of the first pieces of news about the Nationalist party's arrival in the province in 1927 was received when someone came back from the city and reported that there had been a huge meeting to promote the revolution. All kinds of groups and organizations distributed pamphlets; airplanes flew overhead dropping other pamphlets out of the sky. But strangest of all were the women who had cut their hair and others who had no trousers on but were wearing only skirts.[42] Nearly ten years later Liu was still shocked by such costumes. He describes a group of students from the city who had come out to the temples at Jinci on a school trip:

> I left Yongtaiheng shop and went to the lower part of the temple area, where I saw the student travelers running around in total disorder at the water's edge. The boys and girls were both bare-legged, just wearing a pair of shorts. Their legs were completely visible above and below the knees. It was most inelegant to look at.[43]

These students visited Jinci in 1936, on the eve of the outbreak of war with Japan. Knowing the hardships that surely followed for most of them, it is hard not to sympathize with them as Liu catches them relaxing for a brief moment, bare-legged beside the water among the beautiful ancient buildings. But there is also a certain pathos about the old man who watches them so critically, the man who had studied for so many years, but is now an old farmer whose life is divided between his fields and his home. By the 1930s Liu's commitment to the orthodox Confucianism of his youth generated as much amusement as respect. He used to walk past the village's opera stage early in the morning on his way to the fields. One morning after the opera he found himself there,

> And there were cigarette wrappers all over the ground with writing on them. So I collected them up and brought them home, following the ancient teaching that we should respect paper with writing on it. People today do not know this teaching, and actually laugh at me for being so unworldly.[44]

Smoking had long been near universal among all classes in Shanxi, but cigarettes with the brightly colored printed designs on their wrappers were part of the new consumer culture. In picking up the cigarette wrappers and re-spectfully taking them home to burn, the old man was doing no more than following a standard ancient prescription that grew out of a sense of the sa-credness of the written word and the moral teachings it contained. Liu had lived out his life by those teachings, but by the 1930s they no longer made sense to those around him.

Epilogue

In 1937, when Liu Dapeng was eighty years old, war finally broke out between China and Japan. As Japanese troops began to advance southward into Shanxi, Liu would walk down to the bus stop in Jinci to read the news sheets that were pasted up on the wall there. These told of the bloody fighting and occasional Chinese victories, but from the place names it was clear that the Japanese were moving rapidly toward the provincial capital. There were rumors that Japanese airplanes would bomb the area, and Chiqiao people dared not light lamps after dark. Soon there really was bombing in Taiyuan city, and streams of refugees began moving along the main road from the city. Liu's next-door neighbor rented his house out to refugees, but the village would not be safe for long. As the fighting drew closer, Japanese airplanes began bombing the county. The magistrate and his staff abandoned their posts and nearly everyone in Chiqiao fled into the mountains. Liu's grandson Quanzhong took his uncle's two little girls up into Mingxian valley behind the village, where they rented a house for the family, and he was soon followed by his uncle Xiang with the adult women. Liu alone refused to go. In fact, as the bombs fell, he climbed up onto the flat roof of the house to watch the family and make sure they made it to safety. The bombing was followed by looting, often by the retreating Chinese soldiers. Most families, except the poorest of the poor who had nothing worth stealing, returned to find their houses ransacked. But when a group of soldiers threatened to climb into the courtyard and shoot Liu, he stood up and said that he was already very old and he did not care if they shot him. The soldiers passed on.[1]

The looting was followed by a lull while everyone waited for the Japanese to arrive. The county's only remaining official, the prison warden, asked Liu to draft a declaration of surrender to the Japanese and he agreed. He also went down to the county town, where the remaining leaders were holding a meeting to discuss what to do. Then he barricaded the main door of the house with lumps of coal and pieces of furniture and settled down to wait. The Japanese arrived and began to take up quarters in the village. This time Liu was not so lucky. When the soldiers could not get into the house they threatened to burn it down. Some of the villagers climbed over the wall and cleared the entrance so that the Japanese soldiers could get in. Then, while the villagers pleaded with them to have mercy on Liu because of his age, the Japanese beat him. The soldiers stayed briefly in the house, then moved on to Jinci, leaving Liu ill from his injuries and lamenting the loss of the furniture in the shops he owned on the village street: tables, chairs, and benches had all been used for firewood.[2]

Liu spent the rest of his life under the Japanese occupation. For years he had complained of the failure of various governments to deal with the foreign threat. When the Japanese occupied Manchuria and staged a major attack on Shanghai in 1932, he had written: "The Japanese raiders are harassing China more and more, and yet those devils in the revolutionary party do not dare throw themselves at the enemy's spears."[3] The antiquated vocabulary should not deceive us into imagining that Liu did not understand the situation. He read the newspapers in detail, knew about the resistance of Ma Zhanshan in Manchuria and the Nineteenth Route Army in Shanghai, and criticized the failure of the central government to send support.[4] Instead, Liu chose to use certain words because they expressed his opinions about the situation. He called the Japanese "raiders" and "dwarf raiders," but he quickly picked up the new term "the three northeastern provinces," which had been coined by Nationalists to describe the area formerly known as Manchuria.[5] On the other hand he disliked the fashionable term "resistance." As he explained, the government "does not dare speak of quelling the rebel insurrection, but only says that it is using soldiers to resist, which shows how low the party state's morale is."[6] To speak of resistance was to admit the possibility of defeat, which was unacceptable. And Chiang Kaishek's failure to declare war on Japan up until 1937 was a telling sign of the moral weakness of the country's modernizing elite as a whole.

In Liu's opinion the moral failure of China's rulers left him and his neighbors as "the enslaved people of a defeated land."[7] As slaves the people have little choice but to obey their rulers, but nevertheless they should be constantly aware of the shame of their situation. Chiqiao lay on the front line of the Japanese occupation, since the mountain villages were home to Communist guerilla fighters who launched frequent raids on the Japanese. His own experience of Japanese brutality meant that Liu knew from the start the likely outcome of disobedience. As he wrote a couple of years into the occupation, the Japanese treated the people with extreme severity, punishing or killing all those who disobeyed them, so when the Japanese gave an order, no one dared resist it. He himself was occasionally summoned and interviewed about the temples at Jinci by Japanese officers with cultural interests. As this happened only a month after he had been beaten, and he was simply ordered to come to the village office without explanation, the experience must have been frightening. Later he attended a variety of propaganda meetings organized by the Japanese. Indeed he even made a speech at a county meeting to encourage people to respect the elderly and was rewarded with a set of grave clothes. His teenaged grandson Shuzhong had been apprenticed to a wealthy maternal uncle who was a Western-style doctor trained in Japan. As a result of this connection Shuzhong was employed as a military doctor by the Japanese army and eventually became an official in the hygiene department of the puppet government.[8] Liu saw such acts of compliance as the inevitable, though shameful, role of a people who were enslaved. When he saw laborers going back and forth along the road to Jinci as they were summoned to work for the Japanese, he wrote "this is one of the sufferings of an enslaved people."[9] In such a situation the only hope was for survival. That year on the day in early spring when people traditionally made offerings to the god of the granary, he described them lighting incense, kneeling, and begging the god for enough grain to eat so that they could get through the year, since "for a people enslaved not to die of hunger or cold is worthy of celebration."[10]

These attitudes fit easily with those of his neighbors. Shortly after the occupation began, Liu reported that at New Year all the villagers prayed to the kitchen god, who they sent up to Heaven to report on the year's doings, to beg the Heavenly Emperor to quickly destroy the Japanese rebels.[11] The kitchen god, who inhabited a female realm that Liu never entered, was usually beneath Liu's interest, so he is almost certainly reporting something he heard from others but that pleased him. Children's songs were something he had always been interested in, since they were traditionally regarded as omens. He recorded with approval one that went,

> Run away quickly Japanese devils,
> Only the Niangziguan pass is left.
> If you don't go—you'll all be fed to Chinese dogs.[12]

He also records rumors and hopes that all the Japanese will die in China and none of them will ever return to their own land across the sea. These songs, rumors, and prayers were part of a popular culture of resistance that Liu shared with his neighbors. Stories of battles and skirmishes circulated widely as part of this culture. Yan Xishan continued to resist the Japanese in the far south, and Chiqiao children played at being Yan Xishan's forces bombing the Japanese, using maize cobs weighted with stones for bombs. But while Yan Xishan's bombs and airplanes were dramatic, most actual local resistance came from the guerilla forces of the Communist Red Army in the mountains. The popularity of the Red Army's efforts is suggested by the fact that even the Buddhist monk in charge of the big monastery high up in the mountains, who was a friend of Liu's, told him that the Red Army soldiers were orderly and did not harass the local people. Liu reports the most minor skirmishes between the Red Army and the Japanese, emphasizing his own pleasure and that of his neighbors whenever they heard that Japanese soldiers had been killed.[13]

Liu was pleased by the Red Army's successes, and sure that eventually the Japanese would be defeated, but this never undermined his commitment to the moral values of his youth. He continued to see himself as someone whose education gave him a responsibility for his neighbors and the right to be heard by the local government. On one occasion he walked through the mud down to the county town, through the town gates where everyone who passed had to bow to the Japanese soldiers on guard, show a pass and be searched, and on to the county offices. There he urged the magistrate to release all those who had been imprisoned for petty offences. Afterward he complained that the magistrate had not taken him seriously.[14] He was no more effective in his appeals to the village head to reconsider when the Japanese demanded the straw that Chiqiao villagers used to make paper to use as fodder. Liu came across the village head and his deputy looking at the huge piles of straw and wondering how the villagers could survive without it. But when he began telling them how to refuse the Japanese demands, they told him he was interfering. His response to this was to write in his diary:

> I am full of remorse that I do not have the power that comes from virtue to rescue the people of my own village in this chaotic time. I do not have the ability to touch the heart of heaven above or remove the suffering of people below, so how can I comfort the spirits of my late parents in heaven? I am greatly to blame for my lack of filial piety.[15]

Liu had lived his life on the basis that his education and visible Confucian commitment gave him the right to be heard on local matters. He was ignored now because the world had changed: his education and behavior no longer marked him as an upright man, but merely as a relic of an earlier age. Respect for his age may have allowed him to speak, but his Confucian rhetoric meant little to the younger generation, many of whom had not even been born when the old education system was abolished in 1905. Liu's influence was also undermined by his poverty. Liu's family had never been wealthy, but in his youth they had most certainly been comfortably off and respectable. Now they worried constantly where the next meal was going to come from. Like the rest of the family Liu ate porridge made from sorghum, the cheapest of grains, for breakfast, cold sorghum porridge for lunch, and reheated sorghum porridge for dinner. From time to time his wealthy friends sent gifts of maize cobs, sorghum, and even the more valuable millet and wheat flour. Even his former wife's nephew in Beidasi, who was not wealthy, sent root vegetables, politely explaining that they were not worth selling.

Food was the most urgent need, but the family were also short of fuel and clothing. Liu complained that the cold made it difficult for him to sleep because they could no longer afford coal for heating. Shabby clothes, poor food, and the dunning of creditors worked together to undermine Liu's status in the community.[16]

But it was not only the community who ignored Liu; even his own family began to evade his moral values. By 1940 Liu's third and fourth sons, Jin and Xiang, were both drug addicts. They took a compound of morphine, heroin, and caffeine that was widely used in the village, especially by the paper makers for whom it relieved the agony of spending hours standing in an icy river washing pulp in mid-winter. The Japanese occupation made drugs even more easily available, and Jin and Xiang were ruining the whole family. This was worst for Liu's youngest son, Hongqing, who was twenty-one and still not married. (His elder brothers had all married in their teens.) He was hard-working and did not take drugs, but his marriage prospects looked dim since no one would want to marry their daughter into a family with addicts. Hongqing had already suffered from the fact that, unlike his elder brothers, he had only graduated from primary school, since the family had been too poor by then to send him on to middle school. In the scheme of Confucian values that Liu shared, filial devotion and brotherly love were supposed to link families together as a single economic and domestic unit. This was what the family had done up to this point, with Liu, his sons, and grandsons living together, pooling their income, and sharing the same food. Although some of the men went away to find work, their wives and children remained in the family home in Chiqiao, and it was expected that even those who were unmarried would send money home. Family division meant dividing the property between the brothers, making them independent and, in effect, giving them their inheritance. Although it was inevitable that this would happen eventually, Confucian morality urged that it should be postponed as long as possible. In particular, brothers should not divide the family property before the death of the father, since after the division the father became financially dependent on his sons. Family division often gave rise to disputes, and when Liu was called in to mediate he advised against the division altogether. Now his wife and his own sons decided to divide the property, but knowing that he would oppose the division they did not tell him. According to standard practice the property should be divided equally between the sons, and the

responsibility for supporting their parents should also be shared equally between them. In this case, since Liu's second son, Xuan, was still insane, the
property was divided between the four remaining sons, while Liu, his wife
Shi Zhulou, and poor Xuan became their shared responsibility. Since Liu's
eldest son, Jie, was dead, his quarter of the property was divided by his three
sons. The arrangement made it possible for Hongqing, who had received a
quarter of the property, to marry the following year (though his new wife,
who did not want an arranged marriage, ran away shortly after the wedding
and never came back). The main outward sign of the division of property
was that each of the brothers' families now cooked and ate separately, but
since Liu never entered the kitchen and his food was brought to him in his
room, he never knew that the division had taken place.[17]

Liu's beliefs and moral system might be ignored, but he himself went on
pottering round the village. A couple of weeks before his death in 1942, he
was still able to walk over to Jinci, where he dined at one of the shops and
copied down the regulations for a new unified agricultural purchase scheme
posted on the wall there. He chatted to the laborers who passed his door on
their way to Jinci and found that they had been sent to dig fortifications for
the Japanese. In his diary he reported the new Japanese attempt to monop-
olize the local economy and complained, just as he might have done when he
first began writing the diary in the 1890s, that people these days think too
much about money and ignore the demands of proper behavior and a sense
of shame. His last diary entry was about the weather: he noted with pleasure
that rain had been falling steadily all night and that there was now no fear of
drought for the year. Five days later he was dead.

*

Liu was wrong to be optimistic about the weather. The rain continued and
brought with it flooding, which destroyed the crops. Meanwhile the Japanese used the unified agricultural purchase scheme and their monopoly of the
economy to continue to extract grain from the villages. That autumn famine
hit Chiqiao: by the end of the year a hundred people had died in the village.
As usual the paper-making families who relied on the market for food were
worst hit. Liu's own children and grandchildren at least had land and could
grow late vegetables, which kept them going through the winter, but even
so they were impoverished and in the end they had to begin selling the land.

Six years later after the defeat of the Japanese and three years of civil war, the Chinese Communist Party came to power. Their first important action in the villages was to implement land reform, dividing villagers into classes (landlord, rich peasant, middle peasant, poor peasant) and redistributing land from the rich to the poor. By this time three of Liu's four grandsons had left the village: Jingzhong was far away in Shaanxi province, working as a driver in an army unit; Shuzhong was a doctor in Taiyuan city (where he suffered the rest of his life for his collaboration with the Japanese and eventually took an overdose during the Cultural Revolution), and Zuoqing had joined the county police. Thus only Liu's eldest grandson, Quanzhong, and his three younger sons—Jin, Xiang, and Hongqing—remained in the village. Quanzhong had in fact spent most of his working life as a factory worker in Taiyuan city: he had originally been apprenticed to a draper, but soon moved to work in a porcelain factory, and then spent several years in a textile mill, where among other things he was involved in organizing a trade union. When the city fell to the Japanese, he had fled and found work in one of the coal mines in Liu valley, and he ended the war working in an arsenal in a neighboring county town. In the village he had received only one twelfth of the family's property after the family division, which would have meant that he owned less than an acre of land. As a result of his background as an urban worker and the small size of his landholdings, he was labeled a "poor peasant" by the land-reform team and his family received redistributed land. Jin and Xiang had sold the land they inherited to buy drugs and were labeled poor peasants, too, whereas poor Hongqing, who had received less than his brothers all his life but was not addicted to drugs and had therefore managed not to sell the land he had inherited, received the politically disadvantageous label of "middle peasant." These labels remained with the family and their descendants into the 1980s. Meanwhile the family lost touch almost entirely with their daughters, sisters, and aunts, almost all of whom had married into families that now received the worst classification of "landlord." These labels controlled people's lives and when I asked old people in Chiqiao about people mentioned in Liu's diary, unless they were related to the person in question they nearly always answered first in these terms. Such and such a person was a common peasant, a rich peasant, or a landlord. Only further questioning or a chance comment would reveal that the person in question was the village shoe maker, a landless paper maker, or the owner of several coal mines.[18] Chiqiao villagers are seen now, and see themselves, as peasants, but this is to misread their past and that of their village, where for centuries there had been more commerce and industry than agriculture. This vision of the countryside as an agricultural space into which industry and commerce were introduced only by the modern state had its origins in the European ideologies adopted by the modernizers, but it made sense at least in part because by the 1940s so much rural industry and commerce had collapsed and villagers had no alternative to farming.

Since the 1900s modernization had been equated with the development of large-scale urban industry, and this had begun to divide urban and rural populations. But up until the Communist takeover, it was easy enough for Liu's sons and grandsons to find work in the city. Land reform put an end to that. After land reform, all villagers had at least some land and were expected to produce grain and other food. They were not allowed to move to the cities, and identity cards with the classification "peasant" helped to enforce the new regulations. State-subsidized grain and other privileges went to members of the population who were registered as "workers," but only those in large-scale, mechanized, modern industries were considered to be workers. The big coal mines continued to operate, but most of the unmechanized drift mines of Taiyuan county were closed down. The mountains behind Jinci were declared a scenic area: farming was allowed to continue, but not coal mining. Today almost all traces of the mines there have vanished. Paper-making was allowed to continue in Chiqiao after land reform, but was labeled as "handicraft" and "sideline" production, terms which implied that it was both primitive and subsidiary to agriculture. As a result paper makers, like other villagers, were expected to produce grain for themselves and pay grain taxes to the state. Chiqiao had long attracted migrants to work in the paper industry and had considerably more people than could possibly be supported from its land. Land reform had redistributed land between individuals but not between villages, so the 70 percent of the village population who had previously paid for grain by making paper now also had to be supported from the village's limited supply of land. When the whole country suffered from famine in the aftermath of the Great Leap Forward, Chiqiao was particularly hard hit and many villagers died, so that now villagers' accounts of the great famine of the 1870s always include references to 1961. By the 1970s the coarse, handmade paper, which was by then used primarily for toilet paper, was considered unhygienic, and the industry was abandoned. Recently many village men have been buried with the trays they used for molding paper, a mark of the respect they once had for a skill that is no longer needed.[19]

The decline of Chiqiao's industry was part of a process that not only labeled villagers as peasants, but also saw peasants as representatives of an outdated "feudal" way of life that would soon be replaced by the modern industrial age. Peasants were considered "backward" (as indeed was the whole province of Shanxi) and identified in much popular thought with the equally backward and feudal morality of Confucianism. By the 1950s there was hardly anyone left who might have criticized the ideology of modernization at its roots, as Liu Dapeng had done in his dream in 1900, on the grounds that its priorities were not Confucian. Most people have come to accept that modernization and industrialization are essential both to strengthen the country internationally and to raise living standards. The problem with this model for villagers is that as peasants they find themselves marginalized and dismissed by it.

Possibly as a result, since the 1980s there has been a renewed interest in Confucianism. This is not simply a return to the past; Confucianism had spun apart as it was detached from the state and no longer unified by the examination and education systems. The result was that it developed differently in different institutions and social contexts. Confucian interpretations of agriculture have been rendered totally invisible by the Communist state, which set up the urban intellectuals, who were identified with the former scholarly elite, as the absolute antithesis to the peasant farmer. In business Confucian morality continued to be important through the 1920s and 30s because weak enforcement of laws and regulations meant that personal trust and reputation were still vitally important. The imposition of a strong state underwritten by a quite different moral order and with quite different institutions to supply credit and solve disputes removed the need for Confucian morality, though the recent enthusiasm for studies of what is called "Confucian business ideology" suggests that it may well return in some form. Within the family the state's abandonment of Confucianism left the field free for the a highly emotional version of filial piety that emphasized close relations with members of one's immediate family. The intensity of the relationships that grew out of this and their acceptance by the community made the family one of the very few sites of resistance to the extreme state intrusion of the 1960s and 70s. Then when the political situation relaxed in the 1980s, some peasants began to emphasize open displays of filial piety especially through wedding, funeral, and New Year rituals.[20] In Beidasi village, the Wu family have reconstructed their ancestral shrine, and my friend Wu Jiongsheng (who is in his twenties) writes to me that "now there are many sons and daughters who are not filial to their parents, which is a really heartbreaking thing."[21] Wu Jiongsheng's sense of gloom would have made sense to Liu Dapeng, who complained all his life about how unfilial other villagers were. Confucian values in the strict sense were always at odds with ordinary ways of behaving. When the state abandoned Confucianism, it is hardly surprising that it could come to be used in some ways that were in opposition to that state.

The process of modernization rewrote the moral order and in so doing it also reconfigured geographical space. Borders, roads, railways, industries, and cities are created, developed and transformed by political decisions based on government priorities. It is these political decisions, and not necessarily physical geography, that make some places into important centers, and others into remote peripheries. As Pomeranz has argued, political decisions that were at the heart of the modernization project reconfigured China's geography. Some places benefited from this: most obviously the coastal trading cities of Shanghai and Tianjin, but also Taiyuan city, which received massive investment as the provincial capital of Shanxi, and even the town of Yuci, which was on the new railway line. Other places lost out, including Shanxi as a whole, in comparison with other provinces, and especially its rural areas.

Shanxi villagers have not done particularly well out of the process of modernization, but today Chiqiao is relatively prosperous. The political reforms of the 1980s allowed villagers to set up in business again, and Chiqiao families were among the first in the area to take part. Several village women set up enterprises making children's clothes which they sold successfully both in China and, ironically, to Russia through Tianjin. Now the village is about to be absorbed into Taiyuan city, which was once a day's journey away but is rapidly expanding. Most of the village men already work driving taxis or private buses in the city. Huge, expensive housing estates are being built nearby and a new plan has been created which will extend the city boundaries as far as Jinci. The local people will lose their land and be registered as members of the urban population. Jinci itself is to be turned into a major tourist site, a process which will involve demolishing most of the town and all of the nearby village of Beidasi and relocating their populations to newly built apartment blocks. Much of Chiqiao and the other villages round it will probably also be demolished as they are swallowed up by the city. It is perhaps the best and most logical conclusion of the process of modernization that began in the 1900s, given the huge gap between urban and rural living standards that that process eventually created. It will undoubtedly bring more opportunities to the next generation, but it will also uproot people from their homes and destroy communities that have existed for centuries. As has happened from the 1900s onward, change is being imposed by a modernizing state with little regard for the opinions of those involved and at a heavy cost to many who live through it.

Reference Matter

P R E F A C E

1. Chung-li Chang, *The Chinese Gentry*, pp. 6–7.

2. Ch'ü, *Local Government*.

3. Beattie, *Land and Lineage*; Schoppa, *Chinese Elites*; Meskill, *A Chinese Pioneer Family*.

4. Clunas, *Superfluous Things*.

5. But see Smith, *Village Life in China*; Hinton, *Fanshen*; Barr, "Four Schoolmasters"; Yeh, *Provincial Passages*; Hsiung, "Treading the Weedy Path."

6. MacGaffey, *Kongo Political Culture*.

7. Rowe, "Success Stories."

8. Duara, *Culture, Power, and the State*.

9. Liu Dapeng, *Tuixiangzhai riji* (Diary of the chamber for retreat and contemplation) (ed. Qiao), p. 143; Liu Dapeng, Tuixiangzhai riji (ms., Shanxi Provincial Library), 1892/10/15. Where possible I refer to published editions of Liu's works, but Qiao Zhiqiang's edition of the diary is heavily abridged so it is often necessary to refer to the manuscript. References to the manuscript refer to the lunar calendar dates.

10. Liu Dapeng, *Tuixiangzhai riji*, p. 143.

11. Subsequently Chewang has been repaired and redecorated as a tourist destination.

12. Pomeranz, *The Making of a Hinterland*.

13. Harrison, "Village Politics and National Politics"; Paul Cohen, *History in Three Keys*.

14. Liu Dapeng, *Tuixiangzhai riji*, p. 146.

15. This is of course a huge oversimplification. The works of Natalie Davis and others have transformed approaches to European history with their emphasis on individual experience, and I owe much to them. (For an introduction to this literature, see Amelung, *The Flight of Icarus*.) There has also been some work in the field of Chinese history. Spence, *The Death of Woman Wang*, is probably the classic example of the genre here.

CHAPTER I

1. Liu Dapeng, Tuixiangzhai riji, ms., 1925/10/10, 1925/10/25–27; Liu Zuoqing (Liu Dapeng's grandson, born 1926), interview, Taiyuan No. 1 Electric Power Plant, 6th Sept. 1999; Chiqiao, villagers, group interviews and general conversations, Chiqiao 8 Sept. 1997.

2. Chen Zuogao, *Zhongguo riji shilue*, pp. 2–3; *Qingdai riji huichao*.

3. Zeng, *Zeng Wenzheng gong jiashu quanji*, vol. 1, pp. 23–24; Liu Dapeng, Tuixiangzhai riji, ms., 1892/3/14.

4. Liu Dapeng, *ibid.*, 1892/3/4, 1892/3/9, 1892/3/11, 1892/3/12.

5. *Ibid.*, 1892/4/3, 1892/4/21, 1892/4/22.

6. *Ibid.*, 1925/10/10; Luo Zhitian, "Kejuzhi de feichu yu simin shehui de jieti"; Zheng Xianglin (Chiqiao village resident, former Jinci township head), interviews, Chiqiao, 3 Aug. 1999, 2 Aug. 2001. For an example of such an entry, see Liu Dapeng, *Tuixiangzhai riji*, p. 443.

7. Liu Dapeng, Tuixiangzhai riji, ms., 1901/4/13.

8. *Ibid.*, 1915/2/11.

9. Wu Jiongsheng, local historian, letter, 25 Aug. 2000.

10. Liu Dapeng, *Tuixiangzhai riji*, ed. Qiao, pp. 613–15. The surviving material I have found is: *Jinci zhi* (Jinci gazetteer), ed. Mu Xiang and Lu Wenxing. The published text also includes *Liuzi yu zhi* (Liuzi Valley gazetteer), *Mingxian yu zhi* (Mingxian Valley Gazetteer), and "Chongxiu Jinci zaji" (Miscellaneous notes on the Jinci Temple Repairs). The published text also includes abridged versions of "Yiwei gongche riji" (Diary of a journey), and "Qiaozi gongche riji" (Diary of father and son traveling to take the exams) (*Tuixiangzhai riji*, ed. Qiao); "Qianyuan suoji" (Brief notes from Qian garden), abridged in Qiao Zhiqiang, ed., *Yihetuan zai Shanxi diqu shiliao* (Historical materials on the Boxers in Shanxi) (Taiyuan: Shanxi renmin chubanshe, 1980); "Taiyuan xian xianzhuang yipie" (A glance at present conditions in Taiyuan County), and "Gongfei rao Jin jilue" (Brief account of the Communist bandits' harassment of Shanxi), mss., Shanxi Provincial Library; "Jinshui zhi Jin River Gazetteer," ms. owned by Wen Jie, Chiqiao.

11. Liu Dapeng, Gongfei rao Jin jilue, vol. 1, p. 1; *Taiyuan xian zhi* (Taiyuan county gazetteer), p. 1552; *Chongxiu Taiyuan xian zhi* (New edition of the Taiyuan county gazetteer), p. 1713; *Taiyuan xian zhi* (Taiyuan county gazetteer), p. 1826; *Taiyuan xian xuzhi* (Appendix to the gazetteer of Taiyuan county), p. 1882. Cf. S. Amelang.

12. Liu Dapeng, *Jinci zhi*, pp. 1–8, 11; Liu Dapeng, *Tuixiangzhai riji*, p. 447; Liu Zuoqing, interview, 6 Aug. 1999; Luo Houli and Ge Jiayuan, "Jindai Zhongguo de liangge shijie," p. 10.

13. Liu Dapeng, *Jinci zhi*, pp. 656–67.

14. Tao Yuanming, *Tao Yuanming*, p. 370. See also Owen, "The Self's Perfect Mirror"; Kwong, *Tao Qian and the Chinese Poetic Tradition*; Wu Pei-yi, *The Confucian's Progress*, pp. 15–19; Davis, "The Narrow Lane."

15. Liu Dapeng, *Jinci zhi*, p. 1375.

16. *Ibid.*, p. 657.

17. Cf. Fitzgerald, *Awakening China*.

18. Liu Dapeng, *Jinci zhi*, p. 659.

19. Ng On-cho, *Cheng-Zhu Confucianism in the Early Qing*, pp. 96–97; Munro, *Images of Human Nature*, pp. 112–32.

CHAPTER 2

1. The genealogy is no longer extant. Liu Dapeng, *Jinci zhi*, pp. 144–5; Chiqiao villagers, interview 8 September 1997; Liu Zuoqing interview 6 August 1999, 6 September 1999, 28 July 2001; Ying Kui, "Lancun, Zhifang, Chiqiao san cun zhi caozhi diaocha."

2. Zhang Zhengming, *Jinshang xingshuai shi*, pp. 79–82 and passim; Qu Shaomiao and Pang Yicai, *Shanxi waimao zhi*, pp. 29–103; Gardella, "Qing Administration of the Tea Trade"; Li Sanmou, Zhang Wei, "Wan Qing Jinshang yu cha wenhua."

3. Liu Dapeng, Tuixiangzhai riji, ms., 1925/1/8; Williamson, *Journeys in North China, Manchuria, and Eastern Mongolia*, pp. 160–1; An Jiesheng, "Qingdai Shanxi zhongshang fengshang yu jiexiao funu chuxian"; Wu Shouming, *Taigu xian Guanjiabucun diaocha baogao*, pp. 17–18. Presumably men returned home to marry in their early twenties.

4. Liu Dapeng, *Tuixiangzhai riji*, pp. 17, 19; Liu Dapeng, Tuixiangzhai riji, ms., 1892/10/30; Liu Zuoqing, interview 6 August 1999; Beidasi villagers group interviews and general conversation, 2 August 2001; Wu Jiongsheng, letter 25 August 2000. The games mentioned here were all played in the villages of Chiqiao and Beidasi in the 1920s.

5. Liu Dapeng, *Jinci zhi*, pp. 651–2; Liu Dapeng, *Tuixiangzhai riji*, pp. 9, 613; Liu Wenbing, *Xugou xianzhi*, p. 348.

6. Liu Zuoqing, interview 6 August 1999; Liu Dapeng, Tuixiangzhai riji, ms., 1892/9/19. For military degrees see Liu Wenbing, p. 349.

7. Liu Dapeng, *Jinci zhi*, pp. 441–9, 653; Liu Dapeng, Tuixiangzhai riji, ms., 1915/8/26; Shi Yongquan, *Taiyuan shi nanjiaoqu jiaoyu zhi*, p. 5; Liu Wenbing, pp. 347–8.

8. Liu Dapeng, Tuixiangzhai riji, ms., 1892/6/23, 1892/9/25, 1892/11/14; Liu Dapeng, *Jinci zhi*, pp. 651–3, 407–410; Wu Shouming, p. 68; Shi Yongquan, *Taiyuan shi nanjiaoqu jiaoyu zhi*, p. 4.

9. Liu Dapeng, Tuixiangzhai riji, ms., 1892/7/27; Liu Dapeng, *Jinci zhi*, p. 433.

10. Richard, *Forty-Five Years in China*, p. 165; Liu Dapeng, *Jinci zhi*, p. 445.

11. Liu Dapeng, Tuixiangzhai riji, ms., 1914/8/18; Liu Dapeng, *Jinci zhi*, pp. 409–10, 651–4, 1364; Liu Dapeng, *Tuixiangzhai riji*, p. 21, 118–9. For officials from the area see Liu Dapeng, *Jinci zhi*, pp. 586–642.

12. The relevant period is missing from the diary, but see Liu Dapeng, *Tuixiangzhai riji*, pp. 136, 143–4, 184; Liu Dapeng, *Jinci zhi*, pp. 734–5, 1040–2; *Taiyuanshi nanjiaoqu zhi*, p. 843. See also Paul A. Cohen.

13. Cao, "Qingdai Shanxi de niangshi fanyun luxian"; Li Fubin, "Qingdai zhonghouqi Zhili Shanxi"; He, *Guangxu chunian (1876–79) Huabei de da hanzai*, pp. 7–9; Zhang Zhengming, *Jinshang xingshuai shi*, p. 82; Huang Jianhui, *Shanxi piaohao shi*, pp. 139–152; An Jiesheng.

14. Liu Zuoqing, interview 6 August 1999; Liu Dapeng, *Jinci zhi*, pp. 144–5; He Hanwei, p. 32–3; *China's Millions*, September 1878, p. 126; *Report of the Committee of the China Famine Relief Fund*, p. 102; Wesleyan Methodist Missionary Society (London), Archive, Special Series, Biographical, 632 (3), China Papers of D. Hill, David Hill to his brothers, 6 April 1878.

15. *Report of the Committee of the China Famine Relief Fund*, p. 90; Liu Dapeng, *Tuixiangzhai riji*, p. 50; Liu Dapeng, *Jinci zhi*, pp. 1040–2; *North China Herald*, 21 March 1878, p. 297.

16. Liu Zuoqing, interview 6 August 1999.

17. Liu Dapeng, *Tuixiangzhai riji*, p. 118.

18. Liu Dapeng, Tuixiangzhai riji, ms., 1892/6/28.

19. *North China Herald*, 21 March 1878, p. 296.

20. *Famine in China and the Missionary*, pp. 140–2; T. Richard, *Forty-Five Years in China*, pp. 134–5, 137, 168, 173. See also Edgerton, The Semiotics of Starvation.

21. Liu Dapeng, *Jinci zhi*, p. 1042.

22. Liu Dapeng, *Jinci zhi*, p. 1042. For an estimate that only 20–30% of the province's population was supported by agriculture see Zhu Shoupeng ed., *Guangxu chao donghua lu*, vol 1, p. 409.

23. Liu Dapeng, Tuixiangzhai riji, ms., 1892/9/6. Cf. Mann, "The male bond."

24. *Laoye*. Wang Jiaju, "Shanxi daxuetang." When the Chinese half of the university was founded, organization, funding, and teaching staff were transferred from the Lingde Academy. Until 1904 practices in the Chinese half of the university reflected the practices of the old academies. For the argument see Bourdieu, *The State Nobility*.

25. Liu Dapeng, *Tuixiangzhai riji*, pp. 7–8.

26. Liu Dapeng, Tuixiangzhai riji, ms., 1892/10/3.

27. Here I disagree with Woodside who claims that poorer scholars were more likely to emphasize examination passing at the expense of moral self-cultivation. "State, scholars and orthodoxy," p. 176.

28. Liu Dapeng, *Tuixiangzhai riji*, p. 7; Liu Dapeng, Tuixiangzhai riji, ms., 1892/9/23; Zhao Tian, *Suwei zhai wencun*, p. 50. For practical studies (*shixue*) see Ng On-cho, pp. 116, 173–182; Rowe, *Saving the World*, pp. 122–3, 134–5.

29. Ayers, *Chang Chih-tung*; Zhou, *Zhang Zhidong*, pp. 142–4; Liu Weiyi, *Shanxi lishi renwu*, pp. 420–8; Li Yuanqing and Sun Anbang, eds., *Sanjin yibai mingren*, p. 1559; Yang Shenxiu, "Yang Yichun shi yu zougao"; Liang, *Wuxu zhengbian ji*, pp. 99–102; Zhao Tian, pp. 50–2.

30. Li Jupu, *Keshi yulu*, p. 111 and passim (Liu's friend was Hu Ying); Nivison, "Protest against Conventions"; Elman, *A Cultural History of Civil Examinations*, pp. 380–428.

31. Liu Dapeng, Tuixiangzhai riji, ms., 1892/intercal 6/4 and 7.

32. Liu Dapeng, *Tuixiangzhai riji*, pp. 64–5; Liu Dapeng, Tuixiangzhai riji, ms., 1892/11/11.

33. *Ibid.*, 8/8.

34. *Juren* exams were triennial and the 2nd time Liu sat for them was in 1882. He finally passed in 1894.

35. Liu Dapeng, Tuixiangzhai riji, ms., 1892/intercal 6/14.

36. *Ibid.*, intercal 6/24.

37. *Ibid.*, intercal 6/21.

38. Zheng Banqiao, *Zheng Banqiao quanji*, p. 315.

39. Liu Dapeng, *Tuixiangzhai riji*, p. 59 and pp. 55, 101; Liu Dapeng, Tuixiangzhai riji, ms., 1892/11/1, 1901/5/10, 1901/6/28, 1901/7/1–2, 1901/7/21; Liu Dapeng, "Tuixiangzhai riji" in *Jindaishi ziliao Yihetuan ziliao*, p. 782; Liu Zuoqing, interview 6 September 1999.

40. Liu Dapeng, Tuixiangzhai riji, ms., 1892/11/10.

41. Liu Dapeng, *Tuixiangzhai riji*, pp. 77, 131, 138; Chang Shihua, "Yuci Chewang Chang shi"; Zhang Zhengming, *Jinshang xingshuai shi*, pp. 80–1, 229–33; Qu Shaomiao and Pang Yicai, pp. 43, 57, 72–109; Wu Xiufeng, "Taigu jiaoyu zhi." The Chang family's residence is still standing.

42. Liu Dapeng, *Tuixiangzhai riji*, pp. 47–8.

43. Zhang Zhengming, *Jinshang xingshuai shi*, pp. 108–133; Huang Jianhui.

44. Zhang Zhengming, *Jinshang xingshuai shi*, pp. 142–4. Staff held shares that gave them allocation of business profits but did not make them responsible for losses.

45. Liu Dapeng, *Tuixiangzhai riji*, p. 48.

46. Liu Dapeng, Tuixiangzhai riji, ms., 1892/12/4.

47. Liu Dapeng, *Tuixiangzhai riji*, pp. 69, 145.

48. Liu Dapeng, *Tuixiangzhai riji*, p. 48.

49. *Ibid.* Cf. Yu, *Zhongguo jinshi zongjiao lunli*.

50. Liu Dapeng, Tuixiangzhai riji, ms., 1892/12/4.

51. Liu Dapeng, *Tuixiangzhai riji*, p. 20. (1892). Exchange rates between copper cash and silver taels fluctuated wildly. In order to make the figures easier to compare I have converted all sums of money to taels or silver dollars according to rates given in the diary. The conversions are not precise. References for the exchange rate are given with those for the original sum. For the poverty of teachers see: *Report of the Committee of the China Famine Relief Fund*, p. 111.

52. Liu Dapeng, Tuixiangzhai riji, ms., 1892/9/29.

53. Liu Dapeng, *Tuixiangzhai riji*, pp. 62–5; Liu Dapeng, Tuixiangzhai riji m.s. 1901/2/4, 1901/6/13; Hu Yuxian, Wu Dianqi, "Qiao 'Zaizhongtang' jianjie."

54. Liu Dapeng, *Tuixiangzhai riji*, p. 55; Liu Dapeng, Tuixiangzhai riji, ms., 1901/2/17.

55. Liu Dapeng, *Tuixiangzhai riji*, p. 71.

56. *Ibid.*, p. 57.

57. *Ibid.*, p. 198.

58. Cf. Ebrey, introduction to Chenyang Li ed., *The Sage and the Second Sex.*

59. Liu Dapeng, Tuixiangzhai riji, ms., 1892/6/2.

60. Liu Dapeng, *Tuixiangzhai riji*, p. 35.

61. *Ibid.*, pp. 41–2, 592–5.

62. *Ibid.*, p. 595.

63. *Ibid.*, p. 600.

64. *Ibid.*, pp. 40–41.

65. *Ibid.*, pp. 62, 68, 73, 595–6; Liu Dapeng, Tuixiangzhai riji, ms., 1892/4/29. See also Luo Houli and Ge Jiayuan; Luo Zhitian, "Qingji kejuzhi gaige"; Luo Zhitian, "Kejuzhi de feichu"; Luo Zhitian, "Sixiang guannian"; Elman, "The Relevance of Sung Learning."

66. Liu Dapeng, *Tuixiangzhai riji*, pp. 41, 600.

67. *Ibid.*, pp. 57, 58, 66, 83; *North China Herald*, 7 February 1898, p. 174; 14 November 1898, p. 905; 15 May 1899, p. 864; 14 February 199, p. 261.

68. Liu Dapeng, *Tuixiangzhai riji*, p. 59.

69. *Ibid.*, p. 433; Shi Yongquan, *Taiyuanshi nanjiaoqu jiaoyuzhi*, p. 206; Wu Jiongsheng, interview July 2001.

CHAPTER 3

1. Liu Dapeng, *Jinci zhi*, p. 30.

2. *Ibid.*

3. E.g., Liu Dapeng, Tuixiangzhai riji, ms., 1892/7/1.

4. *Ibid.*, 1926/7/26; Chiqiao villagers, interview, 2 Aug. 2001.

5. Liu Dapeng, Tuixiangzhai riji, ms., 1892/9/20.

6. *Xiaojing* (Classic of Filial Piety), ch.1.

7. Liu Dapeng, *Tuixiangzhai riji*, p. 31; Liu Dapeng, Tuixiangzhai riji, ms. 1915/7/15; Wu Jiongsheng, interview 2 Aug. 2001; Liu Zuoqing, interview 28 July 2001. Cf. Kutcher, *Mourning in Late Imperial China*; Li Huaizhong, "Wan Qing ji Minguo shiqi Huabei." The cloths were typical of the area although the wealthy had ancestral shrines with tablets (Liu Wenbing, p. 269). Cf. Myron Cohen, "Lineage Organization in North China."

8. Liu Dapeng, *Tuixiangzhai riji*, pp. 5, 18, 209, 250, 454; Liu Dapeng, Tuixiangzhai riji, ms. 1926/3/19; Zheng Xianglin, interview 2 Aug. 2001; Liu Zuoqing, interview 6 Aug. 1999, 28 July 2001.

9. Liu Dapeng, *Jinci zhi*, p. 626; Kutcher, p. 48; Ebrey, *Confucianism and Family Rituals*, pp. 31–33; Ko, *Teachers of the Inner Chambers*; Zhang Shouan, "Saoshu wu fu, qing he yi kan;" Santangelo, *Le Passioni nella Cina.*

10. Liu Dapeng, Tuixiangzhai riji, ms., 1892/8/15.

11. *Ibid.*, 1892/9/17. See also Liu Dapeng, *Jinci zhi*, p. 113; Liu Dapeng, Tuixiangzhai riji, ms., 1892/9/9.

12. Liu Dapeng, *Jinci zhi*, p. vi.

13. Liu Dapeng, Tuixiangzhai riji, ms., 1908/1/3, 1908/1/6, 1908/6/3, 1908/1/1, 1908/2/3, 1908/2/6, 1908/2/17, 1908/2/27, 1908/2/29.

14. *Ibid.*, 1908/3/2.

15. *Ibid.*, 1908/3/28 to 1908/4/26.

16. Mu, *Jinyang qiu* pp. 516–25.

17. Liu Dapeng, Tuixiangzhai riji, ms., 1892/7/10, 1901/12/11, 1908/3/5; Liu Dapeng, *Tuixiangzhai riji*, p. 118; Wu Jiongsheng, interview July 2001.

18. Liu Dapeng, Tuixiangzhai riji, ms., 1926/6/6.

19. *Ibid.*, 1901/5/1. Chinese ages are reckoned from the New Year and an infant in its first year is counted as one year old.

20. Hsiung, "The Domestic, the Personal and the Intimate." Chang Zanchun, an acquaintance of Liu's, wrote a funeral biography of his daughter who died age seven months. Chang Zanchun, *Xijing caotang ji*, vol. 6, p. 27.

21. Liu Dapeng, *Jinci zhi*, p. 113; Liu Dapeng, Tuixiangzhai riji, ms., 1901/5/18, 1901/12/14, 1926/10/4; Liu Zuoqing, interviews 6 Sept. 1999, 28 July 2001.

22. Liu Dapeng, *Tuixiangzhai riji*, ed. Qiao, p. 21, 357; Liu Dapeng, Tuixiangzhai riji, ms., 1925/3/23, 1925/6/23, 1925/7/17; Ko, *Teachers of the Inner Chambers*; Judd, "*Niangjia*: Chinese Women and their Natal Families."

23. *North China Herald*, 4 Jan. 1895, p. 15 (George Farthing was a missionary in the area). Liu Dapeng, *Jinci zhi*, pp. 569–70.

24. Liu Dapeng, Tuixiangzhai riji, ms., 1925/7/17, 1926/11/8 to 1926/12/10; Wu Shouming, p. 25; Chiqiao villagers, interview, 10 Sept. 1997 (re the 1930s).

25. Liu Dapeng, *Tuixiangzhai riji*, pp. 31, 370. See also p. 408.

26. *Ibid.*, p. 547.

27. Price, *China Journal 1889–1900*, pp. 48, 51; Liu Zuoqing, interview 6 Sept. 1999; Charles Perry Scott, *An Account of the Great Famine in North China*, p. 24.

28. Liu Dapeng, Tuixiangzhai riji, ms., 1901/3/10 to 1901/3/25; An Jiesheng; Wu Shouming, p. 6; *Zhongguo minjian gequ jicheng*, Shanxi, vol., pp. 204, 213.

29. Liu Dapeng, Tuixiangzhai riji, ms., 1901/6/19; Wu Pei-yi; Kutcher, pp. 28–31; Hsiung, "Constructed Emotions"; Santangelo, "Human Conscience and Responsibility."

30. Liu Dapeng, Tuixiangzhai riji, ms., 1892/8/30.

31. *Ibid.*, 1901/4/4.

32. *Ibid.*, 1892/8/15.

33. Liu Dapeng, *Tuixiangzhai riji*, p. 14.

34. American Board of Commissioners for Foreign Missions, Houghton Library, Shansi Mission, Harvard University. Minutes of the Sixth Annual Meeting of the Shansi Mission of the American Board, 1888; Harold Schofield, *Second Annual Report of the Medical Mission at T'ai-yuen-fu, Shansi*, p. 10; Liu Wenbing, pp. 62, 303; Feng, *Zhongguo nongcun jingji ziliao* (a 1929 survey of Jinci and three nearby villages), p. 738;

Zhang Zhengming, *Shanxi lidai renkou tongji*, p. 233 (statistics for 1919); Chiqiao villagers, interviews, 9 and 11 Sept. 1997.

35. Liu Dapeng, Tuixiangzhai riji, ms., 1926/11/26, 1926/12/10.

36. *Taiyuan shi nanjiaoqu zhi*, p. 781; *North China Herald*, 27 Aug. 1902, pp. 419–20; 29 May 1915, p. 586; 10 Feb. 1917, p. 275; 25 March 1892, p. 378; Harold Schofield, p. 10.

37. Liu Dapeng, Tuixiangzhai riji, ms., 1901/1/12, 1908/3/8; American Board for Foreign Missions, Minutes of the Sixth Annual Meeting of the Shansi Mission, 1888. Cf. Elvin, "Who Was Responsible for the Weather?"

38. Liu Dapeng, Tuixiangzhai riji, ms., 1901/1/14.

39. *Ibid.*, 1901/1/23.

40. *Ibid.*, 1901/1/26–7.

41. *Ibid.*, Tuixiangzhai riji, ms., 1901/1/28, 1901/2/5–10, 1901/2/21 to 1901/3/3, 1901/4/14, 1901/4/22, 1901/4/25–7, 1901/5/10, 1901/7/10; Liu Dapeng, *Tuixiangzhai riji*, p. 98.

42. Liu Dapeng, *Jinci zhi*, p. 650; Liu Dapeng, *Tuixiangzhai riji*, ed. Qiao, pp. 304, 349 (the sacrifices took place in other years).

43. Liu Dapeng, *Tuixiangzhai riji*, p. 69.

44. *Ibid.*, pp. 123–24.

45. Liu Dapeng, Tuixiangzhai riji, ms., 1908/1/19, 1908/1/24; *Taigu xian zhi* (1993), pp. 767–68; Ebrey, p. 88.

46. Liu Dapeng, *Jinci zhi*, pp. 654–55.

47. *Ibid.*, pp. 655–56.

48. Liu Dapeng, Tuixiangzhai riji, ms., 1892/9/12.

49. Liu Dapeng, *Tuixiangzhai riji*, p. 16.

50. Liu Dapeng, Tuixiangzhai riji, ms., 1892/9/18.

51. *Ibid.*, 1892/6/6, 1892/6/19.

52. *Ibid.*, 1908/5/23.

53. *Ibid.*, 1915/6/10.

54. *Ibid.*, 1915/4/22.

55. *Ibid.*, 1914/1/3, 1914/1/10.

56. *Ibid.*, 1892/7/4.

57. Liu Dapeng, *Tuixiangzhai riji*, pp. 111, 115; Liu Dapeng, Tuixiangzhai riji, ms., 1892/9/21; Liu Zuoqing, interview 7 Aug. 2002; Luo Zhitian, "Qingji kejuzhi."

58. Liu Dapeng, *Tuixiangzhai riji*, pp. 79, 182; Liu Dapeng, Tuixiangzhai riji, ms., 1908/3/8, 1908/5/7, 1915/7/11; Zheng Xianglin, interview 3 Aug. 1999; Liu Zuoqing, interview 6 Aug. 1999, 7 Aug. 2002. Cf. Messner, "Emotions in Late Imperial Chinese Medical Discourse."

59. Liu Dapeng, *Tuixiangzhai riji*, pp. 115–16, 118–19, 121, 134; Liu Dapeng, Tuixiangzhai riji, ms., 1908/2/7.

60. Liu Dapeng, Tuixiangzhai riji, ms., 1908/2/23, 1908/3/28, 1908/7/15; Hershatter, *The Workers of Tianjin*, pp. 20–24, 29–31; MacKinnon, *Power and Politics*, pp. 152–55.

61. MacKinnon, pp. 145–49.

62. Liu Dapeng, *Tuixiangzhai riji*, p. 138.

63. *Ibid.*

64. *Ibid.*, p. 153.

65. *Ibid.*, p. 182; Liu Dapeng, Tuixiangzhai riji, ms., 1926/1/30; American Board of Foreign Missions. Shansi Mission, 1900–1909; I. J. Atwood, open letter, Fen Cho Fu, 3 Aug. 1906; Hao Shoushen, Shi Yongquan, and Hao Xiu, "Taiyuan xian yigaoxiao ji qi chuangbanzhe"; *North China Herald*, April 1921, p. 299; Liu Zuoqing, interview 6 Aug. 1999.

66. Liu Dapeng, Tuixiangzhai riji, ms., 1925/11/15; Liu Zuoqing, interviews 6 Aug. 1999, 6 Sept. 1999, 7 Aug. 2002.

CHAPTER 4

1. Liu Dapeng, Tuixiangzhai riji, ms., 1901/7/25.

2. Liu Dapeng, *Tuixiangzhai riji*, pp. 156–57; Liu Dapeng, *Jinci zhi*, pp. 1048–9; Liu Dapeng, "Qianyuan suoji," pp. 27–28, 35, 38, 47; Shi Rongchang, "Gengzi ganshi shi"; Gugong bowuyuan Ming Qing dang'anbu, ed., *Yihetuan dang'an shiliao*, pp. 181, 563; *Taigu xianzhi* (1993), p. 631; *Taiyuanshi nanjiaoqu zhi*, p. 956. Liu had taught for Zhang Zishen of Wangguo and maintained a close relationship with him.

3. Liu Dapeng, "Tuixiangzhai riji," in *Yihetuan shiliao*, p. 817.

4. *Ibid.*, p. 818.

5. *Ibid.*, p. 819.

6. Liu Dapeng, *Tuixiangzhai riji*, pp. 102, 146. Cf. Zhao Tian, p. 29.

7. *Ibid.*, pp. 137–38, 151–52, 162.

8. *Ibid.*, p. 177.

9. Liu Dapeng, Tuixiangzhai riji, ms., 1908/3/27.

10. Pomeranz, *The Making of a Hinterland*. Pomeranz dates this change to the 1850s.

11. Liu Dapeng, Tuixiangzhai riji, ms., 1901/8/2.

12. Liu Dapeng, *Tuixiangzhai riji*, p. 144.

13. *Ibid.*, p. 149.

14. *Ibid.*, p. 128.

15. *Ibid.*, pp. 145, 162; *Jinzhong diquzhi*, p. 782; Hu Yuxian and Wu Dianqi; Zhang Zhengming, *Jinshang xingshuai shi*, p. 232.

16. Liu Dapeng, *Tuixiangzhai riji*, pp. 140, 159–60, 180, 186, 614; *Taiyuan shi nanjiaoqu zhi*, p. 430; Luo Zhitian, "Kejuzhi de feichu"; *Shanxi ziyiju diyijie changnian huiyi juean*, fubu 1, pp. 14–16, yifu p. 7. See also Liu Dapeng, Tuixiangzhai riji, ms., 1925/9/23. The volumes of the diary for the period of Liu's participation in the provincial assembly are missing.

17. Liu Dapeng, *Tuixiangzhai riji*, pp. 228, 497; Shi Yongquan, p. 6; *North China Herald*, 20 March 1926, p. 516; Luo Zhitian, "Qingji kejuzhi gaige"; Liu Zuoqing, interview, 6 Aug. 1999; Chiqiao villagers, interview, 11 Sept. 1997.

18. Liu Dapeng, *Tuixiangzhai riji*, pp. 117, 161, 173; Liu Dapeng, Tuixiangzhai riji, ms., 1908/3/15.

19. Liu Dapeng, *Tuixiangzhai riji*, pp. 103, 105, 111, 116; Wang Yeh-chien, *Land Taxation in Imperial China*, pp. 38, 51.

20. Liu Dapeng, *Tuixiangzhai riji*, pp. 126, 143; Luo Zhitian, "Kejuzhi de feichu."

21. Liu Dapeng, *Tuixiangzhai riji*, p. 128.

22. Liu Dapeng, Tuixiangzhai riji, ms., 1915/4/26.

23. Liu Dapeng, *Tuixiangzhai riji*, pp. 118, 153. Cf. Prazniak, *Of Camel Kings and Other Things*.

24. Gillin, *Warlord*, pp. 15–18; Ye Fuyuan, "Xinhai Taiyuan qiyi zhuiji"; Hou, "Xinhai geming Shanxi qiyi jishi"; Shanxi sheng zhengxie wenshi ziliao yanjiu weiyuanhui, *Yan Xishan tongzhi Shanxi shishi*, pp. 6–25; "Taiyuan qiyi mujiji"; Xue Dubi, "Taiyuan qiyi he Hedong guangfu de pianduan huiyi"; Wang Dingnan, "Xinhai geming Taiyuan shangmin zaoshou qiangque de qingkuang"; *Dagongbao*, 27 Dec. 1911, p. 2, 12 Jan. 1912, p. 2.

25. Liu Dapeng, *Tuixiangzhai riji*, pp. 176, 181, 225; Shi Yongquan, p. 231; Li Shiyu, "Hu Ying."

26. Jing Meijiu "Zuian (juelu)," p. 99; Huang Jianhui, pp. 372–94, 436–58. Huang Jianhui estimates that the banks lost an average of 137,000 taels each.

27. Zhang Zhengming, *Jinshang xingshuai shi*, p. 265; Qu Shaomiao and Pang Yicai, pp. 72–96.

28. Liu Dapeng, Tuixiangzhai riji, ms., 1901/7/21, 1914/2/20; *Taigu xianzhi*, vol. 6, p. 6; Zhang Zhengming, *Jinshang xingshuai shi*, p. 260; Chang Shihua. See also Liu Wenbing, p. 160; *North China Herald*, 8 March 1924, p. 358.

29. Liu Dapeng, *Tuixiangzhai riji*, p. 206; Liu Dapeng, Tuixiangzhai riji, ms., 1925/2/9; *North China Herald*, 14 July 1923, p. 89; Liu Zuoqing, interview, 28 July 2001.

30. Liu Dapeng, *Tuixiangzhai riji*, p. 181.

31. *Ibid.*, p. 223.

32. *Ibid.*, p. 204. 1914 is used to translate *jiayin*, one of the years in the traditional 60-year cycle used for dates.

33. Liu Dapeng, Tuixiangzhai riji, ms., 1914/1/1.

34. Liu Dapeng, *Tuixiangzhai riji*, p. 380.

35. *Ibid.*, pp. 176, 186, 614; *North China Herald*, 31 Oct. 1908, p. 294. Cf. Fincher, *Chinese Democracy*, pp. 111–16; Thompson, *China's Local Councils*, p. 86.

36. Liu Dapeng, *Tuixiangzhai riji*, pp. 195, 217, 232; Liu Dapeng, Tuixiangzhai riji, ms., 1915/6/30, 1915/7/8, 1915/7/14 to 1915/8/4.

37. Liu Dapeng, Tuixiangzhai riji, ms., 1915/7/17.

38. *Ibid.*, Liu Dapeng, *Tuixiangzhai riji*, pp. 219, 525; Liu Zuoqing, interview, 28 July 2001; Guo, *Yidai mingchen Wang Qiong*.

39. Liu Dapeng, *Tuixiangzhai riji*, p. 219. Qiao notes that "whole country" is a mistake for "whole province."

40. *Ibid.*, p. 220.

41. Liu Dapeng, Tuixiangzhai riji, ms., 1915/7/24.

42. *Ibid.*, 1915/8/1.

43. *Ibid.*, 1915/9/29.

44. Liu Dapeng, *Tuixiangzhai riji* p. 221. Liu was not the only poor *juren* to write on this topic. See also *Taigu xianzhi* (1993), p. 631.

45. Cf. Fincher, pp. 88, 113–15, 222–24; Luo Zhitian, "Qingji kejuzhi."

46. Liu Dapeng, *Tuixiangzhai riji*, p. 221; Liu Dapeng, Tuixiangzhai riji, ms., 1915/11/14.

47. Liu Dapeng, *Tuixiangzhai riji*, p. 222.

48. Liu Dapeng, *Jinci zhi*, p. 1534.

49. Liu Dapeng, *Tuixiangzhai riji*, p. 265.

50. Liu Dapeng, Tuixiangzhai riji, ms., 1914/5/9; 1914/7/16, 1915/2/18. See also 1915/2/17.

51. *Ibid.*, 1925/12/26, interleaved slip of paper.

52. *Ibid.*, 1925/10/28.

53. Cf. Liu Dapeng, *Jinci zhi*, p. 147; Gu, p. 3.

54. Liu Dapeng, Tuixiangzhai riji, ms., 1914/7/13, 1914/7/19.

55. *Ibid.*, 1914/7/16.

56. Liu Dapeng, *Tuixiangzhai riji*, pp. 277–80; Liu Dapeng, Tuixiangzhai riji, ms., 1925/intercalary 4/19, 1925/intercalary 4/20, 1925/5/1, 1925/5/8.

57. Liu Dapeng, *Tuixiangzhai riji*, pp. 195, 211, 246, 247, 288, 522; Harrison, "Newspapers and Nationalism."

58. Liu Dapeng, Tuixiangzhai riji, ms., 1914/1/1, 1914/2/21.

59. Liu Dapeng, *Tuixiangzhai riji*, p. 160; Liu Dapeng, Tuixiangzhai riji, ms., 1914/7/20.

60. Liu Dapeng, *Tuixiangzhai riji*, p. 199.

61. *Ibid.*, pp. 178–80, 244–7; Wang Yeh-chien.

62. Liu Dapeng, *Jinci zhi*, pp. 1514–17, 1521; Liu Dapeng, Tuixiangzhai riji, ms., 1915/4/24. "Chongxiu Jinci zaji" (Random notes on the Jinci repairs) is in Liu Dapeng, *Jinci zhi*, pp. 1493–1618. See also Strand, "Citizens in the Audience."

63. Liu Dapeng, *Jinci zhi*, pp. 784, 1531–32, 1534–36, 1555, 1558, 1560; Gillin, pp. 15, 26, 43; Huang Guoliang, "Huang Guoliang zishu."

64. Liu Dapeng, *Jinci zhi*, pp. 1616–17.

65. *Ibid.*, p. 1594.

66. *Ibid.*, pp. 1587, 1598–99, 1606–8, 1613, 1617–18.

67. Liu Dapeng, *Tuixiangzhai riji*, pp. 218, 350, 492; Liu Dapeng, Tuixiangzhai riji, ms., 1915/8/29, 1926/5/13–16, 1926/11/10; Liu Dapeng, Taiyuan xian xianzhuan yipie, p Kenqing Shanxi sheng zhengfu.

68. Liu Dapeng, Tuixiangzhai riji, ms., 1926/7/7 (abridged in Liu Dapeng, *Tuixiangzhai riji*, p. 336).

69. Liu Dapeng, Tuixiangzhai riji, ms., 1926/12/23.

70. Liu Dapeng, *Tuixiangzhai riji*, p. 440.
71. *Ibid.*, p. 614; Shi Yongquan, *Taiyuan shi nanjiaoqu jiaoyuzhi*, p. 205; Liu Zuoqing, interview, 6 Aug. 1999.

CHAPTER 5

1. Liu Dapeng, *Tuixiangzhai riji*, ed. Qiao, pp. 44, 182, 186, 188, 190, 194, 197, 200, 228; Liu Dapeng, Tuixiangzhai riji, ms., 1915/1/15, 1914/1/21; Liu Zuoqing, interview 6 Sept. 1999. Kuroda calculates that Liu's landholding was sufficient to feed only three adults for a year. "Nijittsu shoki Taigen gen ni miru chiiki keizai no genki."
2. Liu Dapeng, *Tuixiangzhai riji*, ed. Qiao, p. 252; Liu Dapeng, *Jinci zhi*, pp. 1177, 1340; Taiyuan Xishan kuangwuju Xishan meikuangshi bianxiezu, *Xishan meikuang shi*, pp. 18, 25; *Qingxu xianzhi*, p. 228; *Taiyuan shi nanjiaoqu zhi*, p. 259; Richthofen, *Baron Richthofen's Letters*, p. 132; *Shanxi kuangwu zhilue*, p. 611.
3. Liu Dapeng, *Jinci zhi*, p. 1120.
4. Liu Dapeng, *Tuixiangzhai riji*, ed. Qiao, pp. 178, 322; Liu Dapeng, *Jinci zhi*, pp. 1138, 1379–80; Taiyuan Xishan kuangwuju, pp. 17, 24, 38, 45; Taiyuan shi nanjiaoqu zhi, pp. 531, 819; *Jinzhong diquzhi*, p. 173.
5. Liu Dapeng, *Jinci zhi*, p. 1377.
6. *Shanxi kuangwu zhilue*, p. 113; Taiyuan Xishan kuangwuju, pp. 41–43, 46; Liu Zuoqing, interview, 6 Sept. 1999; Wu Zhenhua and Hao Shoushen, "Feng Yuxiang"; Guo Yuanzhou, "Feng Yuxiang."
7. Liu Dapeng, *Tuixiangzhai riji*, ed. Qiao, p. 202; *Shanxi kuangwu zhilue*, p. 114; Liu Dapeng, *Jinci zhi*, p. 1227; Shi Yongquan, "Kangrizhan qian Taiyuan xiancheng de gongshangye gaikuang"; Wang Shuren, "Taiyuan xian de tuiche"; Chiqiao villagers, interview, 1997.
8. Liu Dapeng, *Tuixiangzhai riji*, ed. Qiao, pp. 6–7, 26; Ying Kui: this survey records 61 percent of families as being paper makers at a time when the industry was already in serious decline.
9. Liu Dapeng, *Tuixiangzhai riji*, ed. Qiao, pp. 32, 46–47, 193, 210–11, 486; Liu Dapeng, *Jinci zhi*, pp. 143–49; Ying Kui; Chiqiao villagers, interviews, 8, 10, 11 Sept. 1997; Liu Zuoqing, interviews, 6 Sept. 1999, 28 July 2001.
10. Liu Dapeng, *Tuixiangzhai riji*, ed. Qiao, p. 312; Liu Dapeng, *Jinci zhi*, p. 1308; *Taiyuan fuzhi*, p. 59; *Shanxi kuangwu zhilue*, pp. 525–26, 542–49; *North China Herald*, 21 Nov. 1914, p. 618; 20 Sept. 1917, p. 729; 15 Dec. 1917, p. 661; *Qingyuan xiangzhi*, vol. 10, p. 17a. Cf. Shi Jianyun, "Shangpin shengchan, shehui fengong yu shengchanli jinbu."
11. Liu Dapeng, *Tuixiangzhai riji*, ed. Qiao, pp. 177, 195, 399; Liu Dapeng, Tuixiangzhai riji, ms., 1914/1/10, 1914/5/12, 1914/10/27, 1915/9/7; Liu Dapeng, *Jinci zhi*, p. 1103; *Shanxi kuangwu zhilue*, p. 111; Liu Zuoqing, interview, 28 July 2001.
12. Liu Dapeng, Taiyuan xianzhuang yipie.

13. Liu Dapeng, *Tuixiangzhai riji*, ed. Qiao, pp. 177, 288; *Shanxi kuangwu zhilue*, p. 111; Taiyuan xishan kuangwuju, pp. 13–16; *North China Herald*, 22 Dec. 1923, p. 816, 5 July 1924, p. 11; Liu Jiansheng and Liu Pengsheng, *Shanxi jindai jingjishi*, pp. 347–48, 363–64. Cf. Wright, *Coal Mining in China's Economy*, pp. 97–101.

14. Liu Dapeng, *Jinci zhi*, pp. 1202, 1234, 1370, 1379–81, 1454, 1556; Liu Dapeng, *Tuixiangzhai riji*, ed. Qiao, pp. 264, 462; Liu Dapeng, Tuixiangzhai riji, ms., 1915/8/21, 1926/4/7–4/14, 1926/5/26; *Shanxi kuangwu zhilue*, pp. 111, 381. Officially the tael was worth more than the dollar, but the value of both currencies against copper cash fluctuated. Both were also subject to inflation. Liu gives local values of one tael = 1,700–2,200 cash in 1914 and one dollar = 1,748–1,830 cash in 1922 (Liu Dapeng, *Tuixiangzhai riji*, ed. Qiao, pp. 195, 298).

15. I am using "trustworthiness" to translate *xin*. Liu Dapeng, Tuixiangzhai riji, ms., 1914/4/17, 1915/2/29; Yu, pp. 140–2; Lufrano, *Honorable Merchants*; McElderry, "Confucian Capitalism?"; Siu, "The Grounding of Cosmopolitans."

16. Liu Dapeng, Tuixiangzhai riji, ms., 1915/4/12.

17. *Sishu wujing Song yuanren zhu*, pp. 80–81.

18. Liu Wenbing, p. 288; Zhang Zhengming, *Jinshang xingshuai shi*, pp. 149–50.

19. Liu Dapeng, *Jinci zhi*, pp. 1611, 1613.

20. *Ibid.*, p. 1598.

21. Cf. Muldrew, "Hard food for Midas."

22. Liu Dapeng, *Tuixiangzhai riji*, ed. Qiao, pp. 156, 188, 193; Liu Dapeng, Tuixiangzhai riji, ms., 1914/6/5–6, 1914/7/25–6, 1914/7/30, 1914/8/1, 1914/8/21, 1914/9/18–21, 1914/9/23, 1914/10/1, 1914/10/6, 1914/10/9. For mediation see Martin C. Yang, *A Chinese Village*, pp. 165–6; Bockman, "Commercial Contract Law"; Philip Huang, "Between Informal Mediation and Formal Adjudication."

23. Liu Dapeng, *Tuixiangzhai riji*, ed. Qiao, p. 228; Liu Dapeng, *Jinci zhi*, pp. 1552–53; Gardella, "Squaring Accounts."

24. Liu Dapeng, *Jinci zhi*, p. 1554.

25. Liu Dapeng, *Tuixiangzhai riji*, ed. Qiao, p. 323; Liu Dapeng, Tuixiangzhai riji, ms., 1926/2/1–3, 1926/2/9, 1926/2/20, 1926/3/25, 1926/3/29. See also Zhang Zhengming, *Jinshang xingshuai shi*, pp. 142–3.

26. Liu Dapeng, *Tuixiangzhai riji*, ed. Qiao, p. 220; Liu Dapeng, Tuixiangzhai riji, ms., 1915/9/8, 1915/10/6, 1915/10/20, 1915/10/24.

27. Liu Dapeng, Tuixiangzhai riji, ms., 1915/10/21. For the distinction between merchant activities and merchant status, see Pomeranz, "'Traditional' Chinese Business Forms Revisited."

28. Liu Dapeng, *Tuixiangzhai riji*, ed. Qiao, pp. 214–15, 219, 331, 333, 341–42, 349; Liu Dapeng, Tuixiangzhai riji, ms., 1915/6/18, 1915/9/20, 1915/11/28, 1915/12/1–4, 1915/12/9, 1926/9/4, 1926/9/11–13.

29. Liu Dapeng, *Tuixiangzhai riji*, ed. Qiao, p. 58.

30. Liu Dapeng, *Jinci zhi*, pp. 1077–1199, 1201–1492.

31. Liu Dapeng, *Jinci zhi*, p. 1470.

32. *Ibid.*, p. 1123.

33. *Shanxi kuangwu zhilue*, p. 381; Liu Dapeng, *Jinci zhi*, pp. 1202, 1310, 1380.

34. Liu Dapeng, *Jinci zhi*, p. 1375.

35. Liu Dapeng, *Tuixiangzhai riji*, pp. 202, 374; Liu Dapeng, *Jinci zhi*, p. 1400.

36. Liu Dapeng, Tuixiangzhai riji, ms., 1914/12/23.

37. Liu Dapeng, *Jinci zhi*, pp. 1377–78.

38. *Ibid.*, pp. 1135–36.

39. Liu Dapeng, *Tuixiangzhai riji*, p. 138; Liu Dapeng, *Jinci zhi*, pp. 1179, 1221.

40. Liu Dapeng, *Tuixiangzhai riji*, pp. 199, 208, 213, 268, 271–73, 276, 279; Gillin, p. 55; Yan Xishan, *Yan Bochuan xiansheng quanji*, pp. 1503, 1516–7; Xiong Xiling, *Shanxi zhengzhi zhi mianmian guan*, p. 1; Liu Zuoqing, interview, 7 Aug. 2002.

41. Liu Dapeng, Tuixiangzhai riji, ms., 1925/2/1.

42. Liu Dapeng, *Tuixiangzhai riji*, ed. Qiao, pp. 318, 322, 330–1, 337, 358, 362, 424, 460; Liu Dapeng, Tuixiangzhai riji, ms., 1926/7/4, 1926/7/26, 1926/11/1, 1926/12/23; Gillin, pp. 110, 116; Yang Wei, "Shanxi nongcun pochan de yuanyin."

43. Liu Dapeng, *Jinci zhi*, pp. 1243–44, 1247, 1388. Cf. Wright, pp. 33–35, 147. In neighboring Yangqu county, by 1935 only small-scale mines using local methods were making any profit at all. See Zhao Bochu "Yangquan mei de buzhenxing tongzhi."

44. Liu Dapeng, *Tuixiangzhai riji*, pp. 281, 474–75; Liu Dapeng, *Jinci zhi*, pp. 1339–41; Liu Dapeng, Taiyuan xian xianzhuang yipie, chapter Bujiu meiyao zhuce zhi jingli; *Shanxi kuangwu zhilue*, p. 611; Shanxi sheng dang'anguan B30/3/119 p. 6; Zhao Binglin, *Kuangtu cehui xuzhi*.

45. Liu Dapeng, *Jinci zhi*, pp. 1339–41; Liu Dapeng, Taiyuan xian xianzhuang yipie, ms. Chapters Cuisui jing, Kenqing Shanxi sheng zhengfu ti'an huiyi zhi tiaojian; Duara.

46. Liu Dapeng, *Tuixiangzhai riji*, pp. 399, 426, 497, 500; Yang Wei; Ying Kui, p. 13; Liu Zuoqing, interview, 6 Sept. 1999; Zheng Xianglin, interview, 3 Aug. 1999; Chiqiao villagers, interview, 4 August 1999.

CHAPTER 6

1. Liu Dapeng, *Tuixiangzhai riji*, pp. 44, 107, 343; Liu Dapeng, Tuixiangzhai riji, ms., 1925/2/25, 1926/9/18. In 1925 Liu paid tax on a total of 41 mu. For land values in Jinci and 4 neighboring villages, see Feng Hefa, p. 726. For conversion of *mu* to acres in Shanxi, see Buck, *Chinese Farm Economy*, p. 21.

2. Liu Dapeng, *Tuixiangzhai riji*, p. 45.

3. Liu Dapeng, *Jinci zhi*, p. 1327.

4. Liu Dapeng, *Tuixiangzhai riji*, pp. 263, 318; Liu Dapeng, Tuixiangzhai riji, ms., 1926/1/29, 1926/2/7–12; *Shanxi ribao*, 10 Sept. 1919, p. 3.

5. Liu Dapeng, *Tuixiangzhai riji*, p. 318; Liu Dapeng, Tuixiangzhai riji, ms., 1901/3/24, 1925/3/12, 1926/2/10, 1926/2/15, 1926/8/1. Cf. Martin Yang, p. 28.

6. The terms are *nong* (farmer) and *shoukuzhe* (farm laborer or tenant). Liu Dapeng, *Tuixiangzhai riji*, pp. 262, 279–80, 320, 322–23; Liu Dapeng, Tuixiangzhai riji, ms., 1925/9/12, 1926/7/30; Liu Wenbing, p. 150.

7. Liu Dapeng, *Tuixiangzhai riji*, p. 324; Liu Dapeng, Tuixiangzhai riji, ms., 1926/2/24, 1926/2/29; *North China Herald*, 3 Jan. 1920, p. 17; *Taiyuan xian xianzheng shinian jianshi jihua an*, n.p.; Sands, "Agricultural Decision-Making under Uncertainty," p. 357.

8. Mu, *Man shan hong*, p. 477.

9. Liu Dapeng, Tuixiangzhai riji, ms., 1914/8/21, 1915/5/23, 1925/6/24, 1926/3/11, 1926/4/4–5, 1926/4/15–16, 1926/4/18, 1926/4/25, 1926/6/8–9, 1926/8/26; Wen Xing, *Shanxi minsu*, p. 295.

10. Liu Dapeng, Tuixiangzhai riji, ms., 1926/6/20.

11. Liu Dapeng, *Tuixiangzhai riji*, p. 125; Liu Dapeng, Tuixiangzhai riji, ms., 1915/5/26, 1915/9/11, 1925/5/15, 1926/8/26; Wen Xing, p. 296. Cf. Martin Yang, p. 33.

12. Liu Dapeng, Tuixiangzhai riji, ms., 1926/6/16, 1925/3/2. The quotation is from the *Shangshu*, vol. 16, Zhou shu.

13. Liu Dapeng, Tuixiangzhai riji, ms., 1925/4/12. The quotations are from *Mengzi*, vol. 9, Wanzhang shang.

14. Liu Dapeng, Tuixiangzhai riji, ms., 1915/6/9, 1915/8/12, 1926/4/5, 1926/5/12; Luo Zhitian, "Kejuzhi de feichu."

15. Liu Dapeng, Tuixiangzhai riji, ms., 1926/6/8; Ng On-cho, p. 95; Munro, pp. 112–37.

16. Wen Guichang, *Shanxi nongyan daquan*, pp. 1–2; Arkush, "Orthodoxy and Heterodoxy."

17. Liu Dapeng, Tuixiangzhai riji, ms., 1926/8/20.

18. *Ibid.*, 1926/5/5, 1926/5/9, 1926/6/2; 1926/8/5.

19. Liu Wenbing, p. 137.

20. Liu Dapeng, *Tuixiangzhai riji*, pp. 15, 23; Liu Dapeng, *Jinci zhi*, pp. 201–3, 1256–57, 1458.

21. Liu Dapeng, *Tuixiangzhai riji*, pp. 184, 232–33; Liu Dapeng, *Jinci zhi*, pp. 156–57; Edwards, *Fire and Sword in Shansi*, p. 307.

22. Liu Dapeng, *Tuixiangzhai riji*, p. 111.

23. Liu Dapeng, *Jinci zhi*, pp. 1075–76. Cf. Pomeranz, "Water to Iron, Widows to Warlords."

24. Liu Dapeng, *Jinci zhi*, pp. 777–991. See also Yoshinami, "*Shinshishi* yorimita Shinsui shi kyo no suiri kangai."

25. Liu Dapeng, *Jinci zhi*, pp. 1057–58; Fullerton and Wilson, *New China*, pp. 87–88.

26. Liu Dapeng, *Tuixiangzhai riji*, pp. 8, 234–35, 428, 545–46; Liu Dapeng, *Jinci zhi*, pp. 21, 189–91, 193–94; Chiqiao villagers, interview, 10 Sept. 1997.

27. Liu Dapeng, *Jinci zhi*, pp. 114, 804.

28. *Ibid.*, pp. xi, 986.

29. "Wu xing yu Wang Zhang liang xing."

30. Liu Dapeng, *Jinci zhi*, pp. 893, 898, 925.

31. *Ibid.*, p. 190.

32. *Ibid.*, *Jinci zhi*, p. xi; Liu Dapeng, *Jinshui zhi*.

33. Liu Dapeng, *Tuixiangzhai riji*, pp. 242, 317, 383; Liu Dapeng, Tuixiangzhai riji, ms., 1915/1/21, 1925/2/9; Yang Wei; Qi, "Dameng, Huangzhai, Qinglongzhen san cun fangwen ji"; *North China Herald*, 10 Nov. 1923, p. 373; Liu Rongting, "Shanxi Qixian Dongzuodun, Xizuodun liang cun ji Taigu xian Yangyi zhen, Pingyao xian Daobeicun jingshangzhe xiankuang diaocha zhi yanjiu"; Chen Han-seng, "The good earth"; "Plight of the Shansi Peasantry" in Feng, pp. 726–28; Liu Zuoqing, interview, 7 Aug. 2002.

34. Liu Dapeng, *Tuixiangzhai riji*, pp. 463, 476–77, 486; Gillin, p. 125; Yang Wei; Chang Chiao-fu, "General Living Conditions," pp. 201–2. Coal production in neighboring Yangquan county dropped from approx. 741,911 tons in 1932 to approximately 476,727 tons in 1933. Zhao Bochu. Farm survey data for Jinci can be found in "Plight of the Shansi Peasantry."

35. Liu Dapeng, *Tuixiangzhai riji*, pp. 431, 495.

36. *Ibid.*, pp. 308, 507; Liu Wenbing, pp. 139–45.

37. Liu Dapeng, *Tuixiangzhai riji*, p. 233; *North China Herald*, 7 Sept. 1894, pp. 408–9, 27 May 1904, p. 1098; A. T. Schofield, ed., *Memorials of R. Harold A. Schofield*, p. 165.

38. Gillin, p. 190; Lu Jun, "Xibei shiye gongsi he Shanxi jindai gongye"; Gillin, pp. 186–87.

39. Liu Dapeng, *Tuixiangzhai riji*, pp. 167, 216, 282, 307, 325, 453; *North China Herald*, 12 July 1924, p. 46, 21 July 1905, p. 170, 13 July 1906, p. 112, 31 Oct. 1908, p. 294, 16 Jan. 1909, p. 131, 9 Oct. 1909, p. 70, 11 Dec. 1909, p. 589, 29 Sept. 1923, p. 900; *Shanxi ribao*, 14 June 1919, p. 2; Mu, *Jinyang qiu* p. 67; Yang Ruo, "Shanxi nongcun shehui zhi yi ban"; Ross, *The Changing Chinese*, pp. 262, 273; Wang Sixian, "Shanxi xuesheng wusi yundong ersan shi"; Liu Zuoqing, interview, 6 Sept. 1999.

40. Liu Dapeng, *Tuixiangzhai riji*, p. 465.

41. *Ibid.*, pp. 476–77; Chang Chiao-fu.

42. Liu Dapeng, *Tuixiangzhai riji*, pp. 357, 497; *North China Herald*, 14 Nov. 1898, p. 905; 28 May 1921, p. 579; 29 Sept. 1923, p. 900; 1 Dec. 1923, p. 592; 12 July 1924, p. 46; *Shanxi ribao* 6 Jan. 1920, p. 3; Wu Shouming, pp. 47–48; Public Record Office, London, FO 228/3022, p. 264; Liu Zuoqing, interview, 7 Aug. 2002.

43. Liu Dapeng, *Tuixiangzhai riji*, p. 496.

44. *Ibid.*, p. 456.

EPILOGUE

1. Liu Dapeng, *Tuixiangzhai riji*, pp. 502, 508–9, 512, 514. Chiqiao villagers, interviews, 9 and 11 Sept. 1997; Liu Zuoqing, interview, 6 Aug. 1999. See also Gillin, pp. 257–63; Mu, *Jinyang qiu*.

2. Liu Dapeng, *Tuixiangzhai riji*, p. 515; Liu Zuoqing, interview, 6 Aug. 1999.

3. Liu Dapeng, *Tuixiangzhai riji*, p. 432.

4. *Ibid.*, pp. 433, 441–3.

5. *Ibid.*, pp. 434, 438.

6. *Ibid.*, p. 473.

7. *Ibid.*, p. 521.

8. *Ibid.*, pp. 519, 536, 560; Liu Zuoqing, interview, 6 Aug. 1999; Chiqiao villagers, interview, 4 Aug. 1999.

9. *Ibid.*, p. 581.

10. *Ibid.*

11. *Ibid.*, p. 519.

12. *Ibid.*, p. 528.

13. *Ibid.*, pp. 521, 527, 535, 566; Liu Zuoqing, interview, 6 Aug. 1999.

14. Liu Dapeng, *Tuixiangzhai riji*, p. 525.

15. *Ibid.*, p. 553.

16. *Ibid.*, pp. 500, 525, 527, 533; Wu Jiongsheng, interview, July 2001; Liu Zuo-qing, interview, 6 Sept. 1999.

17. Liu Zuoqing, interviews, 6 Sept. 1999, 7 Aug. 2002; Chiqiao villagers, interview, 17 Sept. 1997.

18. Liu Dapeng, *Tuixiangzhai riji*, pp. 388, 426, 498, 539; Liu Zuoqing, interview, 6 Sept. 1999. The term *putong nongmin* (common peasant) is used, rather than distinguishing between poor and middle peasants.

19. Cf. Eyferth, "De-Industrialization in the Chinese Countryside"; Zhonggong Shanxi shengwei dangshi yanjiushi, *Shanxi xinqu tudi gaige*, p. 373.

20. Luo Zhitian, "Qingji kejuzhi"; Xin Liu, *In One's Own Shadow*, p. 156; Kipnis, *Producing Guanxi*. I disagree with Potter, "The Cultural Construction of Emotion in Rural Chinese Social Life," which seems to me to reflect the political weakness of villagers and the difficulties of fieldwork in the PRC at the time it was conducted, rather than attitudes toward emotion.

21. Wu Jiongsheng, letter, 23 Feb. 2002.

Amelang, James S. *The Flight of Icarus: Artisan Autobiography in Early Modern Europe.* Stanford, Calif.: Stanford University Press, 1998.

American Board of Commissioners of Foreign Missions, Shansi Mission. *Chinese map of Shansi Province 1881.* Houghton Library, Harvard University, 1881.

___. Minutes of the Sixth Annual Meeting of the Shansi Mission of the American Board, 1988. Houghton Library, Harvard University.

An Jiesheng. "Qingdai Shanxi zhongshang fengshang yu jiexiao funu chuxian" (The custom of emphasizing trade and the appearance of chaste women in Qing dynasty Shanxi). *Qingshi yanjiu*, vol. 1 (2001).

Arkush, David. "Orthodoxy and Heterodoxy in Twentieth-Century Chinese Peasant Proverbs." In Kwang-Ching Liu, ed., *Orthodoxy in Late Imperial China.* Berkeley: University of California Press, 1990.

Ayers, William. *Chang Chih-tung and Educational Reform in China.* Cambridge, Mass.: Harvard University Press, 1971.

Barr, Alan. "Four Schoolmasters: Educational Issues in Li Hai-kuan's *Lamp at the Crossroads.*" In Benjamin A. Elman and Alexander Woodside, eds., *Education and Society in Late Imperial China, 1600–1900.* Berkeley: University of California Press, 1994.

Beattie, Hilary J. *Land and Lineage in China: A Study of T'ung-ch'eng County, Anhwei, in the Ming and Ch'ing Dynasties.* Cambridge, Eng.: Cambridge University Press, 1979.

Beidasi villagers (group interviews and general conversations). Beidasi, 2 Aug. 2001.

Bockman, Rosser H. "Commercial Contract Law in Late Nineteenth-Century Taiwan." In Jerome Alan Cohen, R. Randle Edwards, and Fu-mei Chang Chen, eds., *Essays on China's Legal Tradition.* Princeton, N.J.: Princeton University Press, 1980.

Bohr, Paul Richard. *Famine in China and the Missionary: Timothy Richard as Relief Administrator and Advocate of National Reform, 1876–1884.* Cambridge, Mass.: East Asian Research Center, Harvard University, 1972.

Bourdieu, Pierre. *The State Nobility: Elite Schools in the Field of Power*. Cambridge, Eng.: Polity Press, 1998, and Stanford, Calif.: Stanford University Press, 1998.

Buck, John Lossing. *Chinese Farm Economy*. Shanghai: Commercial Press, 1930.

Cao Xinyu. "Qingdai Shanxi de liangshi fanyun lunxian" (Grain transport routes in Qing dynasty Shanxi). *Zhongguo lishi dili luncong*, no. 2 (1998).

Chang Chiao-fu. "General Living Conditions of the Peasants in middle Shansi." In Institute of Pacific Relations, ed., *Agrarian China: Selected source materials from Chinese authors*. London: Allen & Unwin, 1939.

Chang Chung-li. *The Chinese Gentry: Studies on Their Role in Nineteenth-Century Chinese Society*. Seattle: University of Washington Press, 1955.

Chang Zanchun. *Xijing caotang ji* (Collected works from the West Path hut). 1934.

Chen Han-seng. "The Good Earth of China's Model Province." *Pacific Affairs*, vol. 9, no. 3 (1936).

Chen Zuogao. *Zhongguo riji shilue* (A brief history of Chinese diaries). Shanghai: Shanghai fanyi chuban gongsi, 1990.

China's Millions. 1878.

Chiqiao villagers (Group interviews and general conversations). Chiqiao 8–11 Sept. 1997, 4 Aug. 1999, 2 Aug. 2001.

Chongxiu Taiyuan xian zhi (New ed. Taiyuan county gazetteer), 1713.

Ch'ü T'ung-tsu. *Local Government in China under the Ch'ing*. Cambridge, Mass.: Harvard University Press, 1962.

Clunas, Craig. *Superfluous Things: Material Culture and Social Status in Early Modern China*. Cambridge, Eng.: Polity Press, 1991.

Cohen, Myron. "Lineage Organization in North China." *Journal of Asian Studies*, vol. 49, no. 3 (1990).

Cohen, Paul A. *History in Three Keys: The Boxers as Event, Experience, and Myth*. New York: Columbia University Press, 1997.

Dagongbao. Tianjin. 1911–12.

Davis, A. R. "The Narrow Lane: Some Observations on the Recluse in Traditional Chinese Society." *East Asian History*, vol. 11 (1996).

Duara, Prasenjit. *Culture, Power, and the State: Rural North China, 1900–1942*. Stanford, Calif.: Stanford University Press, 1988.

Ebrey, Patricia Buckley. *Confucianism and Family Rituals in Imperial China: A Social History of Writing about Rites*. Princeton, N.J.: Princeton University Press, 1991.

Edgerton, Kathryn. The Semiotics of Starvation: Famine Imagery in North China 1876–79. Ph.D. diss., Indiana University, 2002.

Edwards, E. H. *Fire and Sword in Shansi: The Story of the Martyrdom of Foreigners and Chinese Christians*. Edinburgh: Oliphant, Anderson & Ferrier, 1908.

Elman, Benjamin A. *A Cultural History of Civil Examinations in Late Imperial China*. Berkeley: University of California Press, 2000.

———. "The relevance of Sung Learning in the Late Ch'ing: Wei Yuan and the Huang-ch'ao ching-shih wen-pien." *Late Imperial China*, vol. 9, no. 2 (1988).

Elvin, Mark. "Who Was Responsible for the Weather? Moral Meteorology in Late Imperial China." *Osiris*, vol. 13 (1998).

Eyferth, Jacob. "De-industrialization in the Chinese Countryside: Handicrafts and develoment in Jiajiang (Sichuan), 1935 to 1978." *China Quarterly*, vol. 173 (2003).

Feng Hefa, ed. *Zhongguo nongcun jingji ziliao* (Economic materials on Chinese villages). Shanghai: Liming shuju, 1933.

Fincher, John H. *Chinese Democracy: The Self-Government Movement in Local, Provincial, and National Politics, 1905–1914.* New York: St Martin's Press, 1981.

Fitzgerald, John. *Awakening China: Politics, Culture, and Class in the Nationalist Revolution.* Stanford, Calif.: Stanford University Press, 1996.

Fullerton, W. Y., and C. E. Wilson. *New China: A Story of Modern Travel.* London: Morgan & Scott, 1909.

Gardella, Robert P. "Qing Administration of the Tea Trade: Four Facets over Three Centuries." In Jane Kate Leonard and John R. Watt, eds., *To Achieve Security and Wealth: The Qing Imperial State and the Economy, 1644–1911.* Ithaca, N.Y.: Cornell East Asia Series, 1992.

___. "Squaring Accounts: Commercial Bookkeeping Methods and Capitalist Rationalism in Late Qing and Republican China." *Journal of Asian Studies*, vol. 51, no. 2 (1992).

Gillin, Donald D. *Warlord: Yen Hsi-shan in Shansi Province 1911–1949.* Princeton, N.J.: Princeton University Press, 1967.

Gugong bowuyuan Ming Qing dang'anbu, ed. *Yihetuan dang'an shiliao* (Archival sources on the Boxers). Beijing: Zhonghua shuju, 1959.

Gu Linzhi. *Shanyou yanyu ji* (Notes on Shanxi criminal cases). 1899.

Guo Yuanzhou. "Feng Yuxiang jiangjun zai Jinci" (General Feng Yuxiang in Jinci). *Taiyuan wenshi ziliao*, no. 6 (1987).

___. *Yidai mingchen Wang Qiong* (Wang Qiong, a famous minister of his age). Taiyuan: Wang shi yanjiuhui, 1991.

Hao Shoushen, Shi Yongquan, Hao Xiu. "Taiyuan xian yigaoxiao ji qi chuangbanzhe" (Taiyuan county Number 1 Primary School and its founders). *Jinyang wenshi ziliao*, vol. 3 (1990).

Harrison, Henrietta. "Newspapers and Nationalism in Rural China." *Past and Present*, no. 166 (2000).

___. "Village Politics and National Politics: The Boxers in Central Shanxi." In Robert Bickers, ed., *1900: The Boxers, China, and the World.* Unpublished ms.

He Hanwei. *Guangxu chunian (1876–79) Huabei de da hanzai* (The great North China famine of the early Guangxu period, 1876–79). Xianggang: Zhongwen daxue chubanshe, 1980.

Hershatter, Gail. *The Workers of Tianjin, 1900–1949.* Stanford, Calif.: Stanford University Press, 1986.

Hinton, William. *Fanshen: A Documentary of Revolution in a Chinese Village.* New York: Vintage, 1966.

Hou Shaobai. "Xinhai geming Shanxi qiyi jishi" (Notes on the 1911 revolution uprising in Shanxi). *Shanxi wenshi ziliao,* no. 1 (1961).

Hsiung, Ping-chen. "Constructed Emotions: The Bond between Mothers and Sons in Late Imperial China." *Late Imperial China,* vol. 15, no. 1 (1994).

___. "The Domestic, the Personal, and the Intimate: Changing Father-Daughter Bonds in Late Imperial China." Unpublished paper.

___. "Treading the Weedy Path: T'ang Chen (1630–1704) and the World of the Confucian Middlebrow." In Kai-wing Chow, On-cho Ng, and John B. Henderson, eds., *Imagining Boundaries: Changing Confucian Doctrines, Texts and Hermeneutics.* Albany: State University of New York Press, 1999.

Hu Yuxian, Wu Dianqi. "Qiao 'Zaizhongtang' jianjie" (A brief introduction to the Qiao family Zaizhongtang). In Lu Chengwen, Qi Fengyi, Nie Yuanyou, *Shanxi fengsu minqing* (Shanxi customs and folklore). Taiyuan: Shanxi sheng difangzhi bianzuan weiyuanhui, 1987.

Huang Guoliang. "Huang Guoliang zishu" (Autobiography of Huang Guoliang). *Shanxi wenshi ziliao,* vol. 3 (1962).

Huang Jianhui. *Shanxi piaohao shi* (A history of the Shanxi banks). Taiyuan: Shanxi jingji chubanshe, 1992.

Huang, Philip. "Between Informal Mediation and Formal Adjudication: The Third Realm in Qing Civil Justice." *Modern China,* vol. 19, no. 3 (1993).

Jing Meijiu. "Zuian (juelu)" (Details of a criminal case [extracts]). In Zhongguo shehui kexueyuan jindaishi yanjiusuo jindaishi ziliao bianjizu, ed., *Xinhai geming ziliao leibian* (Edited materials on the 1911 revolution). Beijing: Zhongguo shehui kexue chubanshe, 1981.

Jinzhong diquzhi (Central Shanxi district gazetteer). Taiyuan: Shanxi renmin chubanshe, 1993.

Judd, Ellen R. "Niangjia: Chinese Women and Their Natal Families." *Journal of Asian Studies,* vol. 48, no. 3 (1989).

Kipnis, Andrew B. *Producing Guanxi: Sentiment, Self, and Subculture in a North China Village.* Durham, N.C.: Duke University Press, 1997.

Ko, Dorothy. *Teachers of the Inner Chambers: Women and Culture in Seventeenth-Century China.* Stanford, Calif.: Stanford University Press, 1994.

Kuroda Akinobu. "Nijittsu shoki Taigen gen ni miru chiiki keizai no genki" (The boundaries of regional economies: the case of Taiyuan county in the early twentieth century). *Tōyōshi kenkyu,* vol. 54, no. 4 (1996).

Kutcher, Norman. *Mourning in Late Imperial China: Filial Piety and the State.* Cambridge, Eng.: Cambridge University Press, 1999.

Kwong, Charles Yim-tze. *Tao Qian and the Chinese Poetic Tradition: The Quest for Cultural Identity.* Ann Arbor: Center for Chinese Studies, University of Michigan, 1994.

Li Chenyang, ed. *The Sage and the Second Sex: Confucianism, Ethics, and Gender.* Chicago: Open Court, 2000.

Li Fubin. "Qingdai zhonghouqi Zhili Shanxi chuantong nongyequ kenzhi shulun" (An account of land reclamation in the traditional agricultural areas of Zhili and Shanxi during the mid- and late Qing). *Zhongguo lishi dili luncong*, no. 2 (1994).

Li Huaizhong. "Wan Qing ji Minguo shiqi Huabei cunzhuangzhong de xiangdizhi—yi Hebei Huolu xian wei li" (The village government system in north China villages during the late Qing and Republic: a case study of Huolu county, Hebei). *Lishi yanjiu*, no. 6 (2001).

Li Jupu. *Keshi yulu* (Sayings of a scholar). Taibei: Shanxi wenxian congshu, 1983.

Li Sanmou, Zhang Wei. "Wan Qing Jinshang yu cha wenhua" (Shanxi merchants and tea culture in the late Qing). *Qingshi yanjiu* (Qing history research), no. 1 (2001).

Li Shiyu. "Hu Ying" (Hu Ying). *Taiyuan wenshi ziliao*, vol. 8 (1987).

Li Yuanqing, Sun Anbang, eds. *San Jin yibai mingren pingzhuan* (Biographies of three hundred famous Shanxi men). Taiyuan: Shanxi renmin chubanshe, 1992.

Liang Qichao. *Wuxu zhengbian ji* (A record of the coup of 1898). Taibei: Zhonghua shuju, 1936 ed.

Liu Dapeng. Gongfei rao Jin jilue (Brief account of the Communist bandit's harassment of Shanxi). Manuscript. Shanxi Provincial Library.

___. *Jinci zhi* (Jinci gazetteer), ed. Mu Xiang and Lu Wenxing. Taiyuan: Shanxi renmin chubanshe, 1986.

___. Jinshui zhi (Jin river gazetteer). Manuscript. Private collection of Wen Jie, Chiqiao, Shanxi.

___. "Qianyuan suoji" (Brief notes from Qian garden). In Qiao Zhiqiang, ed., *Yihetuan zai Shanxi diqu shiliao* (Historical materials on the Boxers in Shanxi). Taiyuan: Shanxi renmin chubanshe, 1980.

___. Taiyuan xian xianzhuang yipie (A glance at present conditions in Taiyuan county). Photocopy of manuscript. Shanxi Provincial Library.

___. *Tuixiangzhai riji* (Diary from the chamber to which one retires to ponder). Manuscript, Shanxi Provincial Library.

___. *Tuixiangzhai riji* (Diary from the chamber to which one retires to ponder), ed. Qiao Zhiqiang. Taiyuan: Shanxi renmin chubanshe, 1990.

___. "Tuixiangzhai riji" (Diary from the chamber to which one retires to ponder). In *Jindaishi ziliao Yihetuan ziliao* (Modern history materials, Boxer materials). Beijing: Zhongguo shehui kexue chubanshe, 1990.

Liu Jiansheng and Liu Pengsheng. *Shanxi jindai jingjishi* (An economic history of modern Shanxi). Taiyuan: Shanxi jingji chubanshe, 1995.

Liu Rongting. "Shanxi Qixian Dongzuodun, Xizuodun liang cun ji Taigu xian Yangyi zhen, Pingyao xian Daobeicun jingshangzhe xiankuang diaocha zhi yanjiu" (Research on an investigation into the present conditions of businessmen in the two villages of Dongzuodun and Xizuodun in Qixian county, Yangyi town in Taigu county, and Daobei village in Pingyao county, Shanxi). *Xin nongcun* no. 22 (1935).

Liu Weiyi. *Shanxi lishi renwu zhuan* (Biographies of Shanxi historical figures). Shanxi sheng difangzhi bianzuan weiyuanhui bangongshi, 1983.

Liu Wenbing. *Xugou xianzhi* (Xugou county gazetteer). Taiyuan: Shanxi renmin chubanshe, 1992.

Liu Xin. *In One's Own Shadow: An Ethnographic Account of the Condition of Post-Reform Rural China*. Berkeley: University of California Press, 2000.

Liu Zuoqing (Liu Dapeng's grandson, b. 1926). Interviews 6 Aug. 1999, 6 Sept. 1999, 28 July 2001, 7 Aug. 2002.

Lu Jun. "Xibei shiye gongsi he Shanxi jindai gongye" (The Northwestern industrial company and Shanxi's modern industry). *Shanxi wenshi ziliao*, no. 63 (1989).

Lufrano, Richard John. *Honorable Merchants: Commerce and Self-Cultivation in Late Imperial China*. Honolulu: University of Hawai'i Press, 1997.

Luo Houli, Ge Jiayuan. "Jindai Zhongguo de liangge shijie—yige neidi xiangshen yanzhong de shishi bianqian" (The two worlds of modern China: political change in the eyes of a country gentleman in China's interior). *Dushu*, no. 10 (1996).

Luo Zhitian. "Kejuzhi de feichu yu simin shehui de jieti—yige neidi xiangshen yanzhong de jindai shehui bianqian" (The abolition of the examination system and the disintegration of the four-class society: social change in the eyes of a local literatus). *Qinghua xuebao*, vol. 25, no. 4 (1995).

———. "Qingji kejuzhi gaige de shehui yingxiang" (The social influence of the late Qing reforms to the examination system). *Zhongguo shehui kexue* 1998, no. 4.

———. "Sixiang guannian yu shehui juese de cuowei: Wuxu qianhou Hunan xinjiu zhi zheng zai si—cezhong Wang Xianqian yu Ye Dehui (The intricate connections between philosophical attitudes and social roles: rethinking the contest between old and new in Hunan before 1898—emphasizing Wang Xianqian and Ye Dehui). *Lishi yanjiu* no. 5 (1998).

MacGaffey, Wyatt. *Kongo Political Culture: The Conceptual Challenge of the Particular*. Bloomington: Indiana University Press, 2000.

MacKinnon, Stephen R. *Power and Politics in Late Imperial China: Yuan Shi-kai in Beijing and Tianjin, 1901–1908*. Berkeley: University of California Press, 1980.

Mann, Susan. "The male bond in Chinese History and Culture." *American Historical Review*, vol. 105, no. 5 (2000).

McElderry, Andrea. "Confucian Capitalism? Corporate Values in Republican China." *Modern China*, vol. 12, no. 3 (1986).

Meskill, Johanna Menzel. *A Chinese Pioneer Family: The Lins of Wu-feng, Taiwan, 1729–1895*. Princeton, N.J.: Princeton University Press, 1979.

Messner, Angelika. "Emotions in Late Imperial Chinese Medical Discourse: A Preliminary Report." *Ming Qing Yanjiu*, 2000.

Mu Xiang. *Jinyang qiu* (Autumn in Jinyang). Beijing: Jiefangjun wenyishe, 1964.

———. *Man shan hong* (The mountains are red). Beijing: Jiefangjun wenyishe, 1978.

Muldrew, Craig. "'Hard Food for Midas': Cash and Its Social Value in Early Modern England." *Past and Present*, no. 170 (2001).

Ng On-cho. *Cheng-Zhu Confucianism in the Early Qing: Li Guangdi (1642–1718) and Qing Learning.* Albany: State University of New York Press, 2001.

Nivison, David S. "Protest against Conventions and Conventions of Protest." In Arthur F. Wright, ed., *The Confucian Persuasion.* Stanford, Calif.: Stanford University Press, 1960.

North China Herald, Shanghai.

Owen, Stephen. "The Self's Perfect Mirror: Poetry as Autobiography." In Shuen-fu Lin and Stephen Owen, eds., *The Vitality of the Lyric Voice: Shih Poetry from the Late Han to the T'ang.* Princeton, N.J.: Princeton University Press, 1986.

"Plight of the Shansi Peasantry." *The People's Tribune*, 16 Jan. 1932.

Pomeranz, Kenneth. *The Making of a Hinterland: State, Society, and Economy in Inland North China, 1853–1937.* Berkeley: University of California Press, 1993.

———. "'Traditional' Chinese Business Forms Revisited: Family, Firm, and Financing in the History of the Yutang Company of Jining, 1779–1956." *Late Imperial China*, vol. 18, no. 1 (1997).

———. "Water to Iron, Widows to Warlords: The Handan Rain Shrine in Modern Chinese History." *Late Imperial China*, vol. 12, no. 1 (1991).

Potter, Sulamith Heins. "The Cultural Construction of Emotion in Rural Chinese Social Life." *Ethos*, vol. 16 (1988).

Prazniak, Roxann. *Of Camel Kings and Other Things: Rural Rebels against Modernity in Late Imperial China.* Lanham, Md.: Rowman & Littlefield, 1991.

Price, Eva Jane. *China Journal, 1889–1900: An American Missionary Family During the Boxer Rebellion.* New York: Scribners, 1989.

Public Record Office. London. FO 228.

Qi Yu. "Dameng, Huangzhai, Qinglongzhen san cun fangwen ji" (Notes on interviewing in the three villages of Dameng, Huangzhai, and Qinglongzhen). *Xin nongcun*, nos. 3–4 (1933).

Qingdai riji huichao (Selections from Qing dynasty diaries). Shanghai: Shanghai renmin chubanshe, 1982.

Qingxu xianzhi (Qingxu county gazetteer). Taiyuan: Shanxi guji chubanshe, 1999.

Qu Shaomiao and Pang Yicai. *Shanxi waimao zhi* (An account of Shanxi's foreign trade). Taiyuan: Shanxi sheng difangzhi bianzuan weiyuanhui bangongshi, 1984.

Report of the Committee of the China Famine Relief Fund. Shanghai: American Presbyterian Mission Press, 1879.

Richard, Timothy. *Forty-Five Years in China.* London: T. Fisher Unwin, 1916.

Richthofen, Ferdinand von. *Baron Richthofen's Letters, 1870–1872.* Shanghai:, North China Herald, 1903.

Ross, Edward Alsworth. *The Changing Chinese: The Conflict of Oriental and Western Cultures in China.* New York: Century, 1912.

Rowe, William T. *Saving the World: Chen Hongmou and Elite Consciousness in Eighteenth-Century China.* Stanford, Calif.: Stanford University Press, 2001.

___. "Success Stories: Lineage and Elite Status in Hanyang County, Hubei, c. 1368–1949." In Joseph W. Esherick and Mary Backus Rankin, eds., *Chinese Local Elites and Patterns of Dominance.* Berkeley: University of California Press, 1990.

Sands, Barbara N. "Agricultural Decision-Making under Uncertainty: The Case of the Shanxi Farmers, 1931–1936." *Explorations in Economic History*, vol. 26 (1989).

Santangelo, Paolo. "Human Conscience and Responsibility in Ming-Qing China." *East Asian History*, no. 4 (1992).

___. *Le Passioni nella Cina.* Venice: Marsilio, 1997.

Schofield, A. T., ed. *Memorials of R. Harold A. Schofield M.A., M.B. (Oxon.) (Late of the China Inland Mission), First Medical Missionary to Shan-si, China.* London: Hodder & Stoughton, 1885.

Schofield, Harold. *Second Annual Report of the Medical Mission at T'ai-yuen-fu, Shansi, North China, in Connection with the China Inland Mission.* Shanghai: American Presbyterian Mission Press, 1883.

Schoppa, R. Keith. *Chinese Elites and Political Change: Zhejiang Province in the Early Twentieth Century.* Cambridge, Mass.: Harvard University Press, 1982.

Scott, Charles Perry. *An Account of the Great Famine in North China, 1876–79, Drawn from Official Sources; Together with an Appendix of Extracts from Private Letters.* Hull: Kirk & Sons, 1885.

Shanxi kuangwu zhilue (A brief survey of Shanxi minerals). c. 1919.

Shanxi ribao (Shanxi daily). 1919–20.

Shanxi sheng dang'anguan (Shanxi Provincial Archives). Taiyuan. Shanxi.

Shanxi sheng zhengxie wenshi ziliao yanjiu weiyuanhui, ed. *Yan Xishan tongzhi Shanxi shishi* (A true history of how Yan Xishan ruled Shanxi). Taiyuan: Shanxi renmin chubanshe, 1981.

Shanxi ziyiju diyijie changnian huiyi juean (Decisions of the first standing committee of the Shanxi Consultative Assembly). 1909.

Shi Jianyun. "Shangpin shengchan, shehui fengong yu shengchanli jinbu—jindai Huabei nongcun shougongye de biange" (Commercial production, social division of labor and improvements in productivity: changes in handicraft industries in modern north China villages). *Zhongguo shehui jingjishi yanjiu*, no. 4 (1998).

Shi Rongchang. "Gengzi ganshi shi" (Poems in response to 1900). *Jindaishi ziliao*, no. 11 (1956).

Shi Yongquan. "Kangrizhan qian Taiyuan xiancheng de gongshangye gaikuang" (The condition of trade and industry in Taiyuan county town before the war of resistance against Japan). *Jinyang wenshi ziliao*, vol. 2 (1990).

___. *Taiyuan shi nanjiaoqu jiaoyu zhi 1840–1990* (Taiyuan city southern suburban district education gazetteer 1840–1990). Taiyuan shi nanjiaoqu jiaoyu zhi bianweihui, 1992.

Sishu wujing Song yuanren zhu (The Four Books and Five Classics with the Song commentaries). Shanghai: Shijie shuju, 1936.

Siu, Helen F. "The Grounding of Cosmopolitans: Merchants and Local Cultures in Guangdong." In Wen-hsin Yeh, ed., *Becoming Chinese: Passages to Modernity and Beyond*. Berkeley: University of California Press, 2000.

Smith, Arthur H. *Village Life in China: A Study in Sociology*. New York: Revell, 1899.

Spence, Jonathan. *The Death of Woman Wang*. London: Weidenfeld & Nicolson, 1978.

Strand, David. "Citizens in the Audience and at the Podium." In Merle Goldman and Elizabeth J. Perry, eds., *Changing Meanings of Citizenship in Modern China*. Cambridge, Mass.: Harvard University Press, 2002.

Taigu xianzhi (Taigu county gazetteer). 1931.

___. Taiyuan: Shanxi renmin chubanshe, 1993.

Taiyuan fuzhi (Taiyuan prefecture gazetteer). Taiyuan: Shanxi renmin chubanshe, 1991.

"Taiyuan qiyi mujiji" (Eyewitness accounts of the Taiyuan uprising). *Shanxi wenshi ziliao*, vol. 1 (1961).

Taiyuan shi nanjiaoqu zhi (Taiyuan city southern suburban district gazetteer). Beijing: Sanlian shudian, 1994.

Taiyuan xian xianzheng shi nian jianshi jihua an (Record of the ten-year construction plan for Taiyuan county administration). 1934.

Taiyuan xian xuzhi (Appendix to the gazetteer of Taiyuan county). 1882.

Taiyuan xian zhi (Taiyuan county gazetteer). 1552.

___. 1826.

Taiyuan Xishan kuangwuju Xishan meikuangshi bianxiezu. *Xishan meikuang shi* (A history of coal mining in the Western Hills). 1961.

Tao Yuanming. *Tao Yuanming zuopin quanji* (The complete works of Tao Yuanming). Gaoxiong: Qiancheng chubanshe, 1985.

Thompson, Roger R. *China's Local Councils in the Age of Constitutional Reform, 1898–1911*. Cambridge, Mass.: Council on East Asian Studies, Harvard University, 1995.

Wang Dingnan. "Xinhai geming Taiyuan shangmin zaoshou qiangque de qingkuang" (How the Taiyuan merchants were robbed in the 1911 revolution). *Shanxi wenshi ziliao*, vol. 9 (1964).

Wang Jiaju. "Shanxi daxuetang chuchuang shinianjian" (The first ten years after the founding of Shanxi University). *Shanxi wenshi ziliao*, vol. 5 (1963).

Wang Shuren. "Taiyuan xian de tuiche" (Taiyuan county wheelbarrows). *Jinyang wenshi ziliao*, vol. 4 (1995).

Wang Sixian. "Shanxi xuesheng wusi yundong ersan shi" (Two or three things about the Shanxi students' May 4th Movement). *Shanxi wenshi ziliao*, vol. 5 (1963).

Wang Yeh-chien. *Land Taxation in Imperial China, 1750–1911*. Cambridge, Mass.: Harvard University Press, 1973.

Wangguo villagers. Group interview, 3 Aug. 1999.

Wen Guichang. *Shanxi nongyan daquan* (Complete Shanxi farming proverbs). Shanxi sheng difangzhi bianzuan weiyuanhui, 1986.

Wen Xing. *Shanxi minsu* (Shanxi folk customs). Taiyuan: Shanxi renmin chubanshe, 1991.

Wesleyan Methodist Missionary Society Archive. School of Oriental and African Studies. London.

Williamson, Alexander. *Journeys in North China, Manchuria, and Eastern Mongolia; with Some Account of Corea.* London: Smith, Elder, 1870.

Woodside, Alexander. "State, Scholars and Orthodoxy: The Ch'ing Academies, 1736–1836." In Kwang-ching Liu, ed., *Orthodoxy in Late Imperial China.* Berkeley: University of California Press, 1990.

Wright, Tim. *Coal Mining in China's Economy and Society, 1895–1937.* Cambridge, Eng.: Cambridge University Press, 1984.

Wu Pei-yi. *The Confucian's Progress: Autobiographical Writings in Traditional China.* Princeton, N.J.: Princeton University Press, 1990.

Wu Jiongsheng [Beidasi village resident, local historian]. Interviews, 3 Aug. 1999, 2 Aug. 2001.

———. Letter 25 Aug. 2000 (reports his interviews with elderly people in Beidasi village).

Wu Shouming. *Taigu xian Guanjiabu cun diaocha baogao* (Report on an investigation into Guanjiabu village, Taigu county). Manuscript. 1935. Collection of Professor Xing Long, Shanxi University.

Wu xing yu Wang Zhang liang xing (The Wu family and the Wang and Zhang families). Inscription in the Wu Family Ancestral Hall, Beidasi village.

Wu Xiufeng. "Taigu jiaoyu zhi (shigao) jiexuan" (Extracts from a draft gazetteer of Taigu education). *Taigu shizhi ziliao xuan* (Selected materials for Taigu historical gazetteer), vol. 5 (1986).

Wu Zhenhua and Hao Shoushen. "Feng Yuxiang jiefang budaiyao" (Feng Yuxiang liberates the sack mines). *Jinyang wenshi ziliao*, vol. 3 (1990).

Xiong Xiling. *Shanxi zhengzhi zhi mianmian guan* (A view of every aspect of Shanxi government). 1925.

Xue Dubi. "Taiyuan qiyi he Hedong guangfu de pianduan huiyi" (Fragmentary reminiscences of the Taiyuan uprising and the 1911 revolution in Hedong). *Shanxi wenshi ziliao*, no. 4 (1962).

Yan Xishan. *Yan Bochuan xiansheng quanji* (Complete works of Mr Yan Xishan). 1928.

Yang, Martin C. *A Chinese Village: Taitou, Shantung Province.* New York: Columbia University Press, 1945.

Yang Ruo. "Shanxi nongcun shehui zhi yi ban" (The situation of Shanxi village society). *Xin nongcun*, vol. 2 (1933).

Yang Shenxiu. "Yang Yichun shi yu zougao" (Memorials of censor Yang Shenxiu). In *Wuxu liu junzi yiji* (Collected writings left by the six martyrs of 1898). Taibei: Wenhai chubanshe, 1966.

Yang Wei. "Shanxi nongcun pochan de yuanyin" (The reasons for the bankruptcy of Shanxi villages). *Xin nongcun*, nos. 3–4 (1933).

Ye Fuyuan. "Xinhai Taiyuan qiyi zhuiji" (Notes tracing the 1911 uprising in Shanxi). *Shanxi wenshi ziliao*, vol. 1 (1961).

Yeh Wen-hsin. *Provincial Passages: Culture, Space, and the Origins of Chinese Communism*. Berkeley: University of California Press, 1996.

Ying Kui. "Lancun, Zhifang, Chiqiao san cun zhi caozhi diaocha" (An investigation into the paper made from straw in the three villages of Lancun, Zhifang and Chiqiao). *Xin nongcun* (Taiyuan), Nos. 3–4 (1933).

Yoshinami Takashi. "*Shinshishi* yorimita Shinsui shi kyo no suiri kangai" (Water utilization and irrigation from the four channels of the Jin river from a reading of the *Jinci Gazetteer*). *Shigaku kenkyu* (Review of Historical Studies), no. 170 (1986).

Yu Yingshi. *Zhongguo jinshi zongjiao lunli yu shangren jingshen* (Modern China's religious ethics and the commercial spirit). Taibei: Lianjing, 1987.

Zeng Wenzheng. *Zeng Wenzheng gong quanji* (Collected works of Mr Zeng Guofan). Shanghai: Dongfang shuju, 1935.

Zhang Shouan. "Saoshu wu fu, qing he yi kan?—Qingdai 'Lizhi yu renqing zhi chongtu' yili" (For a brother-in-law not to wear mourning for his sister-in-law, how can it be endured?—The Qing dynasty debate on "the conflict between ritual and emotion"). In Xiong Bingzhen and Lu Miaofen, eds., *Lijiao yu qingyu: Qianjindai Zhongguo wenhua zhong de hou/xiandai qing* (Neo-Confucian orthodoxy and human desires: post/modernity in late imperial Chinese culture). Taibei: Zhongyang yanjiuyuan jindaishi yanjiusuo, 1999.

Zhang Zhengming. *Jinshang xingshuai shi* (A history of the rise and fall of the Shanxi merchants). Taiyuan: Shanxi guji chubanshe, 1995.

___. *Shanxi lidai renkou tongji* (Shanxi historical population statistics). Taiyuan: Shanxi renmin chubanshe, 1992.

Zhao Binglin. *Kuangtu cehui xuzhi* (Essential knowledge about mineral surveying). Taiyuan: 1918.

Zhao Bochu. "Yangquan mei de bu zhenxing tongzhi" (The structure of Yangquan coal that fails to promote vigorous development). *Zhonghua shiye yuekan* (China industrial monthly), 28 Dec. 1935.

Zhao Tian. *Suwei zhai wencun* (Collected essays from a simple abode). 1919.

Zheng Banqiao. *Zheng Banqiao quanji* (Complete works of Zheng Banqiao). Jinan: Jilu shushe, 1985.

Zheng Xianglin (Chiqiao village resident, former Jinci township head). Interviews. Chiqiao. 3 Aug. 1999, 2 Aug. 2001.

Zhonggong Shanxi shengwei dangshi yanjiushi, ed. *Shanxi xinqu tudi gaige* (Land reform in the new districts of Shanxi). Taiyuan: Shanxi renmin chubanshe, 1995.

Zhongguo minjian gequ jicheng. Shanxi juan (Collected folk songs of China, Shanxi volume). Beijing: Renmin yinyue chubanshe, 1990.

Zhou Hanguang. *Zhang Zhidong yu Guangya shuyuan* (Zhang Zhidong and the Guangya Academy). Taibei: Zhongguo wenhua daxue chubanbu, 1983.

Zhu Shoupeng. *Guangxu chao donghua lu* (Records from the Donghua gate for the Guangxu reign). Beijing: Zhonghua shuju, 1958.

Agriculture: Communist land reform, 166–67; crops, 139–40; day laborers, 138; description of work, 138–42; and drought, 28–31; economic impact of, 151–53; harvest, 141–42; subsistence, 153; value and meaning of, 142–44; water for, 140, 144–51, 154
Alum industry, 117–18, 121
Analects, 25, 122
Ancestral sacrifices, 62–63

Banking, 42–43, 95, 132
Baojin Mining Company, 91
Beijing, 47–51, 85–86, 91
Bicycles, 156
Biyu (daughter), 60
Book of Odes, 127
Book of Rites, 71
Books, respect accorded, 27
Boxer uprising, 7, 12, 63, 67, 77, 78, 84–86, 92
A Brief Account of the Communist Bandits' Harassment of Shanxi (Liu), 13–14, 15
Buddhism, 68–69

Calendar, solar versus lunar, 97–98
Calligraphy, 47–48, 76
Catholic Church, *see* Christianity
Chambers of commerce, 91, 107, 125–26
Chang Chung-li, 2
Chang family, 41–42, 89, 96
Channel heads, 148–51
Chiang Kaishek, 161
Chiqiao: alum industry in, 117–18; Communist social classes in, 166–68; epi-

demics in, 30, 65; famine in, 30–31, 165, 167; Japanese occupation of, 160–63; paper-making industry in, 13, 21, 29–30, 108, 116–17, 167–68; pavilion project in, 108–9; present-day, 1, 6, 169–70; prosperity in mid–19th century of, 23; sacrifices to Holy Mother in, 148–49
Chongxiu Academy, Taiyuan city, 32, 35
Christianity, 67, 84–86, 130
Classic of Changes, 17, 104
Classic of Filial Piety, 25, 52
Classic of History, 142
Clothing, 157
Coal mining: under Communism, 167; deep shaft, 132–33; description of work, 114–16; economic boom in, 119–20; extent of, 114; government regulation of, 133–34; large versus small mines, 132–34; Liu on, 114–15, 127–30; modernization and, 132–33
Communist Party: Red Army, 162; social reforms of, 166–67
Confucianism: and agriculture, 142–43; changes in, 168; in education, 25–26; gentleman's role in, 74, 82; incompatibility with new politics of, 109; modernization versus, 6, 79–80, 86, 88, 97, 109; morality and power in, 20; neo-, 5, 143; prayer in, 145–46; renewed interest in, 168; social role of, 4–5; state abandonment of, 4–5, 80, 86, 93
Confucius, texts by, 25, 26, 122
Conservative politics and thought, 84–86, 93

Consumer culture, 156–58
Cotton, 139–40, 153
Customs: disputes over, 68–69, 72–73; funeral, 68–69; holiday observances, 97–98; irrigation system festivals, 148–49, 154; modern ideals versus, 104; rainfall rituals, 145–46; sacrifices to Holy Mother, 148–49

Daizhou, 80–81
Daoism: Confucianism and, 5; on worldly achievement, 20
Dates, 141–42, 144
Daughters: Biyu, 60; Hongxi, 59–60; Hongyu, 113; relationship to parents of, 61–63
Death, 65
Degree-holders: lives of, 2–3; system of, 2, 25
Deities, Holy Mother, 148–50
Diaries: content of, 10; history of, 10; Liu's preparation of, 10, 15. *See also* Liu Dapeng: diary of
Disease: deaths from, 65–66; treatments for, 66–68
Divorce, 69–72
Dongyue temple, Beijing, 51
Dongyue temple, Jinci, 51–52
Dragon Kings, 28–29, 145
Drinking, 16, 81
Drought, 28–31
Drug addiction, 164

Education: accessibility of, 90–91; cost of, 89–91; male community for, 32–33, 36–37; method of, 26; military degrees, 25; modernization in, 48, 76–80, 86–91; moral content of, 25–27, 38, 88; practical studies in, 35–36; social mobility versus moral indoctrination, 24–25, 38; social status and, 33–35; values of, 27. *See also* Examinations; Teaching; Village schools
Elections, 98–103, 106
Elementary Learning, 25
Elements of Geometry (Euclid), 48
Elite, 2–4
Equality, 79
Essay-writing, 37–38, 49, 76, 78
Euclid, 48

Examinations: abolition of, 86–87; government service and, 25, 102; Liu's sons and, 77–78; national, 47–48; preparation for, 27–28, 36–38; reform of, 49. *See also* Essay-writing

Family: division of property, 164–65; marriage ties of, 62; paper-making roles in, 117; and resistance to state, 168. *See also* Daughters, relationship to parents of; Filial piety; Lineages
Family Sayings of Confucius, 72
Famine, 30–32, 165, 167
Festivals. *See* Holiday observances
Filial piety, 51–82; disputes over, 72–73; education and, 37; importance of, 52–53; and loyalty, 52, 79; modern questioning of, 79, 80; parental love and, 59–61; ritual versus emotion in, 54, 61, 63, 80, 168–69; of Zhang, 69–72
Fines, 131
Food: social status and, 33–34; women's nutrition, 65. *See also* Famine
Footbinding, 63, 65, 80, 131
Foreign incursions, 105, 160
Four Books, 25, 142
Freedom, 79
Friends: Hao Jiqing, 46, 47, 48, 50, 57, 74, 87; Hao Liuji, 120–21, 128; Wang Keqin, 27–28
Frugality, 34
Funerals, 56–57, 68–69

Gazetteers, 14, 36
Gender, village roles involving, 32
Gengzhong (grandson), 65–66
Gentry, 2–4
Gods, Holy Mother, 148–50
Government service: education and, 25, 28, 33, 86–87, 102; elections versus appointments for, 102–3
Grandchildren: Gengzhong, 65–66; Jingzhong, 9, 136, 166; Liu Zuoqing, 60–61; Maoling, 77; Quanzhong, 9, 136, 159, 166; Shuzhong, 9, 161, 166; Xiling, 65–66; Xiluan, 80; Ximei, 65–66; Xiyan, 113
Guo Jing (second wife), 58–59

Hankou, 95, 96

Hao Jiqing, 46, 47, 48, 50, 57, 74, 87
Hao Liuji, 120–21, 128
Harvest, 141–42
Heaven: punishment for wrongdoing from, 62, 65, 66–67; signs of government disapproval from, 103
Hell, 51–52
Hermit, image of, 17, 18, 128–29
Holiday observances, 97–98, 148–49, 154
Holy Mother, 148–50
Hongqing (son), 9, 91, 135, 156, 164–65, 166
Hongxi (daughter), 59–60
Hongyu (daughter), 113
Households, 62
Huang Guoliang, 94, 107–10, 122, 135
Hundred Days reforms, 36, 49
Hu Ying, 48, 76, 94

Irrigation, 146–51, 154

Japan: Chinese-Japanese war of 1937, 159–65; Qingdao occupation in 1914, 103–5; war with China in 1895, 48
Jie (son), 60, 62, 65, 69, 76–81, 113, 123, 126, 142, 145
Jin (son), 91, 113, 135, 145, 151, 164, 166
Jinci: land prices in, 152; present-day, 169; rainfall rituals in, 145–46; revolution of 1911 in, 94; temple repairs in, 107–8
Jinci Gazetteer (Liu), 14–20, 56, 57, 69, 151
Jinfeng coal company, 133
Jingzhong (grandson), 9, 136, 166
Jinyang Academy, Taiyuan city, 35
Journey to the West (novel), 58–59

Kaifeng, 95
Kiakhta, 22, 42
Kitchen god, 162
Korea, 48

Laborers, 138, 139–40, 144
Land reform, 166–67
Li Hongzhang, 48
Lineages, 53–54, 62
Liu Dapeng: autobiographical writings of, 14, 15–20, 45; birth and youth of, 23–24; business career of, 118; and

chamber of commerce, 125–27; character of, 34, 74; children and grand-children of, 59–61, 65–66, 76–81, 135, 164–66 (*see also* Daughters; Grandchildren; Sons); and Chinese-Japanese war of 1937, 159–1; and coal mining office, 126–27; complaints against government by, 110–12; and Confucianism, 4–5; daily routine of, 11–12; daughters of (*see* Daughters); death of, 165; diary of, 7, 10–13, 15; dreams of, 18–19, 45, 58, 64, 74–75, 83–84, 100–101, 111; education of, 24–28, 32, 37–39; and electoral politics, 98–103, 106; examination failures of, 17, 18, 30, 38, 48; family division of property, 164–65; family finances, 113–14, 135, 144–45, 153, 163–64; family history of, 21–23, 53; family status, 8, 23, 96, 163–64; as farmer, 136–58; filial piety of, 52, 54–57, 64–65, 74–75, 81–82; friends of (*see* Friends); gazetteer of, 14–20; government participation of, 106–9; grandchildren of (*see* Grandchildren); grief over father's death of, 57; home of, 1–4, 63; irony toward modernization of, 106; lineage of, 53–54; marriages of, 57–59 (*see also* Guo Jing; Shi Zhulou); as mediator, 123–25; morality of, 4, 11–12, 19–20, 34–35, 45–46, 52; national examination journeys of, 47–50; physical appearance and health of, ii, 2, 137; poetry of, 39, 60; provincial examination passed by, 46; reputation of, 74, 82, 107–10, 118–19, 121–23; and revolution of 1911, 94; sons of (*see* Sons); as teacher, 27, 39–41, 44–45, 87, 90, 96; and temple repairs, 107–9, 122, 124; wives of (*see* Wives); writings (non-diary) of, 13–20
Liulichang, 48
Liu Ming (father), 21–26, 53, 55–57, 63, 74, 92, 96, 113–14
Liu Wenbing, 24
Liu Wuyang, 24–28, 31, 45
Liu Zhiyuan, 21
Liu Zuoqing (grandson), 60–61
Li Xianzhou, 74
Li Yongqing, 37
Lots, drawing, 104

Loyalty: filial piety and, 52, 79; modern
    questioning of, 79
Lu Dongbin temple, Jinci, 104

"The Man Awakened from Dreams"
    (Liu), 18–20, 45
Manchuria, 160–61
"The Man of Wohu Mountain" (Liu),
    15–17
Maoling (grandson), 77
Match factories, 120
Mathematics, 88
Ma Zhanshan, 160
Mediation, 123–25
Millet, 139–41, 144
Miss Liu, 147–48
Modernization: Confucianism versus, 6,
    79–80, 86, 88, 97, 109; consumer cul-
    ture, 156–58; decline of Shanxi during,
    6–7; in education, 48, 76–80, 86–91;
    geopolitical effects of, 169; industry
    and commerce promotion, 91–92,
    154–55; Liu's attitude toward, 49–50;
    money as primary value of, 88; post-
    Boxer rise of, 85; republican govern-
    ment and, 98–103; revolution of 1911
    and, 97; rural areas harmed by, 128,
    154–55, 168–70; in Tianjin, 78–79;
    Zhang Zhidong and, 36
Mongolia, 22, 96, 135
Mother of Liu Dapeng, 55, 63–65, 69
Mountains and mountain society, 127–30
Mourning practices, 52–53
Mu Xiang, 57

Nanxi: Liu as teacher in, 39–43; present-
    day, 6
Newspapers, 105
Niu Yujian, 103, 107–10, 122, 124, 137

Opera, 23, 55, 74
Opium, 81, 131

Paper-making industry, 13, 21, 29–30,
    108, 116–17, 167–68
Pingding, 120
Ploughing, 138–39
Politics, *see* Conservative politics and
    thought; Modernization
Pomeranz, Kenneth, 169

Prayers, 145–46
Privies, 138
Punishment by Heaven for wrongdoing,
    62, 65, 66–67

Qingdao, 105
Qing government: bank problems upon
    overthrow of, 95; Confucianism pro-
    moted by, 5, 26, 72; and 1895 war with
    Japan, 48–49
Quanzhong (grandson), 9, 136, 159, 166
Queues, 94, 131

Red Army, 162
Republican form of government, 98–103,
    106
Revolution of 1911, 93–97, 96
Richard, Timothy, 31
Rituals, *see* Customs
Rural areas, harmed by modernization,
    128, 154–55, 168–70
Russia, 22, 42, 96, 135

Saltpeter, 118, 121
The Scholars (novel), 3
Shaanxi: provincial examinations in, 77;
    trading activity of, 29
Shanghai, 160, 169
Shanxi: banking in, 42–43, 95, 132; Boxer
    uprising in, 63; Chinese-Japanese war
    of 1937, 159; coal mining in, 114;
    under Communism, 168, 169; conser-
    vatism in, 84; decline of, 6–7, 135, 168;
    maps of, ix, x; modernization in, 92,
    97; recession of 1929 in, 152–53; revo-
    lution of 1911 in, 93–95, 97; taxation
    in, 131–32; trading activity of, 22–23
Shanxi Provincial Bank, 132
Shanxi Provincial Library, 13
Shenbao (newspaper), 105
Shimen coal mine, 114–15, 118–20, 121
Shi Zhulou (third wife), 58–59, 165
Shuntian Times (newspaper), 105
Shuzhong (grandson), 9, 161, 166
Smoking, 81, 157–58
Social categories, 3, 142–43, 166–68
Sons: Hongqing, 9, 91, 135, 156, 164–65,
    166; Jie, 60, 62, 65, 69, 76–81, 113,
    123, 126, 142, 145; Jin, 91, 113, 135,
    145, 151, 164, 166; Xiang, 10, 65, 113,

135, 145, 151, 160, 164, 166; Xuan, 60, 65, 69, 76–77, 135, 165
Student protests, 105
Sun Yatsen, 103, 106

Taigu county, 10, 23, 42
Taiwan, 48
Taiyuan city, 154–55, 169
Taiyuan county: coal mining in, 114, 116, 119, 120, 133, 167; revolution of 1911 in, 94–95; taxation of, 131–32
Tao Qian, 17, 18
Taxes: for Boxer indemnity, 85, 92–93; on coal mines, 126, 130; Liu's complaints about, 110–12; for modern education, 89–90; modernization and increase in, 91–93, 130–31; resistance to, 93; in Shanxi, 131–32; student protests against, 105
Teaching: modernization's effect on, 87; salaries for, 43–44, 89. *See also* Liu Dapeng: as teacher
Tenants, 137
Tianjin, 49, 78–80, 169
Tianjin Yishibao (newspaper), 105
Trade: decline of, after Taiping rebellion, 29; with Mongolia, 22–23, 95–96; revolution of 1911 and, 95–96; with Russia, 22–23, 42, 95–96; Shanxi and international, 22–23
Trust, 122–23

Versailles Peace Treaty, 105
Village schools, 24, 28, 87, 89, 91

Wang Keqin, 27–28
War in Europe (1914–1918), 106, 119–20
Wen, King, 128

Westernization, *see* Modernization
Wheat, 139–41
Williamson, Alexander, 22–23
Wives: Guo Jing, 58–59; Shi Zhulou, 58–59, 165
Women: death and health problems of, 65, 81; duties as daughters, 61–63; farming duties of, 136
Writing, respect for, 13, 157
Wuchang, 94, 95
Wu family of Beidasi, 53, 57–58, 149–50, 169
Wu Yanqing, 41, 44, 58, 96

Xiang (son), 10, 65, 113, 135, 145, 151, 160, 164, 166
Xiling (granddaughter), 65–66
Xiluan (granddaughter), 80
Ximei (granddaughter), 65–66
Xiyan (granddaughter), 113
Xuan (son), 60, 65, 69, 76–77, 135, 165

Yang Eryou, 28
Yang Shenxiu, 35–36, 49
Yangyi, 114, 151–52
Yang Zhuo, 120–21, 121, 128
Yan Xishan, 94, 97, 109, 111–12, 126, 131–32, 138, 155, 156, 162
Yuan Shikai, 78, 97, 98, 100, 103, 106

Zeng Guofan, 11, 53
Zhangjiakou, 41
Zhang Zhen, 27–28, 69–72
Zhang Zhidong, 35–36
Zhao Xun, 100
Zhou, Duke of, 142
Zhuangzi, 130
Zuoqing (grandson), 81, 166